IN THE COMPANY OF THEIR PEERS

A Geriatric Peer Counselor Training Manual

Betty Pearson Rogers
Jere G. LaFollette
Wendy Rowe

Skagit Mental Health

Cover: Joann Ossewarde is an artist living in LaConner, Washington.
She created the cover artwork specifically for this book. The piece is titled
"The Seasons of Life."

Illustrations: Gary A. Williams, is the North Sound RSN Area Resource Coordinator
for Whatcom and San Juan Counties. He has been employed in the mental health
field for over 25 years.

The Skagit Community Mental Health Center is a non-profit, United Way Agency
and receives funding for Geriatric Outreach Services from
United Way of Skagit and Island Counties.

For information, write:
Skagit Mental Health Psychiatric and Behavioral Health Services
208 West Kincaid Street, Mount Vernon, WA 98273-4284

Produced by
Veda Vangarde, Inc., 1381-B Highway 9, Mount Vernon, WA 98273
Printed by: Northwest Graphics/Nookachamps Publishers, Inc.

Printed in the USA

ISBN: 9632698-2-8

Cover illustration: Joann Ossewarde
Illustrations: Gary Willams

Funding for the publication and development of this manual has been provided
by the Meyer Memorial Trust of Portland, Oregon.

DEDICATION

This volume is dedicated to the Peer Counselors of Skagit, Whatcom, San Juan and Island Counties and to the Board and Staff of Meyer Memorial Trust whose ongoing support and dedication have made this program possible.

PREFACE

The objective of In the Company of Their Peers

This volume is based upon training developed for a multi-county Geriatric Peer Counseling Program. Over the past eight years this direct service effort has utilized over 225 carefully selected and well-trained seniors as volunteer counselors extending Mental Health Services to a wide range of seriously disturbed older adults. This program has reached over 400 elderly suffering from mental illness.

Due to the success of this program, we believe that the enclosed descriptive and specifically developed training material should be shared with a larger audience within the fields of aging and mental health. It is our hope that this training manual, which includes detailed instructional information, will be of use to others interested in replicating this program or in other ways providing Mental Health services to older adults through trained volunteers. This book attempts to present realistic materials covering all program components from service development to the training curriculum.

The growing number of older adults in need of mental health treatment are universally exceeding service delivery capacities. While a full range of mental health treatment services need to be available to the elderly, we have found that carefully selected, well-trained and closely supervised peer counselors can significantly expand professional staff time in serving older adults. We are convinced that senior volunteers are a resource of extraordinary value. We are grateful for the commitment and enthusiasm of Geriatric Peer Counselors whose work has been so successful in extending mental health care to countless seriously disturbed elderly. In that it is essential for Community Mental Health Programs to look in new directions to meet a growing need, the use of senior peer counselors is one such avenue. It is also a model that enriches not only the lives of clients, but expands the horizons of professional mental health staff with whom senior volunteers work. This manual will provide agencies with an indepth look into possibilities offered by senior peer counselors within mental health agencies.

Some have, at times, minimized the value of "community." However, it is the foundation of this program. It is in "community" that we find change, accomplishment, support, companionship, fellowship, and equality. It is In The Company of Their Peers that both our senior volunteers and our clients experience validation, learn about caring, and find a sense of community.

ACKNOWLEDGEMENTS

The development of the Geriatric Peer Counseling Program and this manual has been a collaborative effort in practice as well as theory. This book reflects the labor, insight and dedication of many friends and colleagues. Their influence has supported this program's success by encouraging growth and not infrequently contributing a dose of reality to the development of this program and accompanying training manual.

Our deep gratitude is extended to all of the Geriatric Peer Counselors who have been part of our training, who have worked with our staff, and given long hours of direct service to their clients. They have committed themselves to sharing their considerable energy with us. We are grateful for the commitment and enthusiasm of Geriatric Peer Counselors whose work has been so successful in extending Mental Health Care to countless seriously disturbed elderly throughout this program.

We also thank the communities of Northwest Washington, the commissioners from Skagit, Whatcom, Island and San Juan counties and the Mental Health Advisory Boards who have reviewed our progress and witnessed for this program in obtaining ongoing and needed funding. Government agencies including the Division of Mental Health, the North Sound Regional Support Network and a wide range of community service providers have also been essential in helping us to create this program and extend it to a four-county area.

The Area Agency on Aging that serves our four-county population is administered by the Northwest Regional Council. Members of the council, their active senior advisory boards and dedicated staff have also been of major help to this program and to Geriatric Mental Health Services in general. This support has been greatly appreciated.

Meyer Memorial Trust Board Members

Senior Service Programs, such as Information and Assistance, have been a major help. We are indebted to the staff of mental health agencies of Older Adult Services from Skagit, Whatcom, Island and San Juan counties for their work in placing and supervising Geriatric Peer Counselor Volunteers. Special thanks go to our Skagit Outreach team: Joan Palmer, Lizbeth Bundy, Lynne Cartland, and Sue Willis, who have provided invaluable assistance and expertise.

Skagit Community Mental Health Center, as well as other Mental Health Programs within our region are members of United Way. In Skagit County, United Way strongly supports Geriatric Mental Health services through outreach services, a multi-disciplinary team and peer counseling.

We are grateful to the Board and staff of the Meyer Memorial Trust for their generous support over the past eight years. The Aging and Independence Initiative of the Meyer Memorial Trust helped to focus our vision, assisted us in establishing realistic goals and funded the development of this program, first in Skagit and later in three adjoining counties. Further, Trust support has allowed us to provide training opportunities throughout the Pacific Northwest. As noted, the Meyer Memorial Trust is responsible for funding the publication of this volume. We remain in their debt for this ongoing support and encouragement.

CONTENTS

PART IV

INTRODUCTION

Services to Mentally Ill Older Adults: Senior Peer Counseling

For most of this century, the proportion of individuals aged 65 or older has increased far more rapidly than the rest of the population. From 1900 to 1990 the number of older Americans has grown from 4 to 13 percent of our nation's people. It is projected that seniors will represent 25% of the population by the year 2030. Such a rapid growth in the number of elderly results in an increasing demand for mental health services for this group, in that they are at high risk for physical and mental health problems.

Mental Health Needs of the Elderly

It is estimated by experts in the field of aging that 10 - 28% of the elderly population have mental health problems that warrant professional intervention. It is also estimated that 10 -15% of older people have clinically significant depression with another 2 - 3% diagnosed with Major Affective Disorder or Bipolar Depression. The following illustrates these mental health needs among America's older adults.

While suicides by young people have captured considerable national attention, suicide among the elderly is generally not highlighted. This is true despite the fact that suicide rates among the elderly are even higher than in younger age groups. Federal figures for 1990 show suicide occurs at the rate of 13.6 per 100,000 persons ages 15 to 24. This compares with 18.1 per 100,000 for persons aged 65 to 74, 26.1 for ages 75 to 84 and 22.5 for ages 85 and above. These high rates may result from the fact that the suicide completion success rates for the aged population is 4 attempts per completion compared to 20 attempts per competion among the general population. The fact that at least 95% of the persons who die by suicide show symptoms of major psychological illness in the weeks before death highlights the necessity for active outreach and case finding services for the elderly.

Severe cognitve impairment affects approximately 5% of the population 65 and over, with senile dementia of the Alzheimer type being the most common cause. By age 80, this rate increases to between 15 to 20%. At least one third of patients with Alzheimer's disease and one half of patients with multi-infarct dementia are affected by coexisting depression or psychosis. At the same time family caretakers of patients with Alzheimer's disease (many of whom are older persons themselves) are highly vulnerable to depression and to stress-related physical and emotional complaints.

About 5% of people age 65 and older are in nursing facilities at any given time, but many more will live in nursing homes during their lifetimes. It is estimated that 43% of people who were age 65 in 1990 will use nursing homes at some time during their remaining years. This elderly nursing home population, though low in numbers in comparison to those living independently in the community, presents a special challenge to the mental health system for the provision of both direct and indirect services, in that the prevalence of mental disorders and behavioral disturbances in nursing homes is estimated to be more than 75%.

Barriers to the Receipt of Mental Health Care for the Elderly

Mental illness, by its very nature can be a crushing experience for persons of any age. At the same time it can be extremely demanding on families, friends, and other caretakers. But, older adults with mental illness are faced with even more challenging experiences. Regardless of the severity or the type of their illness, the elderly find limited access to mental health services, and as a result they are dangerously underserved by the mental health system. While older adults represent about 12% of the population, they rarely represent that same proportion in the caseload of most mental health service providers. This is true in regard to service from community mental health health centers, private practitioners and nursing homes. In fact, it is estimated that countrywide, the elderly (65+) represent only 4-5% of the community mental health center caseloads while psychiatrists in private practice devote only 2% of their time to such patients.

A variety of reasons exists for the under-utilization of community mental health services by the elderly. Older persons may lack the mobility to leave their homes for service. Others may have visual problems which preclude their driving or make it difficult if not impossible to read prescriptions and instructions for treatment. Hearing problems may increase their feelings of isolation, create treatment communication barriers. But perhaps the single greatest impediment to service is that the elderly themselves are often reluctant or resistant to seek or to accept mental health care.

Resistance is often a cover for pervasive feelings of shame, suspicion and fear, while denial renders the elderly consciously incapable of acknowledging problems. Moreover, for the mentally ill elderly a major constraint is the inability to rationally recognize the problem and seek appropriate help. As Ray Raschko, Director of Spokane Older Adult Mental Health Services notes, "it is the very nature of the problems people suffer from - memory loss, and depression - that render them incapable of understanding and reacting." Their mental impairment affects their judgment, desire, and capacity to call for help. At the same time seniors find it difficult to acknowledge the need for emotional support and inconceivable to visit a mental health center for treatment.

Mental health providers share the responsibility for this under-utilization in that they have generally failed to recognize the need to develop innovative strategies for identifying and serving the elderly. Unlike school children or working adults, the elderly have no well defined location where large groups can be reached. Public school systems play a key role in identifying troubled children, especially when families cannot or will not do so. Employee assistance programs identify troubled adults whose work performance is a major symptom. Lacking such sources of identification, it is essential that the mental health system and its providers dedicate more time and resources to the task of active case finding.

Mental health providers also often fail to recognize that the elderly will seldom refer themselves for mental health care. This represents a substantial service barrier. Physical illness or disability is clearly an access problem, mental disability is not. And yet in many instances mental disability is more of a problem. Access problems because of physical disability can be bridged by outreach or in home services. Access problems because of an inability to give consent are virtually ignored. Raschko states that "Multiple visits, persistence and perseverance are all necessary in being able to make contact with people." The unrealistic expectation that the mentally ill elderly will refer themselves to mental health or almost any other service has resulted in community agencies underserving or failing to serve this population despite good intentions.

Despite the fact that so many of the mentally ill elderly are found in nursing homes, there are several factors within the long term care system which reduce the availability and accessibility of mental health services. Nursing homes have historically been designed as medical care facilities that have concentrated on physical ailments. As a result, top priority is routinely given to provision of nursing and rehabilitative services that address these physical ailments. Few dollars are dedicated to the provision of other direct services needed by patient. The same holds true in regard to indirect services such as consultation or training for nursing home staff. The lack of mental health personnel trained in the special needs of nursing home residents further exacerbates this problem. There is a dire need for increased support for undergraduate, graduate and continuing education training, as well as improved linkages between universities and nursing home facilities.

It is also held by many that though there is no scientific proof, there is conscious or unconscious age discrimination within the mental health system that results in this underservice of the elderly. Depending on one's point of view, this may or may not be known as "ageism." Regardless of what it is called, there are some who feel that due to the general scarcity of mental health resources it is a better use of these resources to concentrate on the young and middle-aged populations. This may be a possible explanation for the fact that so few states have mental health appropriations which include funding specifically earmarked for specialized services for the elderly.

It has also been noted that many professionals tend to give higher priority to younger age groups because they believe the elderly are too old for treatment, are resistant to change or are unreachable because of arteriosclerosis or dementia. Older adults are seen as poor candidates for psychotherapy. In this view treatment professionals are clearly mistaken.

Still another factor related to this under-utilization is the lack of sufficient training, sensitivity and orientation of community mental health personnel to the mental health needs of the elderly. As a consequence, mental health professionals tend to avoid working with elderly clients. If these personnel are to play a key role in providing mental health services to older adults, considerable training and motivational efforts will need to be provided to help them define their roles in relation to serving the older patient. They must also learn how to relate to long term care facilities and social and health services that are essential in linking mental health services.

It is also a fact that many older persons cannot afford the price of extended mental health care. At the same time, Medicare and Medicaid inadequately cover these services and to a large extent only do so with many complications to the provider and the recipient of care. Until action is taken at the federal and state levels to make mental health services more affordable for the general population and more fiscally supportive to the mental health service provider, the aged will continue to be under-served.

A Required Array of Services for the Elderly

From a national and statewide perspective, we must recognize that older adults require a full array of psychological and mental health services to address their special needs. They require the same mental health care as younger persons such as diagnostic services, treatment planning, crisis intervention, psychotherapy, etc., but to ensure that adequate and age-appropriate services are delivered on an equitable basis to the elderly, it is essential that these services be tailored to their specific needs and circumstances. In addition, they need specialized facilities and support such as assertive case finding and outreach services, as well as in-home, comprehensive multi-disciplinary evaluation and a full array of residential treatment alternatives. Moreover, they need specialized comprehensive case management to facilitate their interaction with other community-based resources.

Special emphasis should be placed on the homebound and functionally impaired, the homeless, those in nursing homes and other residential facilities. Older adults residing in rural areas and members of poor and minority groups also deserve special attention.

Development of senior peer counseling programs is also needed within the mental health system. Such programs utilize the skills and life experiences of older persons in a self-help approach to mental health. Carefully trained peer counselors can effectively provide supportive counseling under the close supervision of mental health professionals. Not only do troubled mentally ill older persons benefit from such a program, but the peer counselors themselves benefit from any experience that makes their lives more meaningful, and relieves problems of isolation, loneliness, and lack of purpose.

There are seldom easy solutions to the complex problems we find in serving mentally ill older persons. But older adults with mental health problems need and deserve all of the services mentioned above if we are to meet the challenge presented to us by this fastest growing segment of our population. It is, therefore, essential that with a sense of shared responsibility among those concerned about the welfare of the elderly that we dedicate our efforts to improving mental health services for this group. The implementation of Peer Counseling programs, such as is described in this volume, constitutes an important step in that direction.

John D. Piacitelli, MSW, MPH
Washington State Mental Health Division

PART I

Overview of a
Peer Counseling Program

Retired to the County: A Vignette

Frank Miller sat alone at the kitchen table in his trailer house, nestled in the woods, on Samish Island. It was his 81st birthday.

The past several years had not been that good. Frank's wife, Milly, to whom he had been married for 47 years, had died about 18 months ago. During the past several years he had had increasing difficulty getting along with his two sons who seldom came to visit. Although his health was generally good, Frank's vision had become increasingly compromised over the last year due to macular degeneration. After a "fender bender" in the parking lot of a Mount Vernon grocery store, he had lost his license.

Frank had worked as a fisherman, a logger, and a construction worker for most of his adult life. He retired about 10 years ago to a rural area with a little savings and on Social Security.

While the first couple years, fixing up the trailer, taking a few small trips around the area with his wife had been pleasant, her illness, which lasted over several years and eventual death, left Frank alone.

Frank began to hear voices, imagined things. He thought people were living under his trailer home, stealing his things. He had been reported to the Sheriff's Department by a neighbor for brandishing a pistol when his daughter had backed around in his driveway.

The sheriff's visit led to a referral to the Mental Health Center. He was visited at his trailer by a geriatric outreach worker from the center. He had had a physical, but believed the doctor was responsible for him losing his drivers license and refuses to see any doctors.

Over the past several months, he had become more trusting of the outreach worker from the mental health center, allowing her to visit him at the trailer home on a weekly basis. She arranged for Meals on Wheels and helped him connect with the Senior Transportation Program. The social worker had also introduced him to Charlie Ford. Charlie worked with the Mental health Center as a volunteer peer counselor. He was sort of a counselor and friend. Charlie monitored Franks level of anxiety and occasionally encouraged him to see a doctor. He was retired like Frank and used to be a school principal. Charlie would come by once or twice a week, and sometimes they would go shopping or out for coffee. Sometimes Charlie just visited at the trailer house. Frank liked Charlie and liked having him drop by. It gave him something to look forward to, made a difference. Charlie was going to be coming by today . . . tap . . . tap . . . tap . . .

Frank: Yeah, just a minute. I'm coming.

Charlie: Hi Frank. How are you doing?

Frank: Good. Nice to see you. 'They' are really bothering me. Kept me awake all night with trying to take my stuff! So . . . what have you got there? Why, you have a cupcake with a candle in it! Come on in!

• • •

Overview of a Peer Counseling Program
Mental Health Needs Among the Elderly

In a nutshell, Geriatric Peer Counseling involves the use of trained and professionally supported seniors who work on a one-to-one outreach basis with elderly persons experiencing emotional and mental health problems.

Most often peer counseling is conducted in the client's home. Frequently this service is provided in conjunction with other mental health diagnostic or treatment programs.

Through the activities of the Peer Counselors . . . . . . we enhance the ability of a specific elderly person to maintain their independence, and we contribute significantly to the quality of the elderly person's life.

Geriatric Mental Health Peer Counseling is directed toward the accomplishment of several treatment objectives. After working with over 250 geriatric peer counseling clients over the past five years, we have found that this program is effective in:

- Alleviating depression through increased social contact and decreased physical and psychological isolation.
- Assisting an elderly person to develop and utilize a wide range of other community resources as their own support systems decrease over time.
- Providing emotional support and assisting in the development of specific strategies to deal with major life changes such as the loss of spouses, children and friends.
- Bridging the gap between the client and other Mental Health Agency staff also involved in providing services to the older client.

Through the activities of the Peer Counselors in accomplishing objectives, such as those noted above, we enhance the ability of a specific elderly person to maintain their independence, and we contribute significantly to the quality of the elderly person's life.

It has been our experience that all participants in the Geriatric Peer Counselor Program benefit from this effort:

- Clients receive treatment and support services provided by peer counselors.
- Peer counselors themselves receive satisfaction from a role in the community that is both challenging and rewarding.
- Mental Health Center staff benefit from their association with healthy older people and gain specific insight into the areas in which their professional skills can be most useful.
- The Mental Health Center extends Agency services to a significantly greater number of clients.
- The community itself enjoys an increased level of mental health functioning among an important and growing segment of its population.

Agency Services to the Mental Health Needs of the Elderly

A variety of specific problems confront the elderly. These are well known. A brief summary would note that many difficulties facing the elderly are related to their attempts to cope with an increased level of change, often without many of the supports they enjoyed at a younger age.

As we grow older, illness is often more frequent and generally requires longer periods of recuperation. Various physical functions, such as hearing, sight, or mobility, become more difficult. The elderly are beset by degenerative physical conditions and specific ailments, which at one time could be dealt with on a day-to-day basis, subsequently become more problematic. These complicated medical conditions frequently impact the mental health and emotional state of the older person.

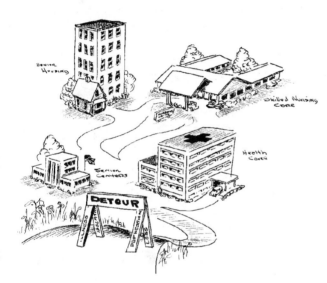

Financial difficulties can arise for the elderly as they move from the role of a wage earner to reliance on pensions, savings, or in many cases government assistance. For many elderly, often on fixed incomes, financial resources fail to keep pace with the rising cost of living. This decline in income or the loss of financial independence can have a major impact on self concept and spirit as well as resulting in true financial hardships.

The elderly encounter many barriers to full social participation and equal status as compared to their younger counterparts. Contemporary society emphasizes youth, not aging. On the basis of age, frequently the lives of the elderly are discounted. Various problems, even those which may be treated, such as drug and alcohol abuse or mental illness, are excused or given less attention on the basis of age. Erroneously, some may suggest that these difficulties are related to the aging process itself, or that the elderly person should not be troubled with attempting to find solutions to various problems in their later years.

Recent changes in our social structure emphasizing greater geographical mobility often take family and friends far away, leaving an elderly person isolated from those sources of support that had previously been very important. This same dispersion of the family and the corresponding shift from the extended to more nuclear family unit, often leaves the older person without a specific role as a contributor, either to society or to a family where they once played a leading part.

The above factors exert a strong influence on the emotional well being and mental health of the elderly. While some disorders, such as Alzheimer's or other dementias, can be associated with the aging process, they are not normal processes of aging, but rather occur with greater frequency as one grows older.

In addressing problems associated with mental health and aging, a number of studies have documented the high level of mental health disorders among the elderly.[1] In 1987 the House Select Committee on Aging estimated that between 15 and 25 percent of Americans over the age of 65 suffer from significant mental health problems.[2] Other studies have echoed these figures. What is more, when levels of more severe mental illness are examined by age, the elderly show a rate of dysfunction approximately twice that of adults in the 18-64 year age group.[3]

This same dispersion of the family and the corresponding shift from the extended to more nuclear family unit, often leaves the older person without a specific role as a contributor, either to society or to a family where they once played a leading part.

The high incidence of mental disorders among the elderly points to the need for the development of a range of mental health services for this group. Based on a prevalence of data, one would expect an over-representation of elderly clients within community mental health programs. Unfortunately, this is not the case. For a variety of reasons, the elderly are generally *under*-represented in mental health caseloads and effective programs for meeting the specific mental health needs of the elderly have been slow to develop.

There is clear documentation that the level of mental health problems besetting the elderly exceed that of their younger adult counterparts. The extent of services provided this elderly group is, however significantly lower. There are a number of reasons for the lack of service for the elderly. These include geographic isolation, resistance on the part of the elderly in asking for help, lack of funds to pay for mental health services, and perhaps, on the part of providers, various prejudices that fail to encourage the provision of service to the elderly.

Providers may feel there is a lack of glamor in working with the elderly. For years the mental health system has emphasized serving the chronically mentally ill. Mobile, and in many ways more demanding, young chronically mentally ill clients may present a more visible problem within the community and thus be more frequently targeted for mental health intervention than their elder counterpart. In that many community mental health services are provided in office based programs, they have not been accessible to homebound or isolated elderly. Due to the often complicated diagnostic picture presented by an elderly mentally ill person, there is frequently a question as to which treatment would be most efficient. Few mental health providers have had adequate training to help them sort out these difficult problems.

1   John Piacitelli, Washington State Mental Health Division Model, Continuum of Mental Health Care for the Elderly, Olympia, Washington, 1988.
2   House Select Committee on Aging, 1987.
3   John Piacitelli, Page 14.

The Development of Geriatric Peer Counseling Services in Skagit County

For a number of years the Skagit Community Mental Health Program has been developing an expanded range of services for the elderly. During the mid-1970's the Agency began a nursing home consultation program. In 1978 a geriatric day treatment program was started. Outreach services to the isolated mentally ill elderly were begun by a professional staff in the early 1980's with the assistance of funding from United Way and the local Area Agency on Aging. With the support of the State Mental Health Division, a Geriatric Multidisciplinary Case Assessment Team was added to Agency services in 1986. That same year, through a grant from the Meyer Memorial Trust, the Center initiated a Peer Counseling Program to enhance home-based mental health care to the elderly living in rural Skagit County.

The establishment of peer counseling as a major component of the Geriatric Mental Health Services was the result, to a large extent, of a fortuitous occurrence. This was the appearance of a particular volunteer, Elmyra Nelson, who in her mid-50's requested the opportunity to provide volunteer counseling or support services to the elderly.

As has been noted, for a number of years the Agency had offered home-based geriatric mental health outreach services. Elmyra's interest in working in this area was stimulated by an article in a local paper describing outreach programs. From the initiation of Geriatric Outreach, there were always more requests for services than could be met. Thus, the need for additional person power in this area was clear.

After meeting with the Geriatric staff on several occasions, Elmyra was assigned a case. The particular person with whom she would be working was a client who had seen a mental health professional for some time and whose problems had received significant attention. While her case was not currently acute, the professional counseling staff felt it would be very beneficial for this client to have ongoing supportive contact with a mental health counselor and remain associated with the professional team at the Center. This initiated a relationship that was to last for several years. It was clear that the client received great benefit from her contact with Elmyra, who not only saw her in her home, but who assisted her in venturing out for coffee or shopping, and for other activities that increased the client's level of more normal community contact.

Experience with this initial peer counselor convinced the agency of the desirability of developing a specific program to train and utilize senior-aged peer counselors in working with the elderly. Through the generous support of the Meyer Memorial Trust, the mental health center has been able to expand this program, training over 225 geriatric peer counselors within a four county area of Northwest Washington State. From it's earliest efforts in using geriatric peer counselors, it was felt that this model was not just a less intense substitute for professional's activity, but rather, provided a new and effective treatment dimension that could stand on its own merits.

From the initiation of Geriatric Outreach, we have always had more requests for services than we could meet. Thus, the need for additional person power in this area was clear.

Integration of the Geriatric Peer Counselor Within a Mental Health Setting

The elderly require a wide range of mental health services and at the community level this includes access to the same set of services that are available to other community residents. 24-hour emergency services; access to short term acute in-patient care; the availability of psychiatric evaluation and medication, and community support/case management to enhance or retain independence, represent services that are needed by all age groups.

In addition to the standard range of mental health services however, the elderly have special needs that require specific attention. Isolation frequently experienced by the elderly has been discussed above. Also noted is the often encountered attitude on the part of the elderly that can contribute to a hesitance to seek mental health assistance. Additionally important are the frequently complicated diagnostic issues as to the origin of what appears to be a mental health problem. These, and other specific issues confronting the elderly require a special mental health services approach.

... the two most critically needed special mental health programs available to the elderly are: (1) home-based outreach service and (2) sophisticated multi-level diagnostic support.

In addition to the standard range of treatment offerings, two most critically needed mental health programs that should be available to the elderly are: (1) home-based outreach service and (2) sophisticated multi-level diagnostic support.

An outreach approach has been part of the Skagit Mental Health Program for a number of years. Home based professional evaluation, counseling and case management has been also offered for some time. More recently, the Agency added a multidisciplinary geriatric case assessment team that provides evaluation for those elderly presenting the more complicated diagnostic situations. The Geriatric multidisciplinary team is funded by the Washington State Division of Mental Health and includes a psychiatrist, a family physician, a psychiatric nurse, a home-health nurse, a geriatric mental health specialist, and a representative from the Skagit County Senior Information and Assistance Program.

The team is coordinated by a geriatric mental health specialist who arranges for various aspects of the evaluation and ensures that team members are able to see elderly clients in their homes or that transportation and other support is provided to enable the elderly person to be seen within a practitioner or agency's offices. The team meets twice monthly to review and develop a collaborative multi-level evaluation and treatment plan.

The availability of more specialized geriatric treatment services—and particularly the geriatric outreach and multidisciplinary case assessment programs—make a vital contribution in meeting the mental health needs of older adults.

Prerequisites for Establishing A Peer Counselor Program

There are several important elements that need to be in place within a mental health agency prior to establishing a Geriatric Peer Counselor Program. These include the availability of geriatric mental health specialists to provide sufficient training and support to the peer counselors, the existence of home-based outreach capacity, diagnostic evaluation services that can ensure that referrals to the peer counseling program are appropriate, and support from the administration and professional staff of the agency.

1. **Availability of Geriatric Mental Health Specialist to Provide Sufficient Training and Support to the Peer Counselor**
   Perhaps the most critical prerequisite for the establishment of a peer counselor program is the availability of mental health specialists to provide sufficient training and support to the peer counselor. If possible, Agency staff should be "geriatric mental health specialists" or mental health professionals with extensive geriatric experience.

2. **The Existence of Home-Based Outreach Capacity**
   To serve the elderly, mental health centers must employ an outreach approach if they are to reach this client population. We have found that peer counselors

can work effectively in providing outreach support services. The outreach model and experience in providing home-based services should be in place prior to the use of volunteers. Supervisory staff must be familiar with cases referred to volunteer peer counselors and have reviewed home settings prior to assignment of a peer counselor.

3. **Sophisticated Diagnostic Capacity**
   Conducting evaluations of the mental health needs of the elderly is a complicated task. A variety of physical, environmental, as well as emotional conditions contribute to the diagnostic picture. An agency should have experience in providing multidimensional evaluations that will assist in identifying that client group for which peer counselors are most appropriate.

4. **Support of the Administration and Professional Staff of the Agency**
   The development of a peer counseling program, as a resource for serving the elderly, requires agency attention at all levels. Volunteers must be viewed as an important resource requiring time, attention, commitment and supervision. It is difficult to develop this support for a peer counselor program if agency administration fails to recognize peer counseling as a significant program. The development and implementation of a geriatric peer counseling program must be a priority particularly at the on-set.

   The following chapters of this manual will provide details on the specific training and day-to-day operation of a geriatric volunteer peer counseling program. In addition, the manual will illustrate program requirements and provide suggestions for operating this important mental health resource for the elderly.

Preview of the Training Manual

This manual has been developed as part of a training program for senior volunteers who provide peer counseling services to homebound elderly. The purpose of peer counselor training is to enhance communication skills, teach basic counseling skills, increase knowledge of mental health issues and provide information on the aging process. The training manual offers the agency and the group facilitator a design to follow when developing a peer counseling program. It also offers a step by step outline for the eight weekly training sessions.

The facilitator is encouraged to use the training manual as a guide, tailoring the areas covered in the manual to the particular needs and resources of their specific program. Each subject area is concisely outlined. It is anticipated that the training facilitator will bring creativity and personal energy in shaping material to the uniqueness of each group. The training manual contains: (boxed information designates handouts and forms.)

- a structure for group interactions
- educational materials
- handouts
- case studies
- group activity ideas
- role playing exercises
- program forms

As this is experiential training which is process oriented, much of the learning develops through the interactions of the peer trainees. While the group facilitator can initiate and structure the learning mode, significant learning comes from the individual's participation in the group experiences and group sharing.

In that this material has been developed for a peer counseling program based within a mental health agency, it is assumed that facilitators using this manual will have considerable skills in group process and experiential learning techniques. Having made this assumption, we do not cover specific philosophies or theories related to training style. We have also omitted introductory information on specific learning models such as experiential exercises, small and large group role play or feedback.

This manual is divided into seven parts, each part focusing on one of several steps necessary in developing an agency peer counseling program. Each part includes the "how-tos" of implementing the program.

Part I	Mental health needs of the older adult and a general description of senior peer counseling within a mental health setting.
Part II	Details for the development of a volunteer program
Part III	Philosophy and format for program implementation.
Part IV	Session by session guide for the training of senior peer counselors, including training recources and ideas.
Part V	Benefits of the program. Program evaluation findings. Statistical results from research period.
Part VI	Additional Resource materials covering aging subject matter.
Part VII	Annotated and general bibliography.

PART II

Critical Elements of a Peer Counseling Program

GETTING OFF THE GROUND: FINDING THE RIGHT VOLUNTEERS THROUGH COMMUNITY ORGANIZATIONS

Thus far we have discussed the administrative groundwork for a Geriatric Peer Counseling Program. Now we turn to several important areas related to attracting, recruiting and screening volunteers which will make this program a success.

1. Community Education to Increase Awareness of Senior Peer Counseling

Local newspapers are often eager for articles about the achievements of "hometown folks." The effective use of this resource will be of great help in publicizing your program and in recruiting potential volunteers.

The Program Coordinator should contact the editor in charge of "Senior News," health sections or other relevant segments of the local paper. Similar efforts should also be directed to senior and retired people's publications in your area. Articles about the peer counseling program, and other agency staff can describe the clients served and the qualifications of Peer Counselors. In order to get the type of recruitment response one hopes for, the advertisement and articles must be in the media eight to ten weeks before the actual start of the training. Articles can also be written for the news media which announce peer counseling as a mental health service for the communities aging population. Emphasis on the use of trained volunteers to augment staff will help to remind the community that the elderly mentally ill is a growing, under-served, and at times, "invisible" group of people.

Volunteerism is honored through such agencies as R.S.V.P, Senior Centers and United Way; these support systems are excellent avenues for advertisements and recruitment of peer counselors. Here again, the coordinator must initiate efforts with these agencies several months before the start of the training program. The coordinator works as the public relations representative for the program. Regular community contacts and presentations bring both recruitment and support for this type of activity. Effective groups for public presentations include the following:

Senior Service Agencies

Area Agency on Aging, Senior Information and Assistance, Senior Centers and Senior Hotlines

Service Groups

Soroptomists, Women's Church groups, Hospital Discharge Planners, Nursing Home Social Workers, Retired Worker's Organizations, Kiwanis, Rotarians, R.S.V.P, Elderhostle, and local community college programs.

Support Groups

Alzheimer's Support Groups, Families and Advocates for the Mentally Ill, and Widow's Support Groups.

These groups usually welcome speakers at their meetings. Such visits from program staff and volunteers link the peer counseling program to important existing community services for seniors. Materials such as flyers and application forms can be left at these meetings and at the service sites.

In our case, we have found that "blitzing" the county through both the news media and personal contacts, eight weeks before the training, has generally resulted in a large number of individual inquiries into the program. This continues to be true, even though we are located in a rural area and we currently have a waiting list for potential Peer Counselors for upcoming trainings.

As our program has become established, the most exciting and rewarding recruitment has come through the Peer Counselors themselves. They tell their friends and their social groups about their experiences and act as representatives of the program. Using their pictures for newspaper articles is particularly effective and a pleasant honor for the Peer Counselor. On the following pages are samples of the our recruitment and advertising programs.

2. Recruitment of Peer Counselors

There are a few fairly specific qualifications that need to be met by the prospective peer counselors. These are as follows:

- •   55 years of age or older
- •   Must have reliable transportation
- •   Must be able to complete the 50-hour training course
- •   Must attend the monthly supervision with Mental Health Professionals.
- •   Must attend the Continuing Education Seminars
- •   Must have genuine interest and be capable of working with geriatric clients with some mental health concerns.

3. Application Process for Peer Counselors

An applicant's first contact is generally with agency receptionist or clerical staff. The receptionist must be made aware of the program, the staff involved and basic information as to the application procedure. Generally, initial calls are referred to the Program Coordinator, who provides further clarification about applicant eligibility, program objectives or other specific issues. An application form is then sent to the individual with instructions to return it as soon as possible.

Our application form acts as an initial screening device. An applicant's motivation to complete the questionnaire and return it serves as an indication of their commitment and often appropriateness for this type of program. Follow up questions may be added by the coordinator if the agency has specific questions. We send a brochure about the program with the application to familiarize the applicant with the program's goals and expectations.

4. Volunteer Screening

As the applications are returned, they are reviewed by the Project Coordinator, for volunteer appropriateness. Special consideration and evaluations should be given to:

- An applicant who has recently (within the past six months) lost a spouse.
- An applicant with questionable transportation.
- An applicant who has a physical disability that limits their mobility.
- An applicant who is looking for a paid job.
- An applicant who expresses unrealistic concerns regarding their own aging process or has dogmatic religious beliefs.
- An applicant expressing an attitude not conducive to learning and group process.
- An applicant who is reluctant to complete the form.
- An applicant who is heavily involved in other volunteer programs.

Applicants who do not meet the basic requirements indicated on the application form or who appear to be inappropriate for the screening interview, are notified by telephone. At this time, a tactful discussion will occur as to why this option for volunteer work might not be the best at this particular time. The coordinator may choose to state specific disqualifying issues, and can also commend the applicant for their interest.

Those who are accepted for the Screening Interview are notified by telephone. The time, place, those involved, and a brief review of the group interviewing process is given to the applicant at that time. This can be followed by a written notice.

5. The Screening Interview

Applicants meet in groups of 4 or 5, with the Project Coordinator, a member of the Program Advisory Committee, and a geriatric mental health professional from the agency. It is important to include staff from the agency that will be providing the Peer Counseling supervision.

These personal, small group interviews are useful in several respects. First, they encourage applicants to interact within a group setting, providing the interview team with information about the applicant's group comfort level and interpersonal skills. Second, through the use of discussion questions, each applicant is given a chance to relate to both professionals and peers in a non-threatening, informal setting.

The interview team can look for the following sample indicators in their evaluation:

- Does the applicant seem to be able to relate to the group members in a direct, spontaneous manner?
- Does the applicant have a healthy attitude towards aging?
- What is the applicant's attitude toward volunteerism?
- Does the professional feel comfortable with the applicant?
- Will the applicant be seen as approachable by other adults seeking service?

The applicants are asked to discuss, amongst themselves, their personal reasons for wanting to be involved in this particular volunteer program. The professionals are encouraged to allow each applicant to express themselves with limited feedback or interruptions during this sequence.

The personal screening interview is a time for the potential trainees to gather more information about the program and the general purpose of mental health agencies, so that they might further decide whether they are interested in this particular volunteer program or wish to be involved somewhere else.

Upon completion of the personal screening interviews, evaluations are discussed by the professionals involved. Congratulatory letters of acceptance into the training program are sent to accepted prospective trainees. Information regarding the training dates, particulars of the training site and other expectations of the trainees are given at this time.

Those not accepted for the training are sent a letter thanking them for their participation and suggesting they continue to explore volunteer work, and find a site where their skills can be used.

It has been our experience that a large majority of program applicants are appropriate for this program. After in-person screening of more than 225 applicants over the past several years, only 12 were felt to be inappropriate for this program.

GRANT SERVES AREA'S SENIORS

A $79,000, two-year grant from the Meyer Memorial Trust has been approved for the Peer Counseling Project through Skagit Community Mental Health Clinic to help senior citizens in a four-county area help other seniors in need.

"These peer counselors are actings as the eyes and ears for the outreach workers and that allows the mental health agencies to see the more acute cases," said Betty Rogers, Geriatric Peer Counseling Coordinator with the Skagit Community Mental Health Center.

*Skagit County's Lucetta Cleveland is a two-year peer counseling volunteer in a program
to train senior citizens to counsel elderly, homebound clients. The four county program is funded
through a $79,000 grant from the Meyer Memorial Trust and administered
by Skagit Mental Health*

Rogers will be conducting an eight-week training course for peer counselors beginning in Bellingham Sept. 26. The training will be held one day a week for eight weeks and then volunteers will be placed with a client to work with, on a beginning basis average of once a week for about an hour and a half.

The course is designed as a hands-on practical approach to learning about the problems which seriously affect the homebound elderly population. Peer counselors often can act as an advocate in some situations and are looked upon by many elderly people as friends.

"The clients these peer counselors see often have severe mental health problems," Rogers said. "They need a lot of support."

The objective of this program is to allow elderly, homebound people needing special attention the opportunity to live at home, without becoming institutionalized."

"Whatcom County is swarming with isolated clients," Rogers said.

The primary problem facing many elderly clients, she said, is depression. In that state, many have isolated themselves from their family and community."

"By bringing in someone closer to their age group, you get better results," Rogers said. And the program has beneficial results for the volunteers themselves. "The peer counselors learn how to more effectively deal with their own aging process," Rogers said. The counselors are regularly supervised by the program geriatric outreach therapist providing them time to discuss client treatment and progress.

One of the expectations of the proposal is to increase the number of peer counselors in the four-county area including Whatcom, Skagit, Island and San Juan counties. With 47 trained peer counselors, the program is recruiting additional counselors to join the program.

"We desperately need more peer counselors in Whatcom County," Rogers said. Thus far, only five applications have been received from Whatcom County residents.

This program of seniors reaching seniors for greater mental health stability and to enhance their quality of life was funded by the grant 1986 and administered by the Skagit Mental Health Center. Last June, the grant was renewed for two more years but Rogers hopes when that money expires, the project will be established and local mental health clinics can pay for the program. Peer counselors receive reimbursement for mileage and if desired, counselors can recieve credits through Skagit Valley Community College.

For more information, call 336-3193 during the weekday working hours and ask for Peer Counseling Coordinator Betty Rogers. An application form will be sent to the potential trainee who will be screened for the training program by individual interviews with the coordinator. Applications must be received no later than Sept. 21.

Reprint from The Skagit Valley Herald, 6-1989

Peer Counseling Training Application

Please fill out this application and return it to Peer Counseling Coordinator at the address below. All information on this application will be considered confidential. Keep your answers brief. You will have ample time in the group interview to elaborate. You will be called to schedule an interview after your application has been reviewed.

Name_____ Date of Birth_____

Address_____

Phone_____

How did you hear about this program?

What do you think are some of the problems of older people?

Have you had experience with aging parents, grandparents, etc.?

How do you feel about your own aging?

Why are you interested in participating in the program?

Do you think participating in the program could influence your personal life in any way? Describe.

Do you believe that one's behavior and attitudes can have an effect on one's health. Explain.

What qualities do you have that you think would help you to become a good counselor?

Describe any experience you have had with counseling or health education.

Describe some of your previous employment or volunteer activities

Organization   Position   Length of Stay

Describe some of your other skills and special interests.

Do you have any health problems that are likely to limit your involvement in the program? Please explain.

Describe any significant "stressor events" in your life within the last eighteen months (changes, losses, gains, retirements, etc.)

What do you use for transportation?

How do you feel about filling out this application?

Any additional comments?

How do I apply to become a peer counselor?

If you would like to become a Peer Counselor, call the Mental Health Center at 336-3193 and ask for an application. You may ask to speak to the Peer Counseling Project Coordinator Betty Rogers to discuss special interests and concerns.

Applications for our next training program should be submitted to:

SKAGIT COMMUNITY MENTAL HEALTH CENTER
PEER COUNSELING PROGRAM
208 KINCAID
MOUNT VERNON, WA 98273

What is the selection process?

Applicants will be contacted by phone and an appointment set for an interview of an hour within the week. The interview will take place in a group setting in the applicant's county of residence. Present will be several applicants, the Project Coordinator, a member of the Project Advisory Committee and staff of an agency offering appropriate volunteer placements and supervision in that county. Most applicants have found this to be an informal, non-threatening and enjoyable process.

VOLUNTEER AS A PEER COUNSELOR
Volunteers counsel senior clients in an individual situation using their training as paraprofessionals.

Volunteer qualifications:
- 55 years or older
- Completion of the 50 hour training course (free to trainees)
- Attend monthly supervision with mental health professionals
- Continuing education with professionals
- Interest in working with geriatric clients who have some mental health concerns

WE'RE LOOKING FOR APPLICANTS FOR OUR SPRING TRAINING
Skagit-Island County Course to being April 9, 1990

Applications must be received as soon as possible

**For more information call: Betty Rogers, coordinator
Skagit Community Mental Health Center 336-3193**

CHARACTERISTICS OF A POTENTIAL PEER COUNSELOR

Attentiveness
evidence that the applicant is listening to others

Genuineness
the degree to which the applicant appears to be freely, deeply, honestly him / herself

Openness
willingness to share personal information with emotional content rather than just facts

Empathy
sensitivity to what another person is experiencing

Expressiveness
ability to communicate feelings in a meaningful, spontaneous way

Reality Orientation
accurate perception of what is going on around him/her

Vitality
spirited enthusiasm about life and its possibilities

Sociability
tendency to relate to and interact with other people

Sincerity
demonstration of a genuine commitment to the program

Peer Counseling Training Letter of Acceptance

Dear Peer Counselor Candidate:

We would like to congratulate you on being selected to be part of our Peer Counseling Training Program. The training will begin Monday September 25th from 9:00 a.m. to 4:00 p.m. We will be meeting at the Anacortes United Methodist Church, 2200 H. Ave. Anacortes (See directions enclosed).

The training sessions are day long so please plan something for the lunch break, (12:00 - 1:00). Trainees can either bring a sack lunch or plan to have lunch at a local restaurant. Please wear casual, comfortable clothing as we want everyone to be as relaxed as possible. Also bring with you writing paper or pad, pens, pencils and a 3-ring notebook or folder.

I'm looking forward to our "journey" over these next eight weeks. There will be hot coffee/ tea and donuts waiting for you!

Again, congratulations, The Skagit Community Mental Health Staff are looking forward to working with you.

Sincerely,

Geriatric Peer Counseling Coordinator

Peer Counseling Training Letter of Non-Acceptance

Dear Applicant:

Thank you for participating in the interview for our Senior Peer Counseling Program. We had many applicants for our training program and it is with regret that are not able to take you into this program at this time.

There are many volunteer placements which could use your skills and we encourage you to continue exploring volunteer work. If we can help you to identify another area you might be interested in we would be happy to talk to you.

Sincerely,

Peer Counseling Coordinator

PEER COUNSELING PROGRAM: CLIENTS, COUNSELORS, GOALS AND THE COMMUNITY

The Peer Counseling Program for older adult clients is composed of several interrelated elements. A successful program needs to address each of these in line with the specific needs of the community. Program elements identified for special consideration include:

1. The elderly target population to be served by the Peer Counseling Program.

2. The characteristics of peer counselors who will be recruited, trained and deployed in serving elderly clients.

3. Program goals, objectives and procedures.

4. Peer Counselor training and supervision to be developed and provided by agency staff.

5   Program relationships and communications with other Human Service providers, particularly those serving the elderly.

1. Identification of the client population

The Agency must make an early decision as to the type of client to be served by the Peer Counseling Program. What are the characteristics of this potential consumer group and what are their needs? What group of elderly in the community could receive the most benefit from this program? What group of clients, on the other hand, may need a different level of intervention?

The Agency must make an early decision as to the type of client to be served by the Peer Counseling Program.

A feel for the type of client who might be appropriate for a peer counselor can be gained through reviewing several cases. The following profiles are geriatric clients now served by the Skagit Mental Health Center through the Peer Counseling Program. These illustrate the type of client and nature of problems most often seen by geriatric peer counselors over the past few years.

Names of clients have been changed in these profiles out of respect for their privacy.

Mary Ann

Mary Ann is a 72-year-old woman who lives alone in a 22-foot travel trailer. She shares five acres of rural, remote property with her son and his family. The client's home has no running water. Water is supplied by a stream and must be hauled by the client daily for cooking and washing. There is electricity which supplies the only source of heat – a small portable heater. The client moved here five years ago from Montana. The client's only source of income is her monthly Social Security check.

Mary Ann was referred to the Geriatric Outreach Program by a friend who lives in the Seattle area. On her first visit, this friend discovered what she considered to be inadequate living arrangements. She also mentioned the client seemed very forgetful and confused. She felt that the woman's family was not adequately prepared to deal with their mother's aging as well as their own responsibilities.

Marvin and Sue

Marvin and his wife live in their own home within the city limits of a small Skagit County town. He is 80 and she is 86. During their 50 years of marriage they have developed a communication style that is aggressive and verbally combative. Marvin's wife, Sue, has macular degeneration and due to a broken hip, now needs the aid of a walker to move about. Marvin also has very limited vision and significant hearing loss. They have become increasingly isolated because of their physical limitations and their social behaviors.

Recently, they were asked to leave both the Senior Center and the Bingo games because of their argumentative and disruptive behaviors. These losses, their isolation and increasing awareness of each other's disabilities has, for both members of this family, caused a significant increase in tension and agitated depression.

It is evident that with the multiple issues described in these vignettes, that before a Peer Counselor can be placed with the geriatric client, the client must first be evualated by mental health professionals and a treatment plan established within the formal structure of the clinic system. Based on that evaluation, a Peer Counselor may be appropriate, depending on the severity of mental health issues at hand.

2. Identification of the Peer Counselor

A second element for early consideration is the type of individual sought as potential senior peer counselors. One needs to consider their backgrounds and ensure that they are capable of learning the skills needed to fit into this clinically based program.

Again, let us present to you, in profile form, several of our peer counselors, giving you an idea of volunteers utilized by our program.

Ellie

Ellie is a 79-year-old widow. Her husband suffered from Alzheimer's disease for ten years. In the later years he was placed in a nursing home and died a year ago. Ellie, herself, had attended Alzheimer's support groups during his illness and is still involved in her own grief process. She read of the Peer Counseling Program in a local newspaper and felt this might be a way for her to become more involved with people. Ellie also felt she had some experiences with chronic illness that might be of use in such a program. Ellie was able to be an active member of the group and often shared, intimately, her own perceptions of loss and grief. She now is seeing a geriatric client who has been widowed for some years and is suffering from dementia and isolation.

Gustavo

Gustavo is 60-years-old, was a business man and quite successful. He told the group about his regrets at retiring so early. "You can only play so much golf" he reported with some frustration and a great deal of boredom in his voice. He was at a point in his personal "growth" of becoming more aware of his need to find out about people. He was ready to learn about communication, empathy and aging. Gustavo visited our Geriatric Day Treatment Program and met a client who for years had been in and out of State Institutions and who seldom spoke to anyone. Gustavo discovered this man's ability to build balsa models and related how he saw this man "beam" and "become alive" when he showed Gustavo his models. Gustavo, himself, was beaming. He has continued to meet with this client on a weekly basis.

At the end of each training program, the Peer Counselor's are asked to write a brief paper stating what the training meant to them. The following is an excerpt from a final paper.

"I have thought a lot of what this class has meant to me. It is difficult (to sum up) because I will be finding out the rest of my life. I have been given a life tool that will grow as I, hopefully, will grow. One direct result was a dream I had – I was in a mirrored tunnel, many mirrors and many reflections of myself. At the end was a glowing, smokey golden light. I felt this showed me I had been through a period of self examination. I sometimes wondered where the lessons were going, but in the end they all fit. I still can't describe what we do with others, but I do know I want to do more."

Peer Counselors who are successful in this volunteer program often comment that they have come to know themselves better through the training and through their experiences with their client. This flexibility and willingness to "stretch" themselves in their own personal growth is essential. Personal characteristics such as vulnerability, curiosity, empathy, honesty and a sense of humor are qualities of an accomplished peer counselor.

Peer Counselors have come from a variety of occupations. We have worked with teachers, nurses, social workers, housewives, businessmen, librarians, farmers and policemen. At the beginning of our project most were retired, however some have gone on to part-time jobs.

Personal characteristics such as vulnerability, curiosity, empathy, honesty and a sense of humor are qualities of an accomplished peer counselor.

One was chosen as a Senior State Legislative Aid for our State Representative; one worked part-time as a VISTA volunteer; three were employed as a direct result of the peer counseling training – one as a Geriatric Day Treatment staff member, one as a

Nursing Home Case Manager for the Mental Health Center, and one as a Senior Center Activities Director. Three of our peer counselors have gone on to facilitate the Alzheimer's Support Groups in Skagit, Camano Island and Whidbey Island. All are supervised by the Peer Counseling Program Coordinator.

3. Program Goals and Procedures

A third element of developing a Senior Peer Counseling Program is the need to develop clear goals and procedures in order to share them with the community and other service providers. Communities often have limited access to mental health professionals. The geriatric homebound are often served essentially by Senior Services, local physicians and churches, even when mental health needs may be evident. When developing services, the Peer Counseling Program must establish clear program guidelines. These should include a written program description, the qualifications and format for referrals, qualifying criteria for the clients served and a clear statement of what other community agencies can expect from the program sponsor. The community itself will need an introduction to the program through the media and additional education regarding the needs of elderly homebound people and related mental health issues.

The establishment of an advisory Committee is of great help in this area. We have used a program advisory committee from the inception of the program in Skagit County. Advisory group functions can include assessing resources, educating the community, creating interest, and giving credibility to the newly developing service. It should be remembered that many elderly maintain inaccurate perceptions or fear of the Mental Health system. Thus, the elderly may hesitate to become involved in Mental Health Programs even as a volunteer.

The community itself will need an introduction to the program through the media and additional education regarding the needs of elderly homebound people and related mental health issues.

Support from established programs – who may be represented on the Advisory Group – such as Senior Services, Area Agency on Aging and Retired Senior Volunteer Program will help reduce elderly apprehension and work toward a successful program initiation.

4. Peer Counselor Training and Supervision

A fourth element of the program is the training of the Senior Peer Counselors. We have offered a Peer Counseling Training Program two times a year in September and in March. Daytime meetings have been appropriate for the initial 8-week, 50-hours of training we provide, as many seniors prefer not to travel after dark. The initial peer counselor training sequence works best when it is held in the sameplace and at the same time over the 8-week period. Often communities will have church buildings or Community Centers that can be used free of charge. We have used a 9:00 a.m. to

4:00 p.m. schedule with a one-hour lunch break, one day per week with what we feel has been good success and consistent attendance from the trainees. This time frame allows for important social interaction between the peer trainees, the establishment of an esprit de corps within the group, and the development of a full discussion on the day's focus or topic.

A "bonding" develops through the group process, with the individuals gaining self confidence and a more in-depth involvement as the weeks progress. The importance of group identification cannot be overstated, as it is this "groupness" which appears to ensure that volunteers continue their service after the training and placements are completed. The group is encouraged to use the democratic process of discussion and negotiation to answer specific needs of its members.

Each geographical area will need to develop meeting times and agendas specifically geared to their community. As has been stated, the groups can be given the responsibility of making some of those decisions. For the group facilitator this offers an excellent vehicle by which to begin awareness of such training issues as empowerment, limit setting, and assertiveness.

> *A "bonding" develops through the group process, with the individuals gaining self confidence and a more in-depth involvement as the weeks progress.*

Supervision of Peer Counselors by professional mental health workers, geriatric specialists or case managers is a critical element of a high quality program. Supervision can be accomplished for an individual or for a group setting. In our experience, group supervision – held at least monthly – appears to be the most effective and efficient. The professional and Peer Counselor work as team members in reviewing and planning services given a particular client. The supervision time, again, is a time for Peer Counselors to learn from the professionals and from each other's experiences. The professional sets a tone of validation for the service provided by the Peer Counselor. At this time other business can also be completed, such as the collection of progress notes and RSVP vouchers or providing program or training announcements.

As professionals, we acknowledge the volunteers by our interactions with them, therefore a variety of support systems may be blended into a Peer Counseling Program. We have used monthly Support meeetings involving all peer counselors and the Peer Counselor Coordinator as a time for sharing joys and frustrations, both personal and programatic. This meeting is a time for Peers to look at their "process" as a volunteer.

A bi-annual continuing education program is also a part of this support system, with Peer Counselors expected to participate. These are day long workshops focused on areas pertinent to the seniors and their clients. Professionals in a number of fields may be invited to present or facilitate the groups. This meeting also may include a pot luck and social time.

5. Community Relationships

The last element to consider in developing a Peer Counseling Program is to establish this unique effort in relation to existing Mental Health Center and other community services. Geriatric Outreach workers, Elder Day Treatment Programs, Multidisciplinary Teams, Senior Information and Assistance, local physicans, Senior Center Directors, emergency workers, nutrition programs, R.S.V.P. and home health care providers should be included and given information regarding the Geriatric Peer Counseling Program. When information is shared, concerns regarding appropriateness of placement and territorialism can be averted and the client will benefit from this coordination of services.

Money won't buy the love I need.
I tell them that, they do not heed;
But bring me pretties and gifts of shoes
And other things I'll never use.
An hour of time you'll never miss.
Just listen while I reminisce
Of flowering gardens
Where I like to toil
Happy with my hands in soil;
Bringing beauty so all could see
The magic of each plant and tree.
I'll tell you of the hush at dawn,
The bird's first sleepy, halting song.
Can you but listen a little while
Before you hasten on your way
And leave me lonely another day?

Florence Brumm (88)
Mount Vernon, Washington
1989

*Illustration from Gerontological & Geriatric Education, 1987-88,
U.S.C. Health Science Campus, Los Angeles, CA, artist unknown.*

PART III

Training Philosophy and Format

GROUP TRAINING PHILOSOPHY AND FORMAT:

The Learning Environment

The Peer Counselor Training material we use comes from a wide range of educational, medical, therapeutic and spiritual systems. Group dynamics and the interactions which take place between the facilitator and the trainees, serves in part, as the model peer counselors will use in their work with clients. The role of the facilitator therefore must be flexible, versatile and open-minded creating a positive learning environment.

Each trainee is encouraged to incorporate this learning within their own life experiences. They are also asked to challenge this new experience and the information presented during the 8-week program. It is our experience that the group members who feel safe to probe this new learning are the ones who, to a greater degree, integrate this information into their own lives and use it in their work with clients. It is this integration of past experiences and new information which creates effective peer counselors.

By encouraging an atmosphere that allows openness and self expressions, a variety of sensitive issues and subjects are able to be covered during the training.

Peer Counselor training and the material presented provides an opportunity for the exploration of issues and feelings in a variety of personal areas. We have always found the groups supportive as members expose their own vulnerability through disclosing various feelings and personal experiences. Recognition of the feelings of others—even when different—is a key element of the training. By encouraging an atmosphere that allows openness and self expressions, a variety of sensitive issues and subjects are able to be covered during the training. The dynamics of the group is one which moves progressively towards bonding, acceptance and increased awareness resulting in effective paraprofessional counseling skills.

Specific Group Training Design

How the training is conducted depends, to some degree, on the size of the group. We have had groups ranging from 6 to 15 trainees. Less than six members does not allow the trainees the valued interactions essential in learning "people skills." The use of dyads and triads is also more difficult with less than six trainees.

More than 15 trainees is difficult for a single facilitator to handle. It is important to give each member of the group time for personal discussion and reflection. With more than 15 trainees and one facilitator the group discussions must be limited and often times less aggressive, shy members can be overlooked and overwhelmed.

Generally, there is about a 5 to 1 ratio of women to men. As the program grows in your community, you may want to seek out male oriented service groups from which to recruit in order to increase male participation. Whether male or female, for their comfort level, be sure to arrange your group to have at least two of the same sex in each training group. A single man with a group of women will most likely drop out.

Our program requires trainees to be at least 55 years or older and there is not an upper age limit. Our oldest trainee is a delightful, energetic 84-year old man. We have, under special circumstances, accepted trainees who are under 55. An important element of the program's success, however, relates to the similarity of peer counselor's ages to the age of their clients. In our experience, the ages of the trainees is less relevant than is their attitude towards their own aging and the aging of others.

The diverse backgrounds and educational levels of the trainees creates the interesting dynamics in the group. We often state that peer counseling is an art, not a science, and therefore intellectual achievements are not the most important requirement. The ability to read and to communicate is, however, essential. We are hoping to encourage bilingual members of our Hispanic community to become trainees, as this is an elderly, homebound population that is often overlooked by services, due to the language barrier. In communities that have a large subculture of non-English speaking members, a Peer Counseling program geared particularly to their cultural needs would certainly be effective and valuable.

In communities that have a large subculture of non-English speaking members, a Peer Counseling program geared particularly to their cultural needs would certainly be effective and valuable.

The wide variety of attitudes, interests, beliefs and experiences on the part of the volunteers gives the agency an advantage when it is time to make a placement. The successful match of a peer counselor to a specific client is often most successful when they can relate to various areas of common experience.

As has been noted, the training occurs within an 50-hour course. It consists of eight 7-hour sessions, 1 day a week for eight weeks. Each session focuses on a specific topic related to the development of counseling skills and mental health education. Each week's training builds on the previous week. Therefore all trainees are asked to commit themselves to faithful attendance throughout the 8-week period.

A variety of subjects are included in the training. Some of this material is designed to increase self-awareness. Other topics are directed towards the demystification of aging or development of counseling skills and techniques. Mental illness, dementia, community support, family systems and case management are each examined in terms of the helper's role as a paraprofessional As the program moves forward subjects are covered with a greater degree of sophistication and depth. Each session builds upon its predecessor and contributes toward the primary learning agenda of enhancing and empowering the peer counselor trainees, by validating their life experiences. A key element of each session is to encourage all trainees to have fun through active participation in the training program. The high rate at which trainees attend all sessions speaks to the success of this model.

The use of handouts, reading lists, field experiences, and journal/workbook activity provides the trainee with a variety of materials to which they can refer during the group discussions. Throughout this manual, handouts are desingated by boxed enclosures. These handouts validate trainees learning experience.

Over the many years that we have presented this course, we have realized that volunteers want to be involved in a project that is purposeful, valid and credible. Our Community College has included this training under its Continuing Education Program, certifying 5 credits in the Human Service Program for completion of the 50-hour course. Our clinic also presents Certification of Achievement

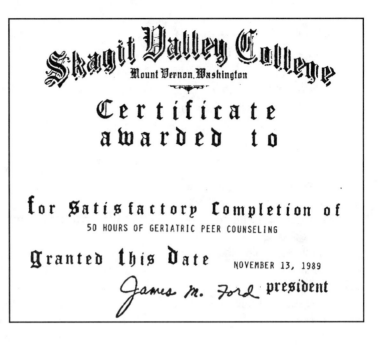

Skagit Valley College
Mount Vernon, Washington

Certificate awarded to

for Satisfactory Completion of
50 HOURS OF GERIATRIC PEER COUNSELING

Granted this Date NOVEMBER 13, 1989

James M. Ford **president**

Awards, signed by the Director of the Agency, to each trainee completing the 50 hours of training. These efforts provide important recognition for participants, giving these volunteers the honor they enjoy and deserve.

The high rate at which trainees attend all sessions speaks to the success of this model.

An informal Graduation Celebration follows the end of the class. We plan a ceremony, ask representatives of our community, state legislators and our Clinic directors to join us. Short speeches, presentation of Certificates of Achievement and congratulations honor the new Peer Counselors. The ceremony is topped off with a potluck and picture taking.

Choosing a Training Facilitator

The agency Program Coordinator may serve as the training facilitator, as is the case in our agency. The value of such a structure allows the trainer to know the agency staff and its system. It allows the facilitator to be involved in the selection of potential trainees and establishes, from the onset, this project as an integral part of the agency's geriatric mental health services.

As the elderly often require a wide range of mental health services, the training facilitator needs to have a strong background in mental health and/or geriatrics. It has been our experience that the training facilitator's tasks are of such a diverse nature that they need to be comfortable with assuming multiple roles, from public speaking to therapeutic interventions.

Basic to a successful program is a facilitator who has had experience as a group leader, who is comfortable with and understands group dynamics and group process.

The facilitator will need to be flexible in their approach to the trainees. They must have the ability to attend to the technical subject matter, as well as the various personal issues raised by group members.

... it is critical to have a professional in this role who truly values the volunteer's work and recognizes the volunteer's potential contribution.

As the tone of the training is set by the facilitator, it is critical to have a professional in this role who truly values the volunteer's work and recognizes the volunteer's potential contribution. Such a coordinator will create a program that becomes a major asset to an agency's mental health program.

The training facilitator represents the Agency to the trainees, as well as to the community, and serves as a role model for mental health services.

An effective role model is one who is spontaneous while creating structure and accepting while setting high expectations. Those personal characteristics which we seek in our peer counselors are very much what we expect from the facilitator; honesty, openness, flexibility, creativity and a high comfort with aging (their own and other's.) The training facilitator will need to be adept at interweaving the trainee's personal concerns with their concerns regarding the new learning materials. The facilitator will need to demonstrate how counseling skills create a relationship which draws from both personal and academic experiences.

The training facilitator must be able to operate independently as well as comfortably with other organizations, as much of the success of this program depends on interactions away from the Agency. A facilitator who knows the community and networks effectively with its many services can bring in the needed adjunct facilitators to the training and lends creditability to the program.

The 7-hour training day is most often intense and demanding for the trainer. They are in the role of teacher, group leader and therapist.

Our agency has chosen to place some consideration on the age of the training facilitator. It has happened that the two coordinators (training facilitators) have been in their 50's and 60's. As this program's philosophy is to use the wisdom of aging and to validate life experience, we choose also to support that philosophy within our own staff. A training facilitator who has had life experiences similar to that of the Peer Counselors can, perhaps, more accurately address the group's needs and style. High energy is also needed by the facilitator in that this position requires the ability to organize a number of concurrent tasks and the ability to work within specific time frames. The 7-hour training day, which occurs one day per week during the eight week training course, is most often intense and demanding for the trainer. The training facilitator acts as a teacher, group leader and therapist.

The facilitator should also be enthusiastic about the training program and the volunteers. This is a vital characteristic. A good facilitator is someone who is able to create an atmosphere of excitement about learning, and one who stimulates the

Graduation Celebration Announcement

Date

Dear Peer Counselor:

You are invited to join the Graduation Celebration for the Fall Peer
Counseling class.

DATE: November 21, 1989

TIME: 1:00 p.m. to 4:00 p.m.

PLACE: Revised Church of the Latter Day Saints, Samish Island
       (please see the map).

Our State Legislator, Representative Harriet Spanel, will be there to speak
and to present the Certificates of Completion. Also present will be representatives of the various Mental Health Clinics.

A Potluck will be served, so please bring your favorite dish. We will provide table service and dessert.

Please come and meet all the Peer Counselors from Skagit, Whatcom,
Island and San Juan Counties.

See You There!

Peer Counselor Coordinator

trainees to take some personal risks while in this program. A facilitator who maintains a sense of humor will give rise to a training program that can deal well with the serious subjects which must be covered in the training.

Adjunct Training Presenters

To add interest to the training classes outside speakers can be used effectively in sharing their expertise with the trainees. This is also an excellent avenue by which to introduce the trainees to other professionals in the field of mental health and senior services. Guest professionals may be from the host agency or from the community. Their presentations add to the trainee's knowledge of networking; which they will need when choosing appropriate services for their clients.

Scheduling of these professionals needs to be prepared well in advance as they are being asked to participate during their work hours and generally with no reimbursement. The following agency staff members and community support services have been presenters for our groups:

- **Senior Information and Assistance**
- **Mental Health Staff**
  Chronic Mental Illness
  Geriatric Mental Health: dementia, depression and chronic pain
  Geriatric Outreach staff
  Mental Health Case Management
  Clinical Record Keeping
- **Senior Center Director**
- **Clergy**
- **Area Agency on Aging Case Management**
- **Retired Senior Volunteer Program (R.S.V.P.)**

Many services that work with older members of the community are excellent resources to bring information to the group and are most eager to do so.

Generally, the time allowed for the adjunct presenter is from one to two hours, depending on the subject being covered.

Post Training Activities

Following the initial training program, peer counselors receive a variety of ongoing educational and supervision experiences. These include:

* Monthly supervision - 2 hours

* Monthly support group - 2 hours

* Bi-Annual Continuing Education - day long workshops

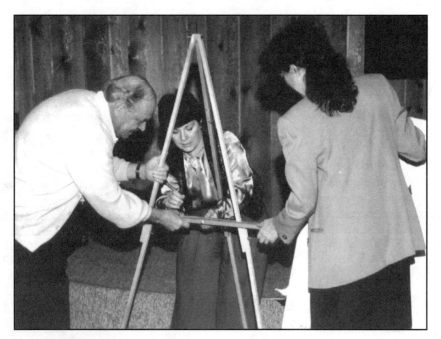

Monthly Supervision

As a clinically based program, mental health staff screen and supervise all cases assigned to the Peer Counseling Program. In many instances, clients referred to peer counselors have been on the case load of a Mental Health professional and are seen as appropriate for transfer to the peer counseling program. All cases have had mental health evaluation and have established treatment plans outlining therapeutic goals and objectives. These are reviewed with peer counselors prior to the transfer and placement.

Ongoing supervision is provided at least monthly, at which time professional staff meet with peer counselors to review treatment progress and assess client treatment goals. The majority of supervision occurs in group meetings involving a staff supervisor and several peer counselors. Each counselor "staffs" his/her client. They are asked to follow an abbreviated, yet formal case presentation style. The peer counselor reports on the client's overall adjustment, specific areas of concern and provides objective observations and life events which may be significant. The peer counselor and supervisor discuss possible treatment plan changes, particularly in areas that may need professional intervention or further action. Supervision is also a time for peer counselors to learn from their supervisors as well as from each other through the case presentation model.

At the monthly supervision meetings, formal progress notes which document each session are turned in and become part of the formal case record. For statistical, as well as clerical purposes, accurate reporting of the peer counselor's clinical contact with clients is required. At the end of each quarter it is exciting to report the extent of direct service the peer counselors have contributed to Agency operations. Our volunteers (over 60) are also registered with R.S.V.P. (Retired Senior Volunteer Program.)

R.S.V.P. involvement allows volunteers to collect mileage reimbursement and receive coverage from the R.S.V.P. auto insurance program. Each peer counselor is asked to turn in monthly R.S.V.P. forms recording their service hours.

Monthly Support Group

Providing homebased counseling to older clients can be rather isolating. Thus it is important to recognize the peer counselor's need for support and contact with other counselors and agency professional staff. We have addressed this need, in part, through a monthly support group which follows group supervision. The peer counselors meet with the program coordinator for a "brown bag" lunch and discussion time. This group is process oriented in contrast to the case orientated supervision time.

The monthly groups can be focused on concerns expressed by the peer counselors or on a generalized subject relating to peer counseling. This group follows the format of the training in that group discussion is encouraged, allowing members to support and validate each other's fears, concerns and successes. This time sustains the feelings of trust and bonding developed during the training and brings experienced peer counselors and new graduates together in a supportive environment.

Thus it is important to recognize the peer counselor's need for support and contact with other counselors and agency professional staff.

Some of the areas of focus have been:

* "Am I doing any good?" * "How do I avoid burn-out"
* "What is this thing called counseling?"
* "How do I get what I need from my Case Manager"

As is evident, this is a time for the Peers to share their frustrations and joys and receive affirmation from each other. Both Supervision and Support Group activity stress the necessity of professional feedback and guidance and are an important part of our model.

Bi-Annual Continuing Education

Bi-annually, the Peer Counseling Program presents a day-long workshop facilitated by an agency or outside professional. The topic may be any of a wide range of issues appropriate to working with geriatric clients and mental illness.

We have presented training workshops on:
* Memory impairment
* Psychotherapy and the Elderly
* Chronic Pain Management
* Stress and Relaxation Techniques/Therapy
* Dementia
* Drug Abuse and Alcoholism in the Aging
* Domestic Abuse in the Elderly

Our workshops always include a grand potluck or catered lunch and time to socialize. In addition to offering formal education, the supervision, support groups, and workshops provide the peer counselors with more informal contact with professional staff. This contributes to the commitment and enthusiasm of the Peer Counselors. We feel the educational and social experiences offered through the Peer Counselor Program are valued by program volunteers and have served as an important factor in maintaining volunteer commitment to this program.

Skagit Community Mental Health Center
COUNSELING AND PSYCHIATRIC SERVICES

March 15, 1980

Dear Peer Counselors,

Our supervision for this month is March 26 from 10:00 – 2:00. Attached you'll find a sample of the progress notes. We hope this will clarify any confusion with these new forms. Please bring your green sheets as we will do a "practice" prog. note during the supervision. If you can't come to supervision please send in your green sheets. Suzy & Liz must have them each month to complete the statistics. Our Continuing Education is Thursday March 29 9 am to 4 pm. Please bring a Pot-luck dish for lunch! Our Speaker is Doug. Uhl m.s. on Counseling skills and Chronic Pain. We will meet at the United Methodist Church in Anacortes, 2200 "H" Ave. We hope to have a very good turn out... Doug is excellent, a therapist and a PHD. Candidate. We has prepared a special training manual for us focusing on this workshop.

See you then,

Betty

40-J

Newsletter

A quarterly newsletter is prepared by the program coordinator and a peer volunteer. It is sent to each of the peer counselors and to supportive community services. The newsletter announces coming events, personal news from individual peer counselors and Agency staff. Specific information on educational events, community workshops and lectures are related to the peers through the newsletter. A message from the coordinator is also included in each issue. The purpose of the Newsletter is to remain informative, informal and personal. It is a fine way to thank and honor individuals for their work and activities.

Contacts with Professionals

The value of a clinic based program is the close supervision and connections between professional staff and peer counselors. Peer Counselors are encouraged to call the Case Manager/Therapist if they have questions or concerns regarding their client. The peer counselor is an important part of the geriatric team and provides a unique and valuable service. Contact with professional staff is also a way for the peer counselor to receive reinforcement and acknowledgement of their effort. We encourage professional staff to take each opportunity to actively connect with the Peer Counselors. It has been our observation that professional staff and peer counselor are both enriched by this contact which relies on the unique perspective of the two parties working together.

Volunteer Placements

We have found that the ideal time to begin placement of Peer Counselors with their first clients is within the last two weeks of the initial training program. At this point peer counselors are eager to try out their newly discovered skills on "real clients." Initial client contact at this time is also helpful to the facilitator in providing information on how trainees have grasped the concepts covered in the training. It allows the trainee in-class time to review their initial meeting with their client, a time to express concerns and feelings within the group, and an opportunity to receive feedback and encouragement.

As in all learning, there is a gap between classroom theory and the actual encounters with the client.

As in all learning, there is a gap between classroom theory and the actual

Skagit Community Mental Health Center

COUNSELING AND PSYCHIATRIC SERVICES

PEER COUNSELING NEWSLETTER

FALL 1989

Dear Peers:

What a memorable four months this has been for me. My emotions have run the gamut from "My God, what have I gotten myself into . . . ." to "This is the greatest job I've ever had!" At this writing, I'm feeling extremely pleased with the training and excited to introduce the new "trainees" to you "veterans." We have 14 trainees in Skagit County. We are sad to report one of our trainees, Patricia Treadwell, suffered a mild stroke and was forced to drop out. The good news is that she is now stronger and gaining some of her vision back. She hopes to be well enough to be a part of the Spring Training.

Whatcom County training session has a class of seven. Yes, I do the Skagit training on Mondays and the Whatcom training on Wednesdays. And yes, I am "pooped" on Thursdays!

I want to thank each one of you for your expressions of warmth and acceptance! With your support, I have been able to "learn" my job with much less stress and with a greater degrees of success.

So . . . thank you! Thank you! Thank you!

TRANSIENT !

This will not come as a surprise to you who have been with us over the past 5 years, but we have again been moved! We are temporarily "housed" in the old Planned Parenthood Building at 1023 South 3rd. Susan, Lynn, Liz and myself are considering putting wheels on our desks! The rumor is that we will be back into the renovated 108 Broadway building some time in January. However, we have a "moving pool" with all of us making odds as to the actual date that we're back in our offices can still reach us at the 336-3193 phone number.

PEANUTS

208 Kincaid, Mount Vernon, WA 98273 • (206) 336-3193

Our Director, Jere LaFollette, Martha Day, Susan Gardner and myself continue to work towards the completion of the Training Manual. Our target date is January 31, 1990.

QUARTERLY CONTINUING EDUCATION EVENT

Judy Lemon, M.A., psychotherapist from Whatcom Counseling and Psychiatric Clinic will facilitate the quarterly workshop for Peer Counselors on Relaxation, Stress management counseling, and Imagery: A "How to" for both you and your client. The date is Tuesday, October 31, at the United Methodist Church in Anacortes (see attached map).

The training day will begin at 9:30 with coffee and a time for the Peer Counselors to meet the "trainees." From 10:00 - 12:00 we will plan and discuss the future support meetings for Peer Counselors, establish criteria for those support groups and gather ideas for the actual implementation of such groups in Whatcom, Island, San Juan and Skagit Counties. We will break for a potluck luncheon at noon, at which time Judy Lemon will join us. She will facilitate the group training from 1:00 - 4:00.

This is the first Continuing Education Workshop since the June program, on Memory, by James De Long. I plan to have the next workshop at the end of January. The workshop will be on Chronic Pain and Counseling. All Peer Counselors on active status are expected to participate. Those on leave are welcome to attend.

Please bring your favorite Potluck dish, and a blanket and pillow to use for the relaxation exercises. Plates, cups, and silverware will be provided.

We understand from Fred Meyer's that they chose the picture of Elmyra Nelson and Evelyn Cornish to put into their Annual Report . . . "Fame Comes To Skagit Valley Ladies!"

A special word of thanks to Lucetta Cleveland, who has begun to select and "sanitize" client information which will be used in the research portion of the Grant. Thanks to Evelyn Cornish, who reviewed articles and books on Schizophrenia and Chronic Mental Illness for us. We may be able to use some in the Continuing Education Workshops.

More thank yous to all of you who posed for the pictures at LaConner Flats. I used many of those pictures in articles for the recruitment of trainees. I'll bring those articles and pictures on Tuesday.

Well, it seems clients have a way of finding their own Peer Counselor. I heard a great story of how Barbara McKechnie was "picked" by one such client. She'll have to tell you about it!

From Whatcom, the news is of Harriet Napecinski's successful stage production. We also understand she has taken on a new client . . . Busy Woman!

George Meintel assisted me in the Whatcom group on "Loss and Grief." Thanks George, for your valuable addition to the group.

There have been some staff changes at Whatcom Clinic, with a new Case Manager, David Tobin, joining Kathy Coe-Vetter and Mike Yeager. They appear to be a good team of supervisors.

Island County Mental Health has also had staff changes. Pat Wold has retired and Kenny Tam is her replacement. His background is in Geriatric Mental Health, so we are very hopeful that the Island County Peer Counselors will be receiving more extensive supervision in the future. Joan and Roger Wilson, Edeath Linderman and Jack Hinton (new trainees) met with I.M.H. to encourage the support of our program.

Warmly, Betty

42-0

encounters with the client. Training and supervisory staff would be wise to keep in mind their own experiences when first out of graduate school and into an agency—how expectations of doing "miracle cures and healings" were overshadowed by anxiety and the fact that often clients did not respond in keeping with the textbook theories. Peer Counselors have the same expectations and fears. It is therefore, most important that staff keep reinforcing the value of the counseling process. The trainer will need to reinforce the concepts unique to working with geriatric mental health clients. These concepts are basic to the training, yet often subtle and difficult for the peer counselors to internalize until they have actually worked with clients for some time.

Reinforcement from professional mental health workers must emphasize that counseling this population means slow, consistent, "being there," often, with little evidence of change. It is particularly important that the peer counselor be reminded of this during the first two months of their initial placement. It's also important that the peer counselor remember the enormous value of maintaining the status of an older client. Making small additions to the quality of their lives through a trusted relationship is a treatment goal.

The peer counselor is asked to review and sign a nine month commitment contract before placement. To begin, each peer counselor is initially assigned to one client. Later, many peer counselors choose to take on a second client. The placements are based on the facilitator's knowledge of the peer counselor and the Case Manager's or Therapist's knowledge of the client. Agency staff attempt to find commonalities between the Peer Counselor and the client, such as nationality, life or work experience, religious background, or physical situation. Successful placement scenarios might be 1) a peer counselor who is placed with a client who worked in the same or a similar industry or occupation; 2) the widow of an Alzheimer's victim placed with a client suffering from dementia, or, 3) with a client suffering from depression due to grief. Placement is often successful when the peer counselor and the client have a common event or experience which they both value.

Our program has recently begun to have peer counselors fill out adjective inventory surveys at the beginning of the training sessions. These inventories are then scored and reviewed when placements are discussed. They supplement the specific knowledge

It is the role of the professional to evaluate the client's needs and areas of concern, in order to most effectively support and guide the Peer Counselor in their interactions with the client.

and observations that the facilitator has gathered during the training period. It serves as useful background information when assessing placements.

Matching the Peer Counselor's and the client's geographic location is also an important placement consideration. Peers travel to the client's homes on a weekly basis, therefore it should be within a comfortable travel distance for the peer counselor. If communities have transit systems, which some Peer Counselors may use, the client's residence needs to be within walking distance of the bus line. Every attempt should be made to make the placement as easy as possible for the peer counselor. In large rural areas with no transit system, the program needs to recruit Peer Counselors from the remote areas.

The supervisor, case manager or therapist must determine if a client can benefit from a peer counselor and how that peer counselor will fit into the client's treatment plan. It is the role of the professional to evaluate the client's needs and areas of concern, in order to most effectively support and guide the Peer Counselor in their interactions with the client. Again we state, as a clinically oriented program, professionals are augmenting their services to clients with peer counselors. The client's needs are always the priority, with the needs of the peer counselor as a secondary concern.

Clinical Accountability

An agency using a Peer Counseling program must instruct the peer counselors in the State regulations related to services, Record Keeping and Confidentiality. This is presented as part of the training and reinforced through the requirements of monthly Clinical Progress Reports. Our agency has developed a Progress Report form for the peer counselors, which gives Peer Counselors indicators to use when documenting the weekly sessions. The peer counselor reports date, length of visit, and a comment as to the context of the visit, then signs the progress note. The format follows the S.O.A.P. type of recording used by most agencies. These Progress Reports are kept in the client's charts and are referred to by professionals when doing 90-day Quality Assurance evaluations or Treatment Plan changes. We stress the importance of the Progress Notes in documenting observations and client treatment as well as serving as basic information from which statistical reports on the Peer Counseling program are prepared.

Confidentiality of the client sessions is emphasized from the first day of training. The model set in the training sessions admonishes that "what individuals share in the group stays in the group." The Peers are instructed to use only their client's first name during the monthly group supervision. Again, this acts as a reminder of the element of confidentiality that must be honored in this work.

Peer Counselors are asked to sign Assurance of Confidentiality forms during the training sessions after they have read the State regulations pertaining to the rights of clients. These forms are kept at the agency in the Volunteer's personnel folder. Some agencies may also choose to have the volunteers sign a Volunteer Agreement form or Commitment Contract.

A Volunteer Personnel Folder contains:

Application form

Dates of training and Completion of Training

Assurance of Confidentiality

Client's Rights form (W.A.C.)

Clinic Volunteer form

Commitment Contract

Termination form

Skagit Community Mental Health Center
208 Kincaid • Mount Vernon, Washington 98273-3193

Barriers and Trouble Shooting

In even the most successful programs, problems can arise that call for evaluation, mediation, or other actions on the part of the agency staff and supervisors. This agency has an established grievance procedure which is available to volunteers in resolving conflicts. First, the peer counselor and their clinical supervisor meet to attempt a resolution of the issue in question. The next step is for the clinical supervisor, the program coordinator and the peer counselor to meet. If no resolution can be arrived at at this level, the peer counselor has the option to request a meeting with the agency director. It is important for the peer counselors to feel that their work is valued to the point that the agency will go to great lengths to assure that they are treated fairly and with consideration for their point of view in every situation.

> *In even the most successful programs, problems can arise that call for evaluation, mediation, or other actions on the part of the agency staff and supervisors.*

drawing by Ken Morgan, SCMHC, 1993

Termination of a Client Relationship

While we strive for compatible placements, there will be some situations which will require the professional to reevaluate the client's need for a Peer Counselor. Some situations that would justify the termination of the client from the Peer Counseling relationship include:

- When a client is abusive or combative towards the peer counselor;

- When a client's condition deteriorates to such a point that peer services are counter-therapeutic;

- When the client exhibits behaviors of pathological dependency on the peer counselor and the prognosis for change appears to be doubtful.

- When a client has increased independence, has resolved the crisis by developing new coping skills, and has created a sufficient support system outside the mental health setting to continue a healthy existence.

Termination of a Peer Counselor

The various screening devices and the demands of the training often are self-screening instruments. However, some situations may lead to the termination of a peer counselor from the program these would include:

- Inability or unwillingness, on the part of the Peer Counselor, to adhere to the treatment plan designed for the client;

- Inability or unwillingness to attend regular monthly supervision or to complete regular Progress Notes;

- Inconsistence or inactivity with the client due to the Peer Counselor's lack of motivation or interest;

- Inappropriate behavior with a client, such as the proselytizing of beliefs, whether religious or political; inappropriate physical contacts; or financial indiscretions;

- Repeated evidence of poor judgement in interactions with the client or support services;

- Breach of confidentiality.

When a volunteer is "counseled out" of the program, it is hoped that it can be for the benefit of the Peer Counselor as well as for the benefit of the program. In our years with this project we have only had one experience in which the peer counselor was terminated as a result of an inability to work within the above established

Review of R.C.W.
and W.A.C. Regulations
Related to Client Rights

I have received a copy of and read:

WAC	275-56-230	- Client Rights
WAC	275-56-235	- Protection of Client Rights
WAC	275-56-240	- Confidentiality of Information
RCW	71.05.360-440	- Rights and Confidentiality
WAC	275-55-241	- Related to Involuntary Treatment

The regulations are related to the protection of client rights and I understand that it is the policy of the Skagit Community Mental Health Center to ensure that these requirements and client rights are adhered to.

_____   _____

Signature   Date

Volunteer Commitment Contract

I agree to:

_____ make a nine-month commitment as a peer counselor;

_____ attend the monthly meeting for peer counselors;

_____ attend Quarterly Workshops

_____ see my client weekly or as stated in the treatment plan;

_____ keep agency paperwork current;

_____ consult with project Coordinator regarding:
- times I am unable to see my clients;
- difficulties I am having with client relationships;
- personal issues that may interfere with counseling;
- termination of cases;

In addition, I agree that all information shared with me about a client or about another peer counselor is to be kept confidential within the program.

I understand this is a contract in good faith between myself and Skagit Communmity Mental Health Center. If, at any time, I am unable to maintain this contract, I will advise the Program Coordinator.

_____   _____   _____   _____
Peer Counselor   Date   Program Coordinator   Date

PEER COUNSELING
Assurances of Confidentiality

As an employee, student, volunteer, or acting in any other capacity in connection with the Skagit Community Mental Health Center, I agree to the following:

1. All charts, notes and other written material concerning clients will be locked up when I am not using them.

2. Discussions regarding clinic clients will be held in staff offices or other places which assure privacy.

3. No privileged information about clients will be discussed with family or friends.

4. Privileged information, written or verbal, which is to be shared with other agencies and professionals, written authorization will first be obtained from the client.

5. Access to client files is limited to Clinic professional and clerical staff and graduate students supervised by Clinic professional staff. Access to client files by anyone else must be approved by the Director.

Date _____ Signature_____

Training Evaluation

In order to develop the best training program available, we rely on your feedback. Please think through each question carefully and give us your honest opinion.

1. Give your overall reaction to this program

very useful   useful   somewhat useful   not very useful   not at all useful

2. In what ways was it particularly effective? (Please be specific).

3. In what ways might it have been more effective? (Give specific examples).

4. Please rate on a scale of 1 to 5 each component of this training. 5 is very satisfied. 1 is unsatisfied. Please comment about each.

a.	Basic Principles of Counseling	_____
b.	Listening /Communication Skills	_____
c.	Transitions in Aging	_____
d.	Issues of Death and Dying	_____
e.	Loss and Grief	_____
f.	Mental Disorders	_____
g.	Stress Management	_____
h.	Family Relationships	_____
i.	Community Resources	_____

5. How satisfied were you with the way your instructor functioned?

very satisfied   satisfied   somewhat satisfied   not very satisfied   not at all satisfied

6. In what ways was your leader particularly helpful?

7. In what ways could your leader have been more helpful?

8. What do you plan to do differently as a result of this program?

9. Comments:

Questionnaire developed by Oakland University Rochester, Michigan

guidelines. Program staff must be aware of the real and personal situations of Peer Counselors. This may mean taking the initiative at times, and raising the question as to the counselor's need for a respite from serving clients.

The Peer Counselor may experience a particularly stressful period or a difficult life event, at which time it is appropriate for the peer counselor to take a Leave of Absence. Clearly, the mental status of the peer counselor will directly determine their effectiveness with program clients. This program is de-signed to enhance the Peer Counselor's mental health and to encourage a sensitivity to their own needs.

> *This program is designed to enhance the Peer Counselor's mental health and to encourage a sensitivity to their own needs.*

Program Evaluations

A necessary part of this program is to constantly review feedback in order to produce quality training and services. As "peer counseling" is a relatively new service model, we are continuing to refine our program to meet the growing demands in the geriatric field.

> *As "peer counseling" is a relatively new service model, we are continuing to refine our program to meet the growing demands in the geriatric field.*

The program is unique because of it's significant use of volunteers within a mental health agency. Therefore, periodical reviews are needed.

The training sessions allow for weekly feedback for the facilitator, who can evaluate the usefulness of the materials covered in the previous week's session. A final paper or evaluation of the program is completed by peer counselors at the end of the initial 8-week training period.

Continuing education evaluations are completed at the end of each workshop. These are compiled and sent to the workshop Presenters for their review.

The monthly Support Groups are designed to allow Peer Counselors to discuss and resolve any issues that may arise concerning their supervision. While this is an informal process of evaluation, it is closely attended to and suggestions raised are acted upon by the coordinator and the clinical supervisors. Personality conflicts or other personnel issues are evaluated in one to one meetings with the Program Supervisor, appropriate interventions are used to resolve issues.

78

LAST WORDS: *How To Stay Alive*

Here is our final advice for those who want to see their community-based volunteer programs continue and grow.

A. Have Conviction

Believe in what you are doing. That belief will be the source of your well of energy. A prime example of what belief can do is our belief that trust in trained volunteers will lead to their evolution as valued team members. There is a cyclical process involved that is illustrated below.

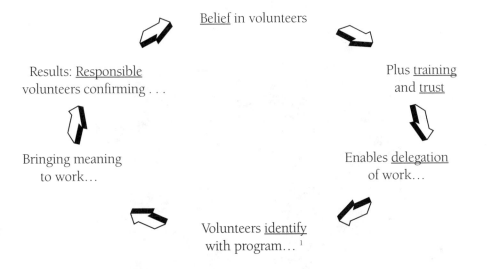

Belief in volunteers

Plus training and trust

Results: Responsible volunteers confirming . . .

Enables delegation of work…

Bringing meaning to work…

Volunteers identify with program… [1]

B. Hustle

Be on the lookout for everything you can get for free – food, transportation, services, facilities, utilities. Adopt the ten rules below as your program modus operandi:

1. Try to get it for nothing.
2. If you can't, try to get it for cost.
3. Do not try to do it yourself. Find the right person to do the job. Recruit people for the specific job.
4. Involve as many people as possible. Do not rely on just a faithful few.
5. Have a plan of action.
6. Have a goal to reach. Be realistic, but exceed the goal if possible.
7. Have a time frame. Keep it short.

1. *The Connection*, Skagit County Volunteer Action Program

8. Always evaluate the process. Involve everyone.
9. Always remember to say "thanks."
10. Keep good records on everything you do. (maintain a "paper trail")

C. Build a Broad base in the community.
Involve volunteers of all sorts and member organizations.

D. Establish a presence.
Do your publicity homework.

E. Become essential.
Using informal feedback and formal needs assessments, design and provide a quality program. Invite other service providers to evaluate you.

Source: "The Connection", Skagit County Volunteer Action Program.

PART IV

Week-by-Week Sessions

Yearly Time Frame for a New Program

Based on a Spring and Fall Training.

JANUARY
* Coordinator to meet with Advisory Committee, Agency Staff and Community Senior Services.
* Arrange for Training Site.
* Secure and schedule training adjunct presenters.
* Review all materials for training, compiling resources.

FEBRUARY/MARCH
* Begin intensive public relations campaign, announcing upcoming training. Begin at least 10 weeks prior to actual training date.

APRIL
* Spring Training Course

MAY
* Bi-annual Continuing Education Seminar.
* Placement of Peers with Clients—last week of training.

JUNE
* Newspaper follow-up articles.
* Follow-up with Senior Support Services.
* Monthly Supervision begins.
* Monthly Support Group begins.
* Quarterly Peer Newsletter.

JULY
* Summer social activity.

AUGUST
* Begin public relations and advertisement for Fall Training.
* Prepare materials for training.
* Arrange for Training Site.
* Secure and schedule adjunct trainers.
* Continue support of experienced Peer Counselors, using them to increase community awareness of program (speaking at meetings, newspaper articles, etc.)

SEPTEMBER
* Fall Training—optimal time is mid-September after Labor Day, as many seniors are vacationing until late September.
* Complete Fall Training before the Thanksgiving holidays begin.

NOVEMBER
* Placement of Peers with Clients—last week of training.
* Quarterly Peer Newsletter
* Newspaper follow-up articles.
* Monthly Support Groups.
* Monthly Supervision.
* Integration of new Peer Counselors into existing group.

FEBRUARY
* Materials review.
* Preparation for Spring Training.

WEEK BY WEEK TRAINING SESSIONS

Sample Training Schedule and Time Frames

Each Training Schedule follows a consistent and routine format, lending structure and comfort for the trainee. While there are a variety of ways your group may want to proceed, the following is the formula we have used with a great deal of success:

Sample Schedule

9:00 - 9:15	Socialization: coffee and donuts.
9:15 - 10:15	1) "Temperature Reading." Check-in time for trainees to clear up issues from last session, to give personal report to group without feedback.
	2) Brief Introduction of day's focus by facilitator. Brief review of day's events.
	3) Handouts (if not in workbook.)
10:15 - 10:30	Break time. Members must have these breaks to stretch, move about and informally interact with peers.
10:30 - 10:45	An experiential exercise to bring active awareness of the day's topic. (If the speaker of the day requires two hours for presentation, this exercise may be omitted.)
10:45 - 11:00	Reflection time or group discussion pertaining to exercise or day's topic.
11:00 - 12:00	Topic of Study or Speaker's presentation.
12:00 - 1:00	Brown bag lunch—try to encourage trainees to include out-of-doors activity or meditation during this time.
1:00 - 3:00	Presentation of day's topic by Facilitator or Speaker. Using group discussions, dyads, triads or role play.
3:00 - 3:15	Break time.
3:15 - 3:30	An experiential exercise on focus of topic.
3:30 - 4:00	Group discussion and closure. Closure is a time for summarizing the day's learning.

We have found that the trainer's anxiety about filling a day-long training session quickly disappears after the first training session. Trainees are so enthusiastic about learning that they can keep a session going with seemingly minor encouragement from the facilitator.

Crabbed Old Woman

What do you see nurses, what do you see?,   What are you thinking when you look at me?
A crabbed old woman, not very wise,
Uncertain of habit, with faraway eyes
Who dribbles her food and makes no reply,   When you say in a loud voice, "I do wish you'd try"
Who seems not to notice the things that you do,
And forever is losing a stocking or shoe
Who, unresisting or not, lets you do as you will,   With bathing and feeding, the long day to fill
Is that what you're thinking, is that what you see?
Then open your eyes, you're not looking at me.

I'll tell you who I am as I sit here so still,   As I move at your bidding, as I eat at your will
I'm a small child of ten with a father and mother,
Brothers and sisters who love one another
A young girl at sixteen with wings on her feet,   Dreaming that soon now a lover she'll meet
A bride soon at twenty - my heart gives a leap,
Remembering the vows that I promised to keep
At twenty-five now I have young of my own,   Who need me to build a secure happy home
A woman of thirty my young now grown fast,
Bound to each other with ties that should last
At forty the young ones will soon all be gone,   But my man stays beside me to see I don't mourn
At fifty once more babies play round my knee,
Again we know children, my loved one and me
Dark days are upon me, my husband is dead,   I look to the future, I shudder with dread
For my young are all busy rearing young of their own
And I think of the years and the love I have known
I'm an old woman now and nature is cruel,   'Tis her jest to make old age look like a fool
The body it crumbles, grace and vigor depart,
And now there's a stone, where I once had a heart.
But inside this carcass a young girl still dwells,   And now and again my battered heart swells.

I remember the joys, I remember the pain,   And I'm loving and living life over again
I think of the years all too few—gone so fast,
And accept the stark fact that nothing can last
So open your eyes, nurses, open and see,   Not a crabbed old woman - look closer - see me.

Anonymous
This poem was found among the possessions
of an elderly Irish woman who had died in a geriatric hospital.

SESSION I

Beginning the Journey Together

Session I

Session Guide To the Trainer

Begin by helping trainees to understand the word "Process". Process is the basis for this training and for developing counseling skills. Process is the journey.

Your style and manner during the first session will be critical to the remaining training sessions. You are the model counselor; what you do and how you relate to the trainees will set the stage for the many interactions which will develop in this group. The trainee will respect your expertise if you present it in a relaxed, easy manner with a willingness to disclose your feelings, thoughts and reactions.

Validation of their comments, reactions and even shyness during these initial exercises will lead to increased risk taking as the training develops.

The experiential exercises begin with non-threatening interactions. While many trainees are willing participants, they are also anxious to "do it right" and are unfamiliar with the therapeutic techniques that are commonplace for the facilitator. Validation of an individual's comments, reactions and even shyness during these initial exercises will lead to increased risk taking as the training develops.

Be the observer as you begin, in order to understand the trainee's interactions styles.

Review the techniques of role playing. Emphasize the sharing of real life experiences and how this is beneficial to the trainee and to the training process. Review the techniques of "Temperature Reading" as developed by Virginia Satir. At the beginning of each session, give each group member the opportunity to clarify issues from the previous week. Allow them to share 2-3 minutes of feelings, thoughts, and observations without feedback from the group.

Session Materials

* Large newsprint flip chart
* Marking pens
* Coffee, cups, etc.
* Workbook - Journals for each trainee
* Easel
* Extra pencils/pens

Session I

Beginning The Journey Together

> *"When the student is ready,*
> *the teacher will appear."*
>
> A Zen Teaching

Today's Goal

- Introduction of peer counseling to the trainees to create allegiance to the program.
- Introduction of group format and structure.
- Encouragement of group interactions to begin bonding process.

Strategy

Validation of each group member by acknowledging individual stories and/or encouraging the expression of fears and expectations. Use experiential exercises to dissipate anxiety and to begin to create the feeling of "membership."

Learning Objectives

- Establish the basic philosophy of the Peer Counseling Program.
- Make "learning" an active participation process.
- Establish the importance of the group's interpersonal bonding.

Handouts and Workbook Materials

Welcome letter
Training syllabus
Class roster
Suggested field experiences
10 Commandments for volunteer
Folklore and nonsense of age

Mental health & aging
Vocabulary of feelings
Guide for successful peer counseling
How We Can Help
What does helping mean?
Enhancement of Self Awareness

And So We Begin . . . Session I

I. Introduction of Staff

A welcome by a representative from your Agency, such as the director or clinical supervisor, etc.

A personal introduction from the training facilitator with a brief background of that individual's education, connection with the Agency and personal history.

Introduction of Trainees

Allow an hour for this activity, giving time for each trainee to share with the group a bit of personal history. Using the following exercise at this time will act as an "ice breaker" and encourage group interaction.

Experiential Exercise - "Ice Breaker"

Trainees form dyads, choosing a member of the group who is least familiar to them. Each member of the dyad is asked to spend 3-4 minutes sharing with their partner how or why they have chosen the Peer Counseling Program as a volunteer interest. Regroup, and ask each trainee to introduce a partner and share one piece of information they learned during their exchange. Ask each trainee to be aware of any feelings they are experiencing during this exercise.

II. Stages of reactions to a new situation

Encourage trainees to identify with any of the following stages (write out stages on newsprint.)

1. Anxiety - results from the natural fear of the unknown.
2. Chaos - seems to prevail because we have never done this before or have no model.
3. Integration - occurs when we have spent some time with this new expe rience and have found ways to manage it and have survived.[1]

Group Discussion

How have you dealt with new experiences in the Past?
What do you see as your "style" of coping with a new situation?
Is there any part you would like to change?

Key Element -

Create an atmosphere that will allow for the expression of differences and the appreciation of the difficulties one experiences in unknown situations.

1. *Effectiveness Training Conference, 1980.*

III. Confidentiality

Peer counselor trainees create a group in which the sharing of personal experiences and self disclosure are essential to the learning process. Stress the need for trust and your expectation that each member will honor the other members' needs for confidentiality.

WHAT IS SHARED IN THIS ROOM, STAYS IN THIS ROOM

Values of Confidentiality

* Encourages openness and honesty in a group.

* Is an integral part of building a relationship.

* Keeps the integrity of the helping relationship in place.
  (Allow for discussion time and questions.)

What is Peer Counseling?

Geriatric peer counseling is a relationship between two people wherein one is trained to give service to the other. They share a common age and common experiences and through that they create a trusting atmosphere. This facilitates change.

• Peer counseling differs from professional counseling in the following ways:

• Peer counseling allows for a more equal relationship and less intimidation.

• Peer counselor's knowledge is often experiential while the professional's knowledge tends to be formal/academic.

• Peer counselors are not able to diagnose or to create treatment plans.

• Peer counseling also differs from friendship in that the relationship is not coming from a mutual point and the client is the focus.

Group Discussion

Using newsprint, have trainees list the many ways in which peer counseling differs from either 1) friendship or 2) professional counseling.

---

*"The best antidote to fear is
to know all we can about a situation."*
John Glenn

IV. Enhancing Interpersonal Relationships With Group Members

Experiential Exercise - "Learning Group Names"

Ask group to stand, join in a circle. Have each trainee state his or her name and the name of the person to their right. Each trainee repeats in turn, all the names of the group members before them in the circle. Since remembering all the names in the group becomes difficult, the group members have fun and are rewarded for their efforts by cheers and applause from the group.

Key Element -

Facilitator sets the stage for the level of energy, encouraging spontenaity and acceptance. A non-judgmental atmosphere is essential. Playfulness is encouraged.

V. Closing

Housekeeping details need to be addressed, such as:

How to handle absences -

Trainees call facilitator if they must miss class. More than two weeks of absences are difficult to make up and interfere with the group dynamics. This needs to be resolved right away.

Concerns regarding evaluations or "tests" -

Dispel such fears with emphasis on the trainee's skills and knowledge they have used to this point in their lives. Help the trainee to focus on the training as a process. Review any questions about the field experience requirement.

VI. Summarization

We encourage a summarization of the day's topics and concerns covered in the first session. Trainees are eager to take home a clear sense of accomplishment and a bit of new knowledge. This builds excitement and leads to increased participation.

Recommended Readings

Alpaugh, P. and Haney M. *"Counseling the Older Adult."* Lexington Books. 1985. D.C. Health & Co., Lexington, Mass.

Weininger, Ben and Eva L. Menkin. *Aging is a Lifelong Affair.* Los Angeles: Guide of Tutors Press. 1978.

SESSION I

Handouts & Workbook Materials

Syllabus

SESSION I
Beginning the Journey Together
Introduction of Peer Counseling
Getting to know each other

SESSION II
Aging, Your Body, Your Mind, Your Emotions
The physiology and psychology of Aging
Confidential forms and Agency Registration

SESSION III
Beginning Communication Skills
Are you listening?
Record Keeping and Case Management

SESSION IV
Levels of the Helping Model
Stage I   Problem Clarification
Stage II   Goals
Stage III Action

SESSION V
Loss, Grief and Mourning
Using counseling skills with loss and grief

SESSION VI
Death and Dying
Grief work and counseling skills
Family and Spiritual issues

SESSION VII
Mental Health Problems of Aging
Depression, dementia and anxiety disorders
Cognitive and behavioral disorders
Chronic mental illness
Affective disorders

SESSION VIII
Synthesis of Counseling Skills
Initial meeting with client

WELCOME TO THE TRAINEES

We celebrate with you the beginning of the training program. We are excited to have you with us in this wonderful learning experience. We believe that you are excited, too.

The weeks to come are designed to provide you with information and skills that build on each other. Blended with the learning and integration of new facts will be the continuing opportunity for each of you to learn more about yourself. It is in the combination of these learnings that we can become more effective in our relationships with one another in every area of our lives. This will, in turn, contribute to our being more effective and satisfying counselors to the clients we see when our training is completed.

Within the training period, we will be providing you with reprints and handouts relating to each session. These will be reminders and reinforcers of the material from the session. You are encouraged to keep your own personal Journal. The combination can become a splendid chronicle of the entire training and a record you might want to refer to later.

The Agency is pleased to offer this training to prepare you for counseling older adults. We are proud to provide a caring service to our older citizens whose lives may be enriched through their contacts with you.

So - Let Us Begin The Journey

PEER COUNSELING PROGRAM
Suggested Field Experiences

As a part of basic training, peer counselors are expected to participate weekly in some type of field experience or observation in their communities until they have a regular assignment. Below are various learning opportunities you might like to try. You may discuss your experiences in our scheduled practice sessions.

- Observe Alzheimer's Support Group. Introduce self and observe. By the end of the meeting, identify at least one need of these families that could be addressed by a peer counselor. Check accuracy of your observation with a member.

- Observe and, if asked, assist with one or more Geriatric Day Treatments. Take brown bag lunch as eating together is an important activity. No more than two at a time.

- Visit one or more Nursing Homes. Establish a working relationship with at least one patient and help him/her tell his/her story to you. Assist with other needs as identified by Social Services Director to the extent you feel comfortable. Observe groups, if available. No more than two at a time here, too. 10:00 A.M. is the best time to arrive.

  Burton's Nursing Home   1036 Victoria, Burlington

  Barth Nursing Home   1407 - 5th, Anacortes

  Mira Vista Care Center   1020 N. 8th, Mount Vernon

- Have lunch at least once at a Senior Center. Make reservation at least a day ahead. Approach an elderly person and get him/her to tell his/her story to you. Try not to sit near anyone you know well.

  Anacortes Senior Center   293-7473
  Concrete Senior Center   853-8400
  Mount Vernon Senior Center   336-5757
  Burlington Senior Center   755-9998
  Sedro-Woolley Senior Center   855-1531

TEN COMMANDMENTS FOR VOLUNTEERS AND PROFESSIONAL STAFF

For Volunteers

1. Understand the job you undertake to do.

2. Accept training appreciatively, and contribute your knowledge and experience.

3. Match your interests to the needs around you and therefore to the job.

4. Serve with faithfulness and continuity, listen for and report new insights about your work.

5. Discover its meaning to the total program of which it is a part.

6. Open yourself to opportunities for growth – in skills, empathy, self-confidence, and responsibility.

7. Value your special two-way role as community interpreter.

8. Contribute to supervision by self-evaluation and a willingness to ask.

9. Give loyalty to your institution, its staff, and its program.

For Professionals

1. Do not describe the job as it is not. Don't minimize the time or ability it takes.

2. Offer well-planned program of training and supervision.

3. Concern yourself with the volunteer as a person, not an object.

4. Expect basic ability and reliability and then build on them sharing understanding. Do not confuse people with jargon. Language is to be used not to confuse, but to enlighten; not to obstruct, but to communicate.

5. Be ready to place when you recruit.

6. Give the volunteer a significant task. Don't equate volunteers with untrained persons.

7. Inform volunteers. Make them insiders too. They are non-paid staff.

8. Evalute the volunteer

9. Trust the volunteer.

10. Give proper recognition.

Source: Adapted from writings of Dr. Daniel Thiersz and Mrs. Leonard Weiner

The Folklore and Nonsense of Aging

Here are a few of the leading examples of folklore about age. A surprising number of people, including doctors and hospital administrators, believe them.

Myth: Most old people live in institutions - hospitals, nursing homes, etc.
FACT: The actual figure is just five percent for all persons over sixty-five.

Myth: Most old people are constantly in bed because of illness.
FACT: They get fewer acute illnesses than younger people, 1.3 illnesses per person per year as against 2.1 for all ages. True, 81 percent of people over sixty-five have some chronic problems, as against 54 percent of all people below that age, but this need be nothing worse than short sight or hay fever.

Myth: After sixty-five everyone goes steadily downhill.
FACT: In a Duke University longitudinal study, 44 to 58 percent of patients who returned for checkups had no detectable deterioration in physical condition, and some had improved over periods from three to thirteen years. True, some people do suddenly get sick and decline, but this can happen in earlier life, too, and is called illness, not aging. For all people over sixty-five, 51 percent rate their health as good, 33 percent as fair, and 16 percent as poor. About half or more of any decline is due to boredom, inactivity and the awareness that it is expected of you.

Myth: Old people typically live alone, abandoned by family and lonely.
FACT: In the United States, 80 percent of people over sixty-five live with someone else; 75 percent say that they are "not often alone," and 86 percent saw one or more relatives during the previous week, according to a typical study done by Dr. Ethel Shanas. It doesn't of course follow that none of these people are lonely or neglected, but the stereotype is clearly way off.

Myth: People should retire at a certain age. Older people cannot do a decent job.
FACT: Quite apart from knocking this statement down with numbers of artists, musicians, writers and other professionals who have done good work until they died, it is more to the point to stress that such persisting usefulness is the rule. Older industrial workers have a 20 percent better absenteeism record than younger workers. They also have fewer disabling and nondisabling injuries.

Myth: You can't teach an old dog new tricks.
FACT: …Learning ability … laying accident or disease aside, doesn't diminish with advancing age. The fact is that in the course of having learned so much, an older person has acquired more finely developed techniques for learning than younger people possess, and this may actually enhance that ability. He or she knows how to go about the task.

Myth: The "Aging" are past their prime.
FACT: What does it mean? At 40, Gaylord Perry won the 1978 National League Cy Young Award. In his middle 40's George Blanda was still a premiere place-kicker. Picasso was producing master works in his 90s. George Burns in his 90s insists: I can't die. I'm booked!" On the other hand, the brilliant Russian gymnast Olga Korbut seems to have passed her prime at age 20.

Myth: Thinking slows up as you age.
FACT: Should ordinary thinking activity slow down or go haywire, it is owing to disease or disorder and not to age. There are too many very bright, very old people around to allow the myth that aging brings a decline in thinking ability to stand.

Myth: Intelligence declines with age.
FACT: Opinion - When older people do poorly on some intelligence tests, it might be because they have trouble taking seriously test material that seems dull, pointless or silly.

Myth: Retirement will kill you.
FACT: The sensible person doesn't really retire. He or she changes activities or occupation. Abandonment kills, not retirement.

Myth: Old people are more likely to become depressed.
FACT: All things considered, of course, growing old in our culture can be a depressing experience. But actually, while depression might be an accompaniment of age, age in itself doesn't cause it.… It is, therefore facllacious to regard the disorder as a condition of age.

Taken from A Good Age by Alex Comfort. © Mitchell Beazley Publishers Limited. 1976. Used by permission of Crown Publishers.

Mental Health and Aging
Facts About the Mental Health of Older Adults

- 15-25% of older adults have significant mental health problems.

- 60% or more of people over 65 living in nursing and residential care homes have some degree of mental impairment.

- 10% or more of people over 65 have some form of dementia, 20% over age 80.

- 16-25% of reported U.S. suicides occur in the 65+ population (1 out of 4 suicides are committed by persons over 60).

- 10% of persons age 65 or over suffer from depression.

- The incidence of psychosis increases significantly after age 65. There is twice the incidence of psychosis after age 75 than in the 25-34 age group.
- Only 1.5% of the over 65 population uses mental health services.
- Only 4% seen at public outpatient mental health clinics are 65+.
- Only 2% of patients seem by private psychiatrists are over 65.

- Losses such as spouse, other family members, friends, independence, enforced retirement, chronic health problems, financial difficulties, poor housing, and nutrition contribute to stress, depression, and other mental problems.

Barriers to Service
- Stigma of "Old State Hospital" patient, or of being thought "crazy".
- Fear of being institutionalized.
- Lack of transportation.
- Fear of paying high fees.

- YAVIS Syndrome (therapist prefers clients who are Young, Attractive, Verbal, Intelligent, Successful).

- Isolation - geographic and social.

- Lack of understanding regarding normal aging vs. disease and mental ills. from service providers from family, friends, clients

- Lack of outreach mental health services (more comfortable for client).

Source: Adapted from Psychology of Aging. Presentation from Santa Monica Senior Peer Counseling Program, Santa Monica, CA

Feelings Vocabulary

abandoned
accepted
affectionate
afraid
alarmed
amazed
angry
annoyed
anxious
appreciated
apprehensive
approved
ashamed
balmy
belittled
belligerent
bitter
bored
bottled up
calm
capable
competent
confident
conflicted
confused
contented
crushed
defeated
depressed
desolate
desperate
despondent
discouraged
disinterested
disparate
dissatisfied
dispassionate
distressed
ecstatic
elated
embarrassed
empty

enthusiastic
envious
euphoric
excited
exhilarated
fearful
friendly
frustrated
furious
futile
grateful
guilty
happy
hateful
helpless
hopeless
horny
humble
humiliated
hurt
identification
inadequate
incompetent
inflamed
insecure
insignificant
jazzed
jealous
joyful
lonely
longing
loved
loving
miserable
misunderstood
needed
negative
neglected
nervous
numb
passionate
pleased

pressured
proud
put down
puzzled
reborn
regretful
rejected
rejecting
rejuvenated
realized
relieved
resentful
sad
satisfied
sensual
serene
sexy
shocked
startled
surprised
tearful
tense
terrified
threatened
thrilled
transcendent
trusting
uncertain
uncooperative
understood
uneasy
unhappy
unloved
upset
uptight
vengeful
vindictive
wanted
warmhearted
worthless
worthy
yearning

How We Can Help

What is a Helper? Someone who:

- knows helping involves a great deal of sensitivity and work

- pays attention to both the physical and psychological in others

- pays attention to body language of self and other

- listens intently

- responds frequently in client's frame of reference

- respects client, non-judgemental

- cares about others

- is not defensive

- integrates:
  helps clients put together information about themselves to help them understand self and behavior

- is not afraid to share about themselves if this will advance helping process

- can confront with care and tact

- does not let themselves and their needs get in the way of helping

- helps client act upon self-understanding

- can enter the world of another with all its distress

- can handle stress and crisis

- does not retreat from own problems, continues to explore own behavior, knows who they are

- knows what it means to be helped

- realizes process should center on person, rather than person's problems since problem may change

Source: Gerald Egan, <u>The Skilled Helper</u>, Second Edition, 1975, Brooks/Cole Publishing Company, Monterey, CA

The Process in the Client
Guides for Successful Peer Counseling

1.   The client moves from guessing what his feelings are, to remembering them in the past, to experiencing them fully in the immediacy of the therapeutic moment.

2.   He moves from fearing and defending himself against his feelings, to letting these feelings be and exist, accepted.

3.   He moves from a role relationship (a "client" in relation to a "therapist") to a real relationship (person to person).

4.   He moves from living by values introjected from others to values which are experienced inhimself in the present.

5.   From existing only to satisfy the expectations of others, and living only in their eyes and in their opinions, he moves toward being a person in his own right, with feelings, aims, ideas of his own.

6.   From poor communication within himself - being out of touch with some aspects of his experience - he moves toward free inner communication, a greater awareness of what is going on from moment to moment within.

7.   Likewise he moves from poor communication with others to freer, more real, and direct communication.

8.   He moves from a distrust of the spontaneous and unconscious aspects of himself to a basic trust of his experiencing, of his organism as a sound instrument for encourntering life.

9.   He moves from rigidity and defensiveness to an inner flow of experiencing in the moment.

10. From behavior which is at odds with what he consciously desires, he moves toward behavior which is an integrated expression of a more integrated self.

Variation on an exercise from <u>100 Ways to Enhance Self-Concept in the Classroom</u>.
Jack Canfield, Harold C. Wells. Englewood Cliffs, New Jersey. Prentice-Hall 1976

What Does "Helping" Mean

FOR UNDERSTANDING	FOR SUPPORT AND CRISIS INTERVENTION	FOR POSITIVE ACTION

FOR UNDERSTANDING

1. Listening
   Attending, parapharasing clarifying, perception checking
2. Leading
   Indirect leading, direct leading, focusing, questioning.
3. Reflelcting
   Feelings, content, experience.
4. Summarizing
   Feeling, content, process.
5. Confronting
   Describing feelings, expressing feelings, feeding back, meditating, repeating, associating.
6. Interpreting
   Explaining, questioning, fantasizing.
7. Informing
   Giving information, giving advice, suggesting.

FOR SUPPORT AND CRISIS INTERVENTION

1. Supporting
   Contacting, reassuring, relaxing
2. Crisis Intervention
   Building hope, consoling controlling, developing alternatives.
3. Centering
   Identifying strengths, reviewing growth experiences, recalling peak experiences.
4. Referring

FOR POSITIVE ACTION

1. Problem solving and decision making, Identifying problems, Changing problems to goals, analyzing problems, exploring alternatives and implications, planning a course of action, generalizing to new problems.
2. Behavior changing.
   Modeling, rewarding, extinguishing, desensitizing.

Source: Adapted from The Helping Relationship, Process and Skills, *Lawrence M. Brammer, University of Washington, Prentice-Hall, Inc., Englewood Cliffs,f New Jersey, 1985*

Enhancement of Self Awareness

"The degree to which I can create relationships which facilitate the growth of others as separate persons is a measure of the growth I have achieved in myself."
Carl F. Rogers
Perceiving, Behaving and Becoming

Statements That You Can Reflect On and Complete if You Wish . . .

1. In general, counseling is…
2. This training is …
3. My best quality is …
4. The thing I like best about my work is …
5. Something I'd like to tell my supervisor is …
6. I don't like people who …
7. I like people who …
8. I'm at my best when I …
9. Right now I feel …
10. People I trust …
11. The best thing that could happen to me is …
12. When I don't like something I've done I …
13. When I do like something I've done I …
14. When I'm proud of myself I …
15. I'm very happy that …
16. I wish my colleague knew …
17. Someday I hope …
18. I would like to …
19. Five adjectives that describe me are…
20. Three qualities I'd like to develop as a counselor are.

Variation on an exercise from 100 Ways to Enhance Self-Concept in the Classroom. Jack Canfield, Harold C. Wells. Englewood Cliffs, New Jersey. Prentice-Hall 1976

Like Being Born

When I reached 80, occasionally some younger friend would ask me how it feels to be old. Not 50 or 65, but really old.

I'll tell you how it feels, It feels like spring again after a long cold winter. You find yourself looking around the corner for romance once more. Just one sweet affair. You begin pushing back the dead leaves of your past life searching for Johnny-Jump-Ups and Jack-in-the-Pulpit.

Somewhere in there, deep down, the grass is getting greener. Beneath the moss, beside a log covered with lichens, you come suddenly on ferns uncurling their tiny fiddles. The great god Pan is rousing from sleep, and we are about to strike up the band. The pipes of Pan. Hope springs anew. There is, after all, something to look for ward to. Young Lochinvar may yet come riding. You listen deep, and the brook confides its song to you, whispering under the ice. Your heart starts dancing. Being old feels like being just born. It feels like a colt trying to stand on wobbly legs and not quite making it.

All at once you become actuely aware of the pitiful adolescence of persons in their 20's and 50's. Still in the acne stage. Compassion wells up for them - their uneasy existence, troubled as they are by inconsequential things. Playing the mating game. Preoccupied by sex. Craving they know not what: power, position, wealth. So dead serious about it all.

It pains me to see them suffer. I would rather laugh than cry for them, but they never seem to get the point of the joke. You wait for them to realize life is a comic strip, and we are all Charlie Brown, out there alone on the pitcher's mound. God smiles gently on fools.

How it feels to be old is, after all, my own affair. And what an affair I'm having! I hope to make my passionate involvement in it last, at least until the day I kiss a frog and it turns into a prince.

Elizabeth Landeweer
Skagit County, Washington

SESSION II

Aging: Your Body, Your Mind, Your Emotions

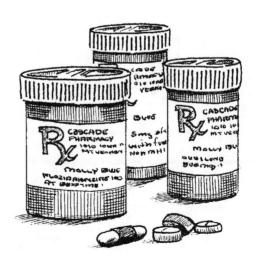

AGING: YOUR BODY,
YOUR MIND, YOUR EMOTIONS

Session II
Session Guide To The Trainer

This session will deal with exposing the myths of aging. The trainee may express the stereotyping common in our culture even while feeling its effects. Their personal stories regarding aging and their reactions to it will bring energy to the discussions.

Review the Myths of Aging quiz with the trainees, allowing for questions and challenges from the group (30 minutes). Correct misinformation or beliefs that may interfere with the trainee's abilities as a potential peer counselor. Another effective tool is to have the group list common myths about older people in a brainstorming session.

As the group discussion develops, it is the facilitator's responsibility to encourage those who are reluctant to speak up and to limit those members of the group who monopolize the conversation. In the latter situation, the facilitator may use such feedback as "you have many thoughts and are excited to share them, however I want to be sure every member of the group gets a chance to share. Perhaps you and I could talk further during break." Calling on shyer members is also effective in bringing out those members of the group. We encourage trainees to "speak up" rather than raising their hands and waiting to be called on. Each session is set up to increase the assertiveness of the trainees, to empower each member and to help them become more aware of communication styles.

Reflecting and reminiscing is used as a tool to help trainees increase their awareness of attitudes regarding aging

Reflecting and reminiscing is used as a tool to help trainees increase their awareness of attitudes regarding aging. Encourage them to look at how their families regard aging and older people.

Session II also deals with getting to know the system -

1. Have the trainee sign up for R.S.V.P. (Retired Seniors' Volunteer Program). You may want to invite the R.S.V.P. coordinator to explain the benefits of being registered and to gather registration forms (30 minutes).

2. Review Agency confidentiality agreements and sign.

3. Review State Administrative Code requirements (W.A.C) and sign.

These forms are collected and kept at the agency.

The "Give & Take" exercise can be very powerful and somewhat disturbing to the trainees. The facilitator's awareness of each member's comments, and allowance for closure, is important. The trainees are being asked to become aware of their own feelings. It is a therapeutic exercise for the group and will raise many feelings and questions from the participants. It is the facilitator's task to help the trainees learn to empathize with feelings their clients might experience by becoming more aware of their own emotions.

Session Materials

- Newsprint   • Easel   • Marking pens   • Agency forms
- Coffee, etc   • Loose change (pennies, nickels, dimes)
- Agency library books on aging, counseling, etc.   • Tissue box

SESSION II

Aging: Your Body, Your Mind, Your Emotions

How old you be if you didn't know how old you was?

Satchel Paige

Today's Goal

- Review, discuss and sign Agency forms.
- Raise awareness of the myths surrounding aging and their effects on the elderly.
- Begin to introduce awareness of feelings, communications and values.

Strategy

Training credibility increases with trainee's signing of formalized agency documents. This gives the trainees the sense of involvement in a well thought-out volunteer program.

Their experiences of aging, expressed to the group, are empathized with and accepted. This allows trainees to get in touch with their feelings about their own aging.

The "Experiential" exercise helps them investigate their personal motives in becoming a "helper." It shows the subtleties which can be present in human interactions.

Learning Objectives

- Gain factual information regarding physical and psychological elements of aging.
- Dispel myths of aging.
- Gain self-awareness of the connection between personal growth, attitudes and counseling.

Handouts and Workbook Materials

Assurance of confidentiality
Administrative Code, regulations, client's rights
Physiology and psychology of aging handouts
Erickson's 8 stages of man & chart
Helpful Hints for Working with Impairments

And So We Invite Awareness In . . . Session II

I. "Temperature Reading" [1]

Allow each member of the group to speak for 2-3 minutes. Since this is a new experience for most trainees, the facilitator may start by modeling her/his temperature reading. Limit any attempts by group members to respond. Trainees may also be reluctant to join in on this first temperature reading. Consideration for their comfort level and response time should be honored. As the weeks progress, even the most timid will join in, realizing how good it feels to have others listen to them.

Key Element -

Counseling skills develop out of respect, empathy and appreciation of others.

II. Introduction to agency forms

Discuss rules, regulations, and laws as related to both professional and peer counselors within a mental health agency.

Review liability; no doubt someone will want to discuss "malpractice." Dispel fears and rumors by addressing your agency's policy on legal and ethical issues.

Have trainees sign forms and registrations (R.S.V.P., college credit registration, etc.) These are to be kept in the trainee's personnel files—some trainees may want copies for their own files.

III. Myths of Aging

Ask the group to identify myths they have heard about the elderly. List answers on newsprint, such as:

Old people are: "set in their ways"   "have no power"   "non-sexual"
"dumb"   "should be respected"   "smarter than others"

Group Discussion

- Where or how might some of these myths have developed? How does our society differ from others in its attitudes towards aging?

- If there is "ageism" in our society, how is it being promoted in the media, in politics, in religion, in families?

- What is "ageism," and in what ways does it correspond to "racism" and "sexism?"

1. Virginia Satir, Conference, 1975.

Key Element -

*Venting a personal experience of "ageism" increases the group's awareness
level of their own difficulties or accomplishments in regard to aging.
This lends to the empowerment of the group.*

Group Discussion

- Myths of Aging - facts v.s. fiction

- Review the questions and answers on the quiz with each trainee reviewing
  their own paper. Spend time on questions that stimulate conversation.

IV. "Experiential" Exercise: "Give & Take"
(Allow one hour for this exercise).

The purpose of this exercise is to create a state of "beneficial uncertainty"
which can be useful to the trainees. Time must be allowed for the process and for
closure of the feelings this exercise will bring up.

Have the group form a circle, either seated on the floor or seated at a large
table. Have them remove all materials from in front of them except for paper and
pencil. Instruct the trainees that they are to remain silent throughout the exercise.

Silence may be difficult for trainees. The facilitator may need to remind the
group that they will be allowed to talk after the exercise.

The exercise has three parts. After each part the trainees are instructed to
silently and independently write down any feelings, impressions or thoughts they
had about the exercise.

Without further explanation, the facilitator requests each person to take a
hand full of coins from their purse or pocket and place the coins in front of themselves. If anyone is without coins, they may take some from the basket of coins the
facilitator has set in the center of the circle. After each member has a pile of coins
in front of them, the facilitator removes the basket of coins.

With the group silent, the facilitator begins. "You are now each asked to distribute the coins in front of you in any way you choose. One person at a time, please
go around the circle and distribute your coins. It does not matter whether you give
them all to one person or divide them among members of the group. When one
person has completed going around the circle, the next person may begin.

The facilitator remains silent, observing the trainees as they distribute their
coins. Make mental notes of any actions that you may want to discuss afterwards.

The group is then asked to jot down their thoughts or feelings about the activity just completed. There should be no talking.

The second part of this exercise also requires group silence. Each trainee is asked to circle the group, one at a time taking any amount of coins from any or all group members. The choice belongs to the trainee. The trainee will then take the coins she has gathered back to her seat and place them on the table at their seat. When they are seated, the next person may go. After each member of the group has had a chance to take coins, ask the group members to write out any feelings, impressions or thoughts about this part of the exercise.

Group Discussion

How did this exercise feel?

What part was hardest?

Why do you think you were uncomfortable?

Where might the discomfort stem from?

What does this say about how we are able to give and take in life situations?

Some examples of group reactions might be:

"I didn't like it" . . .

"I don't get it" . .

"What are the rules, the purpose?"

"It was easier to give out the coins than to take them."

If the facilitator noticed a particular action by a trainee, encourage the trainee to share his thoughts or feelings. For example:

A trainee carefully organized and remembered who gave him each coin and during his turn to give, he gave each coin back. During the taking part, he tried to remember exactly how much he had in his pile to begin with and took only that amount back. An interesting discussion developed on the difficulties this trainee had made with "keeping_score" and how the compulsive sense of "fairness" often interfered with his ability to be spontaneous.

The exercise stimulates thoughts about our cultural attitudes (especially in the aging population) regarding giving and taking.

Women, particularly, reflect on their discomfort at taking and how they were taught that "needing" was somehow "sinful".

What to do with the piles of money? This is the third and final part of the exercise. Group discussion, group negotiation and democratic voting finalizes the decision as to what to do with the money. One group decided to put all the money into a donut fund for the next week. This was a clear statement of just how uncomfortable the group was with individual desires.

Again, group discussion will center on how this might relate to counseling clients. Help the trainees focus on how they felt during this exercise. What do their reactions to the exercise imply about their attitudes toward "giving and taking." Help trainees be aware of how their client might feel about receiving services and why they might act resentful or unpleasant when given some service. Increase their awareness about honoring and respecting their client's feelings.

Key Element -

> *Accept behaviors. Encourage attending to individual needs and desires.*
> *Be sensitive to feelings beginning to emerge.*

V. Closing

Review handout materials for next week. Some of the materials are for the trainees to read at their leisure. Identify those articles which they need to read in order to pre-pare for next week's topic. If you have a speaker for the next session, remind trainees at this time.

Housekeeping duties of this second session become more specific and feedback becomes more spontaneous.

The class is now beginning to be a cohesive unit. Facilitator listens for state-ments and clues from them to use in the summarization.

VI. Summarization

The experiential exercise today is successful if the trainees continue to think about it and discuss it with their family and friends. The facilitator compliments the trainees on their willingness to participate and upon their risk taking. This reinforcement by the facilitator is vital to the trainees comfort. "Your contribution was wonderful and you are so brave" is like an A+ from the teacher.

Agism and the pain it causes is connected with counseling in order that the trainees can better understand their client's feelings of oppression.

> *Aging as a physical change is relatively unimportant*
> *compared with aging as a social nonevent.*
>
> Mitchell Beazley

Recommended Reading

Moore, Pat and Charles Conn. *Disguised.* Texas: Wonderbooks, 1985

A Good Age. Mitchell Beazley, Publishers Limited, 1976, p.31

SESSION II

Handouts & Workbook Materials

PHYSIOLOGY OF AGING

Impact of Neurological and Cognitive Changes and Problems in Aging

- Learning ability may decline because of increased distractibility, poor motivation and decreased ability to organize information.

- Problem-solving difficulties may be caused by an increased concreteness of thought and lower level of schooling.

- Decision-making requires more time, especially if multiple choices are involved.

- Lengthy and detailed instructions take longer for elderly to follow. Lack of motivation, practice and/or experience is often a factor.

- Greater predisposition to confusion because of the reduced reserve capacity of the brain from gradual loss of nerve cells with age.

- Increased susceptibility to falls and injury.

- Problems communicating with others.

- Misperceptions of environment, activities, intent of others, etc.

- Decreased ability to cope with stress.

- Decrease or loss of ability to care for self.

- Decreased sense of self-esteem.

- Impact of increased need for direction, supervision, assistance, protection and care on family and/or elderly spouse.

Source: Senior Respite Care Training Manual, Alzheimer's of Washington and Senior Information and Assistance

Some Helpful Hints for Communicating with a Person with Cognitive Impairment

1. Call the person by name. Expect a response.

2. Because the person with cognitive impairments have a short attention span, expect to have to repeat ideas.

3. Use short sentences with simple ideas.

4. Use pictures, poetry and music to reach a person. Often old humns, prayers and Bible verses come through when other things do not.

5. Always approach a person from the front and explain who you are and why you have come. Use a calm tone of voice.

6. Make sure that hearing aides are in and working, that you talk to a person's good ear. Also make sure that person has their glasses on if they need them. Check to make sure that a person's glasses are clean.

7. Stand where a person can see you and read lips if need be. Don't stand where the light will turn you into a shadow.

8. Use a gentle orientation to reality. But, if they don't agree with you, don't argue.

9. Use touch. Remember that non-verbal communication comes through even when cognitive ability is gone.

10. Make an attempt to talk to the person . . . not around them. Be at their eye level as much as possible.

11. Remember that it is the ILLNESS that makes persons forget. They are not attempting to make life difficult for you on purpose.

Source: Marty Richards, ACSW, University of Washington, Seattle, Washington

Tips for Talking with the Hard-of-Hearing

1. Face the hard-of-hearing person directly.

2. Never talk to him/her from another room

3. Reduce background noises. Turn off the radio, stereo, or television.

4. Keep your hands away from your mouth while speaking. If you are eating or smoking, your speech will be more difficult to understand.

5. Speak in a slightly lower than normal tone of voice. Do not shout; it will only distort sounds.

6. Avoid positions in which the light is shining in the eyes of the hard-of-hearing person.

7. If a hard-of-hearing person does not understand what you are saying, find a new way to say the same thing. Do not repeat the same words. Use shorter, simpler sentences.

8. Always treat the hard-of-hearing person with respect. It could be you!

Source: Adapted from Healthy Lifestyles for Seniors, published by Meals for Millions/ Freedom from Hunger Foundation © 1981.

History Assessment of the Senior Citizen

Vision - Sudden loss of vision is immediately referrable. Changes in vision occurring more rapidly than every three to five years or uncorrected by spectacles should arouse suspicion. Sudden loss of vision almost always signifies a retinal vein thrombosis or a retinal artery occlusion. Pain and watering of the eye should be inquired about.

Ear - The important part of the history of failing hearing is its duration, whether there have been any sudden episodes of deterioration or whether or not tinnitus is present.

Speech - Persons with Parkinson's Disease usually have a soft voice, monotonous pitch and somewhat slurred and often rapid speech.

Laryngeal Disease - Any older person remaining hoarse despite proper care of the nose and throat and restricted use of the voice over a period of two weeks should be seen by a laryngologist. Cancer of the larynx occurs mainly in the older male patient and tends to be neglected in the early stages because of the usual well-being of the patient and the absence of pain.

Absence of teeth is a common and simple cause of difficulty with articulation in the elderly person, but both the patient and his relatives will know that his speech is normal for him when he has not got his teeth in.

Back - In assessing pain in the back, any pain that is of recent onset or pain following a fall is much more likely to be due to a fracture or a metastatic deposit. Pain in the lower lumbar spine and sacrum usually is caused by a benign cause. Severe and persistent lumbo-dorsal pain unaffected by movement or by coughing which is present continually day and night and often relieved by sitting up and bending forward - suggest the possibility of a retroperitoneal lesion (pancreatic cancer).

If a patient complains of severe back pain and is able to move only with obvious stiffness of the back and pain, it is most likely that the pain is due to structural disease of the vertebrae.

Respiratory System

If a patient smokes, it would be necessary to determine a smoking history - inquire with the patient what he is smoking at present and what he has smoked in the past. It is frequently useful to inquire about the largest number of cigarettes per day that has been smoked for any long period. Inquire about the age at which smoking was started. An accurate smoking history enables a more accruate focus to be placed on signs of chronic bronchitis and cough. Cough or sputum produced every day for three months or more in a year for three or more years in succession indicates chronic bronchitis. Inquire if a patient does have smoker's cough. It is useful to inquire how long the patient has had the smoker's cough.

Recent deterioration and the development of breathlessness during dressing, walking or even talking in bed should be established. It should be indicated whether a person is suffering from orthopenea. This usually indicates a cardiac element. In an elderly patient with respiratory diesease the recent onset of extreme fatigue usually signifies the onset of an acute infection of congestive heart failure.

If a patient complains of a cough, inquire into the strength of the cough. Anyone with a weaker cough is in greater hazard of serious trouble from respiratory infections.

Ask patient about color of sputum. If the sputum is mostly mucoid, there is no severe current infection. Hemoptysis indicates bronchial ulceration or damage to alveoli. Blood stained mucoid sputum is frequently due to pulmonary infarction. Blood stained purulent sputum may be due to bronchial carcinoma.

Cardio-Vascular System

Cardiac pain the elderly is usually frequently much less severe although its site and radiation are identical as in a younger patient. Dyspnea of cardiac origin in elderly patients may be much modified so that the principle symptom may be extreme fatigue. In assessing a cough in an elderly patient, anyone who has a cough that goes back many years or is associated with a recent head cold should not be as alarming as a cough of pulmonary congestion which is usually of relatively recent onset.

Irregularities of heart rhythm are frequent in the elderly. The patient should be asked if they are receiving digitalis because the irregularity of rhythm may represent a toxic effect of the drug rather than a failure of the drug.

Any febril illness and a wide range of commonly prescribed drugs can result in postural hypertension. Consider left sided heart failure when there are rales, tachycardia, and gallop rhythm. Consider right sided congestive heart failure when there are extended neck veins and tachycardia, hepatojugular reflex, and sacral edema.

Gastrointestinal System

Since pain sensation is diminished in the elderly large gastrointestinal lesions may occur without classical symptoms. If a person complains of loss of appetitie, it is important to establish the duration of the symptom. If loss of appetitie is only of a few days duration in a person who previously ate well, consider a systematic infection or an acute gastrointestinal disorder. Loss of appetite that has a gradual onset over weeks or months suggests the possibility of a peptic ulcer, neoplasm of the gut, or elsewhere or depressive illness.

Difficulty in swallowing of more than a few months duration is more likely to be benign than malignant in origin. Difficulty in swallowing first solids and then fluids is more likely to be due to a malignant obstruction. It is also important to consider this symptom in relation to all the symptoms the patient gives because difficulty in swallowing may also be due to a neurological disorder.

If a patient complains of abdominal pain which is related to food intake or associated with vomiting, the origin is more likely to be in the stomach or the small bowel. If abdominal pain is relieved by defecation or associated with altered bowel habits, then one should consider that the problem is arising from the large bowel. Having the patient identify the site of abdominal tenderness is more reliable in locating the site of pain than verbal description.

Headache should be assessed in relation to the duration. Headache that has been a frequent complaint over many years is most unlikely to have any sinister cause. The new appearance of this symptom in a person who is not usually subject to headache may be due to some new physical or psychiatric condition. Purely occipital headaches may be caused by severed cervical spondylosis. Severe headache of sudden onset may indicate the presence of an intracranial hemmorrhage or meningitis.

Lower Limb

If a patient complains of pain in the calves and the thighs, this may accompany severe vericose veins and may be due to the increased volume of blood in the vericose veins themselves. Pain in the feet may most commonly be due to simple lesions such as corns and bunions. Also, persistent severe pain in the feet may be due to vascular changes.

Source: Adapted by Rita Moses from Assessment of the Elderly Patient, *F. I. Caird and T.G. Judge (Philadelphia, J.B. Lippincott, Co., 1974.)*

MEDICATION PROBLEMS IN THE ELDERLY

I   Introduction and "Stats":
   - A. >65 average 12-15 prescriptions yearly versus 7 prescriptions for all ages.
   - B. Hospitalized elderly use 8-12 meds.
   - C. 31% of all prescriptions consumed by elderly.
   - D. 75% take at least one prescription drug.
   - E. Over 90% take a medication on a regular basis. 70% take O.T.C. drugs.
   - F. Over 20% mix alcohol with their medications.
   - G. 18% of hospitalizations are secondary to drugs.

II. Problems:
   - A. Patients take generics and brand names at the same time.
   - B. Trade medications, hoarde, reduce or increase dose, etc.
   - C. Physicians unaware of:
     1. O.T.C. drugs (75%);
     2. Other physician prescription drugs;
     3. Total number of drugs (5x more).
   - D. Medical complications:
     1. 30,000 hip fractures;
     2. >200,000 hospitalizations;
     3. >150,000 with brain impairment;
   - E. Little is known about multiple drug interactions.

III. Physical Changes in Aging:
   - A. Smaller bodies
   - B. More fat as a % of total body weight - many drugs attracted to fat.
   - C. Reduction in liver and kidney (1/3 reduction) function.
   - D. Brain "sensitivity" changes.

IV. Medications:
   - A. Most commonly used medications in older patients-"living chemistry sets":
     * 1. Diuretic - hydrochlorothiazide, furosemide, combinations;
     * 2. Digoxin (Lanoxin);
     * 3. Antacids - cimetidine (Tagamet), ranitidine (Zantac);
     4. Nitroglycerin;
     5. Potassium;
     6. Blood pressure and heart medications:
        * a. Methyldopa (Aldomet);
        * b. Prazosin (Minipress);
        * c. Propranolol;
        * d. Nifedipine (Procardia).
     7. Arthritis medications:
        a. ASA;

```
    *        b.  Non-sterioid anti-inflammatories
         8.  Oral antidiabetic medications;
    *    9.  Psychotropic medications.
```
May cause adverse CNS reactions - confusions, dizziness, delirium.

V. Psychotropics:

    A. Antidepressants:

        1. Types:

            a. Heterocyclics - amitriptyline (Elavil), desipramine, nortriptyline, imipramine and others;

            b. Monoamine Oxidase Inhibitors -phenlzine (Nardil) and others;

            c. Non-H.C.'s and -MAOI's - trazodone (Desyrel), fluoxetine (Prozac), buproprion (Wellbutrin);

        Effective in 80% of Major Depressive Disorders.

        Increases brain neurotransmitter levels.

        Dosage - must be individually adjusted:

        a. Lower doses in the elderly;

        b. May take 4-6 weeks for full effect.

        Problems:

        a. Heterocyclics > MAOI > newer medications - trazodone, fluoxetine, bupropion;

        b. Significant side effects: dryness, consitpation, urinary retention, visual problems, confusion;

        c. Inadequate dosing.

        2. Used also in Panic, Obsessive-Compulsive Disorder, Bulimia.

    B. Antipsychotics (neuroleptics, major tranquilizers):

    Often used in elderly for paranoia, mania, psychosis, behavioral control, confusion.

        1. All have similar effect at equivalent doses.

            a. High potency - haloperidol (Haldol)and thiothixene (Navane) - less sedation, more neuromuscular toxicity;

            b. Low potency - thiorikdazine (Mellaril) and chlorpromazine (Thorazine) - more sedation, less neuromuscular toxicity, decreased blood pressure.

        2. Effectiveness - better with confused patients.

        3. Dosage:

            a. Must be individually adjusted;

            b. Some long-acting preparations.

        4. Problems - falls, increased confusion.

    C. Anxiolytics (tranquilizers, sedatives):

        1. Used to treat generalized anxiety, panic attacks, agitation, mania, insomnia.

        2. Commonly used tranquilizers:

     a. Benzodiazepines:
       1. diazepam (Valium)
       2. alprazolam (Xanaz)
       3. lorazepam (Ativan)
       4. chlorazepam (Tranxene)
       5. chlordiazepoxide (Librium)
     b. Meprobamate (Miltown, Equonil)
     c. Hydroxyzine (Vistoril)
     d. Barbiturates
     e. Buspirone (Buspar)
  3. Commonly used sedatives:
     a. triazolam (Halcion)
     b. temazepam (Restoril)
     c. flurazepam (Dalmane)
     d. barbiturates
     e. antihistamines
  4. Effective - particularly the benzodiazepines.
  5. Dosage - individualized.
  6. Problems:
     a. May be addicting;
     b. Falls;
     c. Increased confusion;
     d. "Too effective" - anxiety universal.
D. Non-compliance: 25-90% for advice
                          25-50% for drug therapy.
E. Most strking in long-term care. Drugs are the "high tech" of long-term care.
  1. More stats that bear on compliance issues:
     a. Elderly use 32% of all prescription medications.
       Lots of drugs!
     b. Use 18 or new refilled prescriptions per year.
     c. Nursing home patients - 33% receive > 8 drugs daily.
     d. Non-nursing home patients receive 2-4 drugs daily.
     e. 65% of prescriptions are for chronic care.
     f. 50% default on therapeutic regime.
     g. 40% decrease drug within first year.
     h. 31% commit drug error.
     i. 12-17% of admission secondary to drug problem.
     j. 40% receive drugs from more than one M.D.
     k. 21% take non-currently prescribed medication.
F. Compliance errors:
  1. Failure to obtain prescription.
  2. Improper administration.

        a. M.D. - inadequate or improper dose;

        b. Patient - reduction or increase in dose.

   3. Premature discontinuation - antibiotics.

   4. Physician-related:

        a. Incorrect dosage, improper dose schedule, inadequate warning about side effects.

G. Factors associated with compliance problems:

   1. Severity of disease;

   2. Duration of disease;

   3. Associated psychiatric disorder or brain disease;

   4. Primary psychiatric disorder;

   5. Poor drug response;

   6. Alcohol abuse;

   7. Number of drugs;

   8. Frequency of dose;

   9. Side effects - CNS toxicity;

   10. Cost;

   11. Intelligence and education;

   12. Physician or therapist involvement, number of M.D.'s or therapists, waiting time, number of visits;

   13. Home or institutional support.

H. Consequences of poor compliance:

   1. Adverse reactions and increased morbidity;

   2. 23% of nursing home admits are secondary to poor compliance;

   3. Increased manpower;

   4. Increased costs;

   5. Misinterpretation of disease process.

I.   What can be done?:

   1. Attitude change:

        a. Past: authority figure knows best - - >patient submits;

        b. Present: therapeutic alliance or assisted self-care. Education - - > understanding - - > action - - >reinforcement.

           i. patient judgement important - - Is drug really doing anything? Are side effects intolerable?

          ii. "intelligent non-compliance" -- no ego problem. "These are the benefits and risks."

   2. Communication and education -- teaching versus learning.

        a. Use more than one sense: verbal, visual, hard copy, tactile (hands-on).

        b. Short haul: acute, self-limiting disease - patient focused education - gets them started.

        c. Long haul - chronic disease - patient and social support oriented - uses cues, rewards, reminders - keeps them going.

3. Focus on potential problem patients.
   EXAMPLE: Seventy-year old irritable, depressed post-stroke male with high blood pressure. He lives alone in low-income housing. Given anti-hypertensive and antidepressant medications. Past history of alcohol abuse. Told to return to clinic in one month.
4. Mental Health personnel and medical/medicine compliance.
   a. Is non-compliance a mental health problem?
      i. Success depends on what patients really believe about their illness and therapy.
      ii. Depends on their relationship with provider.
      iii. Depends on their provider continuity.
      iv. Depends on their ability to gather and process technical information.
      v. Depends on their ability to hear and take action under stress.
      vi. Depends on their ability to maintain social/family/ institutional supports.
      vii. Depends on mental health and medical types' ability to cooperate.
   b. What will it take to improve compliance in a mental health setting?
J. Antimanic medications:
   1. Used for manic phase of Bipolar Disorder or secondary mania secondary to medical disorder or drugs.
   2. Lithium carbonate:
      a. Standard drug, effective for acute illness or maintenance;
      b. Side effects - tremor, ataxia, confusion.
   3. Antiseizure drugs:
      a. Carbamazepine (Tegretol);
         i. Used for maintenance;
         ii. Side effects - low WBC, dizziness, drowziness, confusion.
      b. Clonazepam (Klonopin);
         i. Used for acute treatment and maintenance;
         ii. Side effects - ataxia, falls, sedation.
      c. Antipsychotics (see above).

VI. Compliance:
   A. Major problem with any therapeutic effort. Leads to: increased dose, medication change, more potent drugs, chronicity, changed diagnosis, changed doctor or therapist, anger behavior all around.

Source from a lecture by Robert E. Wills, M.D., Consultant, Community Home Health Care, Seattle, WA., Geriatric Mental Health Certification Program, University of Washington, 1990.

The Common Types of Dementing Disease and Their Relative Frequency

Dementing Disease	Relative Frequency, %
Cerebral atrophy, mainly Alzheimer-senile dementia (ASD)	50
Multiinfarct dementia	10
Alcoholic dementia*	5-10
Intracranial tumors	5
Normal pressure hydrocephalus	6
Huntington's chorea	3
Chronic drug intoxications	3
Miscellaneous disease (hepatic failure; pernicious anemia; hypo- or hyperthyroidism; dementias with Parkinson's disease; amyotrophic lateral sclerosis; cerebellar atrophy; neurosyphilis; Cushing's disease; Creutzfeld-Jakob disease; multiple sclerosis; epilepsy)	7-10
Undiagnosed types	3
Pseudodementias (depression, hypomania, schizophrenia, hysteria, undiagnosed)	7

Frequency varies with incidence of alcoholism in the population studied.

Source: C. Wells (ed), Dementia, New York, Davis, 1977.

VULNERABLE ELDERLY DEFINITION

An older person is considered vulnerable if he/she meets the following criteria:

A. Is unable to perform one or more of the Activities of Daily Living listed below without assistance due to physical or mental impairment:

- Ability to independently obtain needed social and health services and benefits.
- Ambulation
- Bathing
- Cooking
- Dressing or undressing
- Eating or preparing meals
- Housework
- Laundry
- Manage medical treatments (prescribed exercises, change dressings, injections, etc.)
- Manage medications (what to take, when to take, how to store properly, etc.)
- Manage money (budgeting, check writing, etc.)
- Personal hygiene and grooming
- Shopping
- Telephoning
- Toileting
- Transfer (getting in and out of bed/wheelchair)
- Transportation

OR

B. Has behavioral or mental health problems that could result in premature institutionalization or has problems that could result in the person not being able to remain in his/her own home (e.g., eviction) or in being transferred to a more restrictive level of care. These problems include:

- Not providing for own health and safety, although physically able to do so.
- Suicidal
- Threatens and/or physically assaults others
- Damages or destroys property
- Dementia
- Depression

AND

C. Lacks an informal support system: Has no family, friends, neighbors or others who are both willing and able to perform the service(s) needed or the informal support system needs to be temporarily or permanently supplemented.

Source: from a lecture by Ronna Loerch, R.N., M.A., Bellingham, WA 1992

Erickson's Eight Ages of Man

Erikson identifies eight central psychodynamic issues that each person must resolve sequentially. Each issue is viewed as having either an adaptive or a neurotic resolution which affects adaptation to subsequent life stages. Five of these eight stages occur in childhood or adolescence; only three are identified for the later years. These stages are defined by the central issues of concern rather than by a clear age parameter.

1. *Basic Trust vs. Basic Mistrust:* In early infancy, children gain security and trust in the world through having their physical needs met lovingly. This early experience develops a positive trust in the goodness of the world. Without such early security, a baby emerges from infancy with a basic mistrust of the social environment.

2. *Autonomy vs. Shame and Doubt:* Beyond the first year of life, the baby can either be encouraged to take control of her or his anal functions, or toilet training can occur in a coercive atmosphere that encourages shame and doubt of one's own capacities.

3. *Initiative vs. Guilt:* The oedipal period (around age 3-5) becomes the background for the development of independent actions as the child seeks to establish gender identification. The child's feelings towards her or his parents at this age can be accepted, or the parents may reject these expressions and make the child feel guilty of them.

4. *Industry vs. Inferiority:* During the early school years that make up the latency period (ages 6-12) the child can invest much energy in learning, if the social environment supports her or his efforts toward competence. On the other hand, a child in an overly critical, demanding environment will emerge with feelings of inferiority about her or his capabilities.

5. *Identity vs. Role Confusion:* During adolescence, the child grapples with the establishment of an identity independent of her or his parents. If such efforts are thwarted by the parents, the child emerges into adulthood without having clarified personal values or goals for the future.

6. *Intimacy vs. Isolation:* The urge to establish meaningful bonds with others becomes central during young adulthood. If one cannot achieve true intimacy and sharing at this time, future relationships will be superficial.

7. *Generativity vs. Stagnation:* Between young adulthood and old age, a person's major energies are directed toward full engagement in major life roles. A feeling of successful contribution is necessary for adjustment during this central adult period. Without the reward of feeling productive, a person experiences stagnation.

8. *Integrity vs. Despair:* In old age, awareness of approaching death leads to a search for the meaning of one's life. If the aged can view their past experiences with pride and satisfaction, they can face the end of their life with acceptance. If they regret their choices and involvements, they will feel a pervasive sense of disillusionment and failure.

Source: Eric, Erickson, The Healthy Personality, Identity and the Life Cycle, W.W. Norton & Company, New York, N.Y., 1980. and Robert Peck, 1955.

Psychosocial Crises

	1	2	3	4	5	6	7	8
Old Age VIII								Integrity vs. Despair, disgust. WISDOM
Adulthood VII							Generativity vs. Stagnation. CARE	
Young Adulthood VI						Intimacy vs. Isolation. LOVE		
Adolescence V					Identity vs. Identity Confusion. FIDELITY			
School Age IV				Industry vs. Inferiority. COMPETENCE				
Play Age III			Initiative vs. Guilt PURPOSE					
Early Childhood II		Autonomy vs. Shame, Doubt. WILL						
Infancy Basic I	Trust vs. Basic Mistrust.							

Source: Erik Erikson, Identity & the Life Cycle, W.W. Norton and Co., 1980 N.Y. London

Theoretical Perspectives on Development In Late Adulthood

Erik Erikson's Theory

In this final crisis of ego integrity versus despair in the Eriksonian progression through life. ego integrity implies, a "love of the human ego - not of the self - as an experience which conveys some world order and a spiritual sense." (Erikson, 1963, pg. 268) This love of the ego embraces an acceptance of the life that one has lived, without major regrets for what could have been or for what one should have done differently. It includes acceptance of one's parents as people who did the best they could and thus are worthy of love, even though they were not perfect. It implies an acceptance of one's approaching death as the inevitable end to life lived as well as the individual knew how to live it. It implies, then, an acceptance of the imperfection of oneself, one's parents, and one's life.

The person who does not achieve such acceptance is overwhelmed by despair in the realization that the time is too short to start another life and try out alternative roads to integrity must outweigh despair for the successful resolution of the crisis, some despair is inevitable, according to Erikson. He asks "How could anyone have integrity and not also despair about certain things in his own life, about the human condition. Even if your own life was absolutely beautiful and wonderful, the fact that so many people were exploited and ignored must make you feel some despair." (in Hall, 1983, Pg. 27).

Erikson also sees old age as a time to play, to recapture a childlike quality, which is essential for creativity. Although the time for procreation is over, creation can still take place. He maintains that the creative potential and the sexual energy of old people have both been underestimated and that both can achieve expression in old age. (in Hall, 1983)

Robert Peck's Three Crises of Old Age

In Peck's (1955) expansion of Erikson's discussion of physiological development in late life, he emphasized three major crises that old people must resolve for healthy psychological functioning.

1. Ego-Differentation versus Work-Role Preoccupation
The chief issue in this crisis lies in the question each person must ask: "Am I a worthwhile person only insofar as I can do a full-time job; or can I be

worthwhile in other, different ways - as a performer of several other roles, and also because of the kind of person I am? 11 (1955; in Neugarten, 1968, pg. 90) This is a crucial question to ask in old age. Upon retirement, people often need to redefine their worth and recall activities they can paint to with pride; they may be more successful in maintaining their vitality and sense of self. The woman whose major work has constituted serving as a wife and parent faces this issue when her children leave home or her husband dies. Whether a career was centered on the marketplace or the home, those adjusting to its loss need to explore themselves and find other interest to take the place of those that formerly gave direction and structure to life. They need to recognize that their egos are richer and more diverse than the sum of their tasks at work.

2. *Body Transcendence versus Body Preoccupation*

The physical decline that generally accompanies old age signals a second crisis. Perople who have emphasized physical well-being as the axis of a happy life maybe plunged into despair by any diminution of their faculties or any appearance of bodily aches and pains. Those who can instead focus on satisfaction from relationships with people and from absorbing activities that do not depend on a peak state of health are able to overcome physical discomfort. An orientation away from preoccupation with the body needs to be developed by early adulthood, but it is critically tested in old age. One of the goals of life may well be the cultivation of mental and social powers that can increase with age, along with attributes such as strength, beauty, muscular coordination, and other hallmarks of physical well-being that are likely to diminish over the years.

3. *Ego Transcendence versus Ego-preoccupation*

Old people need to deal with the reality that they are going to die. Successful adaptation to the prospect of death "may well be the most crucial achievement of the elder years" (1955, in Neugarten, 1968, pg. 91). How do people transcend their ego of the here and now to gain a positive viewpoint toward the certainty of their coming death? By recognizing that the way they have led their lives will help them achieve enduring significance, through the children they have raised, the contributions they have made to culture, and to personal relationships they have forged. Essentially, they transcend the ego by contributing to the happiness or well-being of others, who says Peck, "more than anything else differentiates human living from animal living" (Pg. 91).

Source: Robert Peck

GROUP FACILITATION WITH SUCCESS:
Remember . . .

1. Trust takes time and is necessary for group work to be effective. It can be recognized in the spontaneity and level of involvement of the group members.

2. Group facilitators must insure emotional and physical safety.

3. Peer pressure is extremely powerful - use it.

4. Facilitators don't always have to have the answers!!!

5. Humor is important - have fun.

6. Therapy groups evolve and take time to become effective. The less functional the members, the more time that is required.

7. New members who "bare their souls" frequently leave treatment.

8. Processing patterns of behavior is more effective than focusing on content issues.

9. New groups often demand more structure and direction from the leaders.

10. Suggestions for facilitating process . . .

    a. Make expectations explicit.
    b. Be consistent (but flexible) with format, time, etc.
    c. Attend to everyone (if possible).
    d. Be aware of your own reactions and dilemmas and share them.
    e. Use voting as non-verbal comments.
    f. Occasionally use activities to change the tone and for new material to process.
    g. Change the seating arrangement.
    h. Periodically take the intiative in bringing up issues regarding specific group members.

SESSION III

Beginning Communication Skills

Session III
Session Guide To The Trainer

The group is starting to jell, and they are eager to learn counseling skills. This session is about the importance of case management and how the peer counselor is involved with case management, record keeping and use of community resources. Our agency works closely with Senior Information and Assistance. We have a speaker from their office come with information about community resources. The majority of trainees will not know the many services communities have for seniors or how to access those services. You may want to incorporate such a speaker into a beginning session. Good case management depends on the peer counselor's awareness of community resources, in order to help their client.

Good case management depends on the peer counselor's awareness of community resources, in order to help their client.

The agency outreach therapist defines "case management" and instructs the trainees on the multifacetted aspects of serving the elderly. While the peer counselor's job may not include setting up these services, the peer counselor will evaluate the client's needs for additional services.

Record keeping causes fear in most trainees. The facilitator can lessen this fear by using concrete examples. Having the trainees practice writing "Progress Notes" in class as a part of the practice counseling triads also reduces fear. We have enclosed sample progress notes, but you may want to use your agency's form.

We teach counseling skills starting with learning communication skills, attending skills, listening skills and recognizing verbal and non-verbal cues. The trainees will be instructed to practice these skills throughout the remaining sessions and in their personal lives. Nervous chatter, laughter and resistances are cues which the facilitator must acknowledge, validate and attend to. The facilitator's style will be modeled by the trainees.

We begin role playing at this session. Take some time to help trainees understand the purpose of role playing.

We encourage trainees to role play from their personal experiences. Role playing situations and the outcomes need to be realistic.

Trainees often get confused when role playing, preferring "pretend" scenarios rather than role playing from personal experiences. We encourage trainees to role play from their personal experiences. Role playing situations and the outcomes need to be realistic. The facilitator guides the group feedback discussions. If you have a co-facilitator, this is an excellent time to model role playing for the trainees.

Several theories of introducing counseling skills have been used in this training. Gerard Egan's <u>Skilled Helper</u> presents basic counseling skills in terms of levels with Stages I and II for paraprofessionals. (1)

Stage I   Attending, Listening, Probing, and Understanding
Stage II Summarizing, Information Giving, Confrontation, Self-sharing

Allen Ivy's Basic Attending Skills introduces the four components of active listening. (2)

1) Minimal encouragements   2) Paraphrasing
3) Reflection of feelings   4) Summarization

And Carl Rogers' "Client-Centered Therapy" adds feedback, responses and supportive clarification to this composite of counseling skill modalities.

The most effective theory will be the one with which the facilitator/trainer has the greatest comfort level. We have chosen to use some parts of several theories to teach Basic Communication Skills.

1) Gerard Egan: <u>The Skilled Helper</u>, Brooks/Cole Publishing Company, Wadsworth, Inc., Belmont, CA.1975, 1982
2) Allen E. Ivy & Norma B. Gluckstern: <u>Basic Attending Skills</u>, 1974, 1976, Microtraining Associates, North Amherst, Massachusetts.

SESSION III

Beginning Communication Skills

"Listening is a magnetic and strange thing, a creative force ... The friends that listen to us are the ones we move towards, and we want to sit in their radius as though it does us good, like ultraviolet rays ... When we are listened to, it creates us, makes us unfold and expand. Ideas actually begin to grow in us and come to life ... It makes people happy and free when they are listened to ...When we listen to people, there is an alternating current, and this recharges us so that we never get tired of each other. We are constantly being recreated... I just listen with affection to anyone who talks to me, to be in their shoes when they talk."

-- Clark Moustakas

Todays' Goal

- Introduction of trainees to record keeping and case management.
- Awareness of verbal and non-verbal cues.
- Introduction of communication skills and role playing techniques.
- Practice of active listening and empathic listening.

Strategy

Use modeling by the facilitator to clarify role playing. Give examples. Use dyads to practice the role playing of communication skills such as the awareness of non-verbal cues. Help trainees begin to identify feelings by name (they can refer to the list of feelings words). Facilitator joins each dyad for a short time, giving feedback and assisting the trainees. Start with non-threatening scenarios prepared by the facilitator. This exercise is new and unnatural for the trainees, so your reassurance is imperative.

Learning Objectives

- Practice basic communication skills, becoming familiar with role playing as a learning tool.
- Conceptualize case management.
- Practice clinical record keeping.
- Establish new ways of active listening.
- Introduce the concept of constructive feedback.

Handouts and Materials

Charting - Defining S.O.A.P.
Article: What Would It Be Like To Have No Records
Sample - Clinical Progress Notes
I & A Vocabulary - Your Secret Decoder
Beginning Counseling Skills
Materials on Active Listening
Empathetic Conversation Leads
Why Empathetic Listening Works

Are You Listening? . . . Session III

I. "Temperature Reading"

Allow 2-3 minutes for each member to clarify issues from last week. There may still be discussion from the "Give and Take" exercise. Allow interactions while observing styles of communication.

Key Element -

Time spent encouraging the free expression of feelings will give the trainees a sense of how important it is to be heard. Do not hurry these beginning sessions. Allow them to develop in order to bring personal clarity for each trainee.

II. Introduction to Record Keeping

Using the handouts and sample progress notes, review the S.O.A.P. definitions. Present examples of each component. An agency may also use a 4-step reporting form including client's affect, objective information, content of session, and a plan. The secret is to keep this simple and non-threatening.

Experiential Exercise - "Progress Notes"

Have trainees form triads. One member will represent the client, another member will play peer counselor, and the other member will be the observer. The observer will take notes. Have each member of the triad act as observer at some point. Allow time at the end of the exercise for everyone to write a progress note.

For this exercise the facilitator can use scenarios from the case samples we have included in the manual. Review the progress notes as a group, in order to clear up misconceptions.

Remind the trainees they are noting the progress of the client . . . not the peer counselor! This task is incorporated into each triad throughout the remaining sessions. By the end of the training the members will be less anxious when recording information on assigned clients. Instructions about the date, mode, length of service, and signature needs to follow the requirements of each individual agency.

III. Case Management

Our agency uses case managers (therapists) in the Geriatric Outreach Program. As the State demands more case management from mental health professionals, this modality will become the accepted service title. Your speaker may be a mental health professional who is a case manager.

Review the elements of case management. List types of services available, i.e. Senior Information and Assistance, "Meals on Wheels", vision services, chore workers, book mobile, senior health checks, Visiting Nurses, Home Health Care.

Group Discussion

How is case management related to counseling with the geriatric population?

List multiple services a homebound elderly client might need or use.

How can a case manager and peer counselor help identify appropriate services for the client?

To what degree is the peer counselor involved in case management?

IV. Introduction to Communication Skills

Review the handouts with the trainees, discussing the beginning stages of counseling, non-verbal cues, active listening and empathic listening.
Explore the rules of role playing, offering support for this new task in the Feelings Vocabularys handout,
Review Egan's articles on role playing, and Empathic Conversation Leads. Facilitator can model role playing with a trainee, encouraging, and dispelling the anxiety that arises when trainees begin this task.

Group Discussion

Becoming aware of non-verbal cues means attending to the other person's body communications. Words can be heard from many different perspectives, often denying or ignoring feelings; but the body never lies. Our job is to become more understanding of these body cues in order to communicate better with the client.
The following are behaviors for group discussion. One or more trainees may want to role play a client who exhibits some of these behaviors. Have the rest of the members interpret and discuss the behavior and its message.

1. The "client" sits very rigidly in a chair. He does not make eye contact. He "drums" his fingers on the arm of the chair. He speaks very quickly and with no emotion. (Possible client feelings: anxious, angry, defensive, annoyed, or embarrassed.)

2. Client slouches in a chair, looks listless, preoccupied, and does not appear to hear what you are saying. (Possible client feelings: afraid, depressed, annoyed.)

3. Client's face is flushed and her eyes glare at you. Her lips are narrow and her jaw bone moves up and down occasionally. (Possible client feelings: angry, tense, scared, uncomfortable.)

Questions to aid trainees in understanding non-verbal communications:

How does the client look?

How does the client speak?

How does the client sit or stand?

What is the client doing with his/her hands or feet?

What feelings do these behaviors imply?

Experiential Exercise - "Observing Non-verbal Cues"

Have trainees form dyads with one partner role playing the client and one partner role playing the peer counselor. Allow 10 minutes for this activity. Each member of the dyad is instructed to practice his/her listening skills by attending to the "client's" non-verbal cues as the "client" role plays a particular "emotion" or "feeling".. At a 4-minute interval have the partners change roles. The trainee may still be reluctant to role play their own experiences, but the facilitator can help with encouragements to role play any situation to which they have an emotional reaction. It may even be their reaction to role playing.

Key Element -

The purpose of this exercise is to help the trainee become aware of what feelings they are experiencing and to communicate those feelings to their partner.

Active Listening

Review and discuss the basic components of attending:

1. Minimal encouragements: Open and closed questions, head nods, restatements, and "uh-huhs.

2. Paraphrasing: Clarification as a function for the peer counselor to focus on the content of the client's statements.

    (Facilitators may need to discuss the difference between content and feelings.)

3. Reflection of feelings: Responding to another's emotional experiences. Selective attention to the affect of the client's statement and body language. Labeling emotions helps trainees get in touch with their own emotional experience.

4. Summarization: Gathering the strands of thought from the client to provide a clearer understanding of the client by the trainee.

152

Group Discussion

What is the difference between Open and Closed statements?

Give examples, practice reframing a Closed question into an Open Statement.

How are clients "empowered" by peer counselor's listening ability?

Key Element -

Practicing each listening skill many times in dyads and triads adds to group relaxation and participation. Attending is a way of saying "I am with you. It is worth my time and effort to help you." Remember "unconditional positive regard" as a way of showing respect.[1]

Empathic Listening

In group, the facilitator instructs trainee in paraphrasing techniques with the use of the conversation leads listed on large newsprint. As trainees begin to understand that their job is to remain receptive in order to better understand their client's needs, the task becomes easier. The facilitator can increase the trainee's willingness to put forth effort to learn these difficult concepts by strengthening the trainee's expectations of themselves.

Ways in which trainees sense empowerment:

Success: to act and see their efforts producing results.

Modeling: seeing others do it and being encouraged to try it themselves.

Encouragement: facilitator and group supports their efforts.

Reducing fear and anxiety: work with situations that reduce fear to help heighten the trainee's sense of self confidence.[2]

Experiential Exercise - "Listening Skill Building"

Have the group form dyads, choosing someone they have not worked with extensively, using the following case study. Role play client and peer counselor using the three skills previously discussed:

1. Carl Rogers, 1967
2. Egan, The Skilled Helper, 1975, p. 14, and Bandura, 1977a.

Minimal encouragements

Reflection of Feelings

Paraphrasing

Allow five minutes for each partner to role play the scene.

CASE STUDY

Martha is an 80-year old widow who lives in a rural part of the county. She recently lost an old neighbor who had been her friend for many years.

Martha now states that she is all alone and cries often about her friend's death. Martha has always been independent and able to care for herself. Martha lives off her husband's social security, but expenses for new glasses and medicine for her bronchitis have caused her increased anxiety. Martha cooks her own meals, is able to shop if she can get a ride into town. Martha's family lives on the East Coast, but are supportive and worried about her. Martha does not want to move. Martha states she has not been sleeping well and occasionally is frightened.

<u>Group Discussion</u>

What did it feel like when playing the client?

What things did the peer counselor do or say that gave you the feeling they were interested in you?

As the peer counselor, did you feel temped to try to solve her problems?

What are the benefits of helping people solve their own problems rather than solving the problem for them?

Describe the biggest danger in trying to solve other's problems.

As the peer counselor, what was the hardest part?
What was the most comfortable for you?

Key Element -

This is the beginning of basic counseling skills: practice, practice, practice. Encourage trainees to move past embarrassment by risk taking in their role playing.

V.   Closing

Review handouts for next week, make assignments.

Ask for feedback, modeling the elements of listening, paraphrasing, relfection of feelings and summarization..

VI.   Summarization

This is a very full session with many parts to introduce and begin to work on. Encourage, support, and remind trainees that this is a process which they will continue to work on for the rest of their lives. Remind them that they will become more comfortable with these communication skills as they practice using them. Their homework is to practice these skills with friends and family. These are the basics of counseling to which the course will refer throughout the remaining sessions. Peer counselors are becoming "change agents".

"If I can listen to what he tells me, if I can understand how it seems to him, if I can sense the emotional flavor which it has for him, then I will be releasing potent forces of change within him."

-- Carl Rogers

Recommended Reading

Moustakas, Clark E. *Loneliness and Love.* Englewood Cliffs, N.J. Prentice-Hall, 1972.
Rogers, Carl. *A Way of Being.* New York: Houghton Mifflin, 1980.

Session III

Handouts & Workbook Materials

Beginning Counseling Skills

As a peer counselor helper you can be most effective when you are paying close attention to your feelings and to the feelings of your client.

Beginning level communications lie in self-respect and self-trust. Often we become embarrassed or worried about "performing" and forget to respect ourselves. It is only to the degree that we value ourselves that we can value our clients.

Two basic lessons essential to counseling skills, are increased listening awareness and enhanced self awareness.

Listening Awareness is the key to hearing. This is a simple statement, yet perhaps the most difficult skill for new helpers to develop. Active listening requires attending to words, tones, feelings, and non-verbal indicators.

Self Awareness is what you do with your interpretations and judgements. It is for you, the helper, to understand your own fears and keep those separate from the fears of your client.

Your job is to learn to listen. There is little point in talking about yourself or to propose solutions when you listen to your client. Your job is to help them access their own solutions.

Your _Intention_ will be felt when you are truly listening and involved with your client. If your intention is to bring clarity to the conversation and to enhance the quality of your client's moments with you, "Be still, listen and do no harm". In this way your good intentions will shine through regardless of your style of communications.

A simple skill? No, but the key element is to Practice, Practice, Practice. Begin with your communication among friends, neighbors, and family.

Guide for Peer Counselors:
Ways You Can Help

1. Listening - giving a person time to talk.
2. Understanding - saying that we understand what it is like to feel sad or angry or afraid.
3. Praising - acknowledging what a person has done or is doing that shows strength.
4. Encouraging - recognizing a person's strengths and suggesting that these strengths can help with this problem too.
5. Reassuring - saying that others have experienced the same, "You are not alone."
6. Caring - showing that we care by non-verbal expressions of interest and concern as well as by words.
7. Giving information.

An Examination of Listening

Active listening, as described by Thomas Gordon, in <u>Parent Effectiveness Training</u>, is the process wherein the receiver feeds back "only what he feels the sender's message meant . . . nothing more, nothing less." Carl Rogers' "Client-centered Therapy" requires feeding back to the client what you heard him/her say. Still others use reflective-empathy to focus on the client's feelings, restatement to paraphrase what the client is saying and open-ended questions to seek additional information from the client through non-judgemental questions.

The use of these skills can be further enhanced as you use all dimensions of your person, such as eye contact, attentive body language, and verbal following.

Source: Campbell & Chenoweth, <u>Peer Supports for Older Adults</u>, Turner Geriatric Clinic, University of Michigan Hospital, Ann Arbor, Michigan, 1981.

WHY EMPATHIC LISTENING WORKS

1. THE OTHER PERSON SETS THE PACE. You let them take the lead in the conversation. You don't push them faster than they want to go. This builds trust.

2. THE OTHER PERSON IS COMPLETELY FREE TO BE NATURAL. That's a rare opportunity. The other person will probably take advantage of it by relaxing and behaving in the ways that are most real and honest. When you show that you can be trusted, other persons are free to tell you about their hurts, their secrets and their ambitions. The result - you can really know them.

3. THE OTHER PERSON GETS MORE SELF-UNDERSTANDING. In a mirror, you can see things about your physical self that cannot otherwise be seen. In the same way, empathic listening serves as a mirror in which persons can see their behaviors and attitudes more completely. This helps them understand themselves better and forces them to decide whether or not they like themselves the way they are, or if they want to change.

4. TO EMPATHICALLY LISTEN IS TO GIVE SOMETHING VALUABLE. Empathic listening is hard work and the other person knows it. When you listen with empathy, you prove to the other person that you care.

5. IT KEEPS YOU OUT OF TROUBLE. While you are engaged in empathic listening, you will not do anything that is punishing, painful or hurtful to the other person.

6. EMPATHIC LISTENING CLARIFIES AND REDUCES CONFUSION.

7. EMPATHIC LISTENING CREATES A RELAXED, TRUSTING ATMOSPHERE AND REDUCES THREAT.

8. EMPATHIC LISTENING ENCOURAGES "CONNECTED" COMMUNICATION.

Source: Peavy, 1977 P.O.P.S. Polishing Our People Skills, Good Samaritan Hospital and Medical Center, Portland, Oregon, 1986.

EMPATHIC CONVERSATION LEADS

Sometimes it is difficult to know just how to start an empathic reply. If you have some reason to believe that the person with whom you are talking is receptive and wishes to be understood, then some phrases, which are useful "leads" in empathic responding, are:

You feel . . .

From your point of view . . .

It seems to you . . .

In your experience . . .

From where you stand . . .

As you see it . . .

You think . . .

You believe . . .

What I hear you saying . . .

You're . . . (identify the feelings: angry, sad, happy)

I'm picking up from you that you . . .

I really hear you saying that . . .

Where you're coming from . . .

You figure . . .

You mean . . .

Source: <u>Empathic Listening Workbook</u>, Victoria, B.C., Adult Counseling Project, University of Victoria, 1977.

Twelve Typical Communication Blocks

1. Ordering, directing, commanding. Telling the other person to do something - giving him/her an order or command.

2. Warning, admonishing, threatening. Telling the other person what consequences will occur if s/he does something: alluding to the use of your power.

3. Moralizing, preaching. Telling another person what s/he should or ought to do.

4. Advising, giving suggestions or solutions. Telling the other person how to solve a problem, giving him/her adivce or suggestions, providing answers or solutions.

5. Lecturing, teaching, giving logical arguments. Trying to influence the other person with facts, counter-arguments, logic, information, or your own opinions.

6. Judging, criticizing, disagreeing, blaming. A negative judgement or evaluation of another person.

7. Praising, agreeing. Offering a positive evaluation or judgement.

8. Name-calling, ridiculing, shaming. Making the other person feel foolish.

9. Interpreting, analyzing, diagnosing. Telling a person what his/her motives are or analyzing why s/he is doing or saying something; communicating that you have him/her figured out or diagnosed.

10. Reassuring, sympathizing, consoling, supporting. Trying to make the other person feel better, talking her out of her feelings, trying to make her feelings go away, denying the strength of her feelings.

11. Probing, questioning, interrogating. Trying to find reasons, motives, causes; searching for more information to help you solve the problem.

12. Withdrawing, distracting, humoring. Trying to get the other person away from the problem; withdrawing from the problem yourself; distracting the person, kidding her out of her feelings. pushing the problem aside.

Source: Counseling the Aged, American Personnel and Guidance Association, Washington, D.C. 1979, Page 183

Common Mistakes in Empathic Listening

1. Sounding like a parrot or a robot.

2. Talking about content only, ignoring feelings.

3. Giving cheap advice.

4. Using poor attending skills. You sound good, but you look like you could care less.

5. Shifting attention to yourself. Talking instead of listening.

6. Having no energy. You must be as intense in your words and emphasis as the other person.

7. Sliding into non-helpful replies such as joking, making judgments, reassuring, etc.

8. Using empathic listening when it is not the best method.

Source: Peavy, 1977 P.O.P.S. Polishing Our People Skills, Good Samaritan Hospital and Medical Center, Portland, Oregon, 1986.

Vocabulary - Your Secret Decoder

AAA
Area Agency on Aging - 4-county regional planning and funding agency for senior programs - Senior I&A, HDMs, Senior Screening, Respite, Nutrition, VCP, and others.

AAFS
Adult & Aging Field Services - the division of DSHS in charge of Chore, COPES, NH placement, APS (not Food Stamps or Medicaid).

APS
Adult Protective Services - part of DSHS - investigates elderly abuse, exploitation, neglect.

CAA
Community Action Agency - provides help to low income, emergency housing, energy assistance and many programs for infants, etc.

COPES
Community Options Program Entry System - a DSHS program that provides in-home help for people who qualify (1) medically for nursing home care and (2) financially for Medicaid.

CSO
Community Services Office - the local DSHS office - on Continental Place by Cinema 5.

DSHS
Dept. of Social & Health Services - huge state dept. in charge of many programs including "welfare", Food Stamps, Nursing Home licensing and inspection, Medicaid, Chore Service, APS.

EAP
Energy Assistance Program - a program of CAA providing help with heating bills for low-income people (all ages).

ECIP
Energy Crises Intervention Program - a CAA program for help with heating cutoffs, hookups and repairs.

I & A
Information & Assistance - a program of Skagit County Senior Services - concentrating on services and issues of concern to the elderly.

Vocabulary - Your Secret Decoder

I & R   Information & Referral - a program of CAA with information and programs for low-income of all ages.

MEDICAID   State health insurance. Must be low-income, very low assets. Apply DSHS. Provides "medical coupons" which cover nearly all medical expenses - Drs., prescriptions, glasses, equipment, dentures, nursing home care.

MEDICARE   Federal health insurance program tied to Social Security for over 65 (or on Social Security Disability 2 years or more) covers most hospital and about 50% of doctor bills. Nearly all seniors are covered.

RSVP   Retired Senior Volunteer Program - a program of Skagit County Senior Services - placing and supporting volunteers over age 60.

SCOA   Skagit Council of Aging - private, nonprofit agency - operates senior transportation and supports senior centers and other senior programs.

SOCIAL
SECURITY   Federal retirement or disability income benefit based on a person's work history (or a spouse's).

SSI   Supplemental Security Income - a federal/state welfare program for the very poor - brings monthly income up to $396. Apply at Social Security.

Source: Donna Sitts, B.A., Director Skagit County Senior Information and Assistance

What Would It Be Like To Have No Records?

"I have only eight working hours in a day and the most important thing is seeing clients and their families. I can't afford to waste valuable time writing about what I do—the main thing is that the job gets done." Such was the harried comment of a busy social worker. Ah, Utopia. No records. No paperwork. No supervisors getting after you because you're behind in your recording. All those extra hours that can be spent seeing clients. Let's join the Utopia Hospital's Medical Social Service Department and experience the absence of records.

8-9 a.m. Thirty workers, three supervisors, and one director struggle into the office, followed by one secretary and fifteen social work students. The phone rings. A nurse on East Wing 18 wants to know if the social worker has seen Frank Appleman yet. Since there are no master card files, the secretary calls out "Who here is working with Frank Appleman?

Meanwhile, social worker Sally Smith is sitting in her office trying desperately to remember what she was trying to do with Mary Browns case. She saw Mrs. Brown last week and they had a rather intense discussion and she's sure there was something she was supposed to follow up this week. Half an hour goes by and she still can't remember.

In strides an important looking man with a large brief case who has a paper to give one of the supervisors. It is a court subpoena. One of the students made an offensive remark to a patient and the patient is suing and holding the supervisor responsible. As the supervisor heads for the director's office for a hasty consultation, she is heard muttering, "But I didn't even know about the incident—how can I be held responsible—I can't know what my student does all the time.

The director tells the supervisor he can't see her until later because he has an important meeting with a group of doctors. In fact, they come in as the distraught supervisor exits. What do the six M.D.'s and three head nurses want with the director? Well, it seems that the social worker assigned to their area has been "goofing off" at least as far as they can tell, because few patients are being seen. One doctor shoves across the desk a paper with the figure $192,816.12 written on it. "That," points out Dr. Englebert, "is what Medicare owes this hospital and refuses to pay because there is no social work recording in our charts." He goes on to explain that he has recommended to the hospital administrator that this amount be deducted from the Social Service Department's budget over the next three years to recoup the loss. Meeting adjourned.

In comes the secretary with the morning mail. What have we here? Copies of two letters addressed to the hospital director. They are from two important accrediting agencies. One explains, "Since your Social Service Department has failed to implement its own internal peer-review mechanism, we have set up the following system for you to follow." The other letter contains more cheery news. The Joint Commission on Accreditation is coming to the Social Service Department tomorrow and wants to see the following: "departmental procedure manual, minutes of all in-service training activities, departmental statistics for the past fiscal year, and a random sampling of fifty records that document social work involvement.

The director's phone rings. It is Supervisor Hennessy explaining that worker Jones called in sick today. "Do you by any chance know what he was doing with the Horace Williams case? It seems Williams is being discharged, and the doctor wants him placed in a nursing home today."

Meanwhile, Supervisor Young is having problems of her own. She recently hired a new MSW graduate to do counseling and is beginning to suspect that his skills aren't all that great. How can I be sure about my assessment? How can I find out what areas I need to help him with? I wonder if he will agree with my observations? Her thoughts are interrupted periodically as the secretary bellows: "Anyone here know anything about Mary Ratz on North Wing 8?" Who was the last person to see Roberta Mugs?"

Worker High-volume struts into the office to announce he's seen fifteen patients today—only two fewer than he had seen by this time yesterday. "Yessir, this department really gets things done when we don't have to record!" Everyone knows Mr. High-volume is pushing hard for a special merit increase next month.

At 4 p.m. the director receives a phone call. It is the hospital director's secretary announcing an emergency meeting. It seems that the Social Service Department's budget request for the coming year is being denied. In fact, the hospital can no longer justify maintaining the department at its present size. Thus, effective in two weeks staff will be reduced to eight social workers, no more than half of whom shall be M.S.W.'s. The hospital director makes it quite clear that "We'll hire a couple of M.S.W.'s because the powers-that-be say we have to, but otherwise we're going to go with the B.A.-level person who can do the same job at a much reduced cost."

As the dejected director returns to his office, he is met by Worker Adams, who shoves a subpoena under his nose. It seems that she reported a case of suspected child abuse and there is going to be a hearing to ascertain whether the child should remain with the parents. The court is asking worker Adams to "come and bring with you all records which would substantiate the report of suspected child abuse and your recommendations RE: placement of the child." Worker Adams is frantic. "What an I going to do? I just know the parents are beating that child!" The director's advice is brief and to the point: "Don't worry about it, Miss Adams— in two weeks neither of us will be here and it won't matter."

Source: Record Keeping, Wilson, I., 1980
reprinted by Roy Walker, M.S.W., Area Agency on Aging, Northwest Regional Council.

Charting - Defining SOAP

S   Stands for subjective symptoms:
Information you can't measure. Problems from patient's point of view; i.e., weakness, paralysis, pain, constipation, shortness of breath.

O   Stands for objective symptoms:
Information you can measure. Direct physical observation; what you see, smell, feel, i.e., bleeding, pallor, skin conditions, vital signs, edema, respiratory distress, flaccid extremities on the right side.

A   Stands for assessment:
Diagnostic criteria; your impression, conclusion - ruling in and ruling out problems.

P   Stands for plan of action:
Method of working on the problem; nursing actions, goals, referrals, plans for therapy.

E   Stands for evaluation of the plan:
Identify problem with number and area.
Always refer back to problem list so you don't initiate a new problem.

EXAMPLE:

S   Patient states, "I can't move my right arm and leg."

O   No grip in right hand.
No voluntary movement in right arm and leg.

A   Right sided paralysis.

P   Notify physician. P.R.O.M. every shift. Position to prevent external rotation of the right hip and flexion of the right arm and fingers. Teach patient how to turn in bed. Complete motor and sensory testing. Establish bowel and bladder program.

PROGRESS NOTE

1. Patient presentation; appearance, affect.
2. Significant life events and patient's
   responses since last session.
3. Content and/or process of sessions.
4. Plan

INCLUDE: Client visits,
important phone calls,
consults, cancellations,
no-shows.

NAME_____

DATE	MODE	SIGNS	LENGTH OF SERVICE	COMMENTS/INTERVENTIONS/PROGRESS NOTES
9-21-89	1:1		2:00	10:30 — 12:30
				All was happiness and joy with B today, even though I got her out of bed at 11:00. As she hurried to dress and have her breakfast, she told me about her job.
				---The college has taken over the Wee Care ~~building and is turning it into the college daycare~~ center. B was told about this and hied herself in to see if she could get a job. She volunteered 4 days, washing, cleaning, and painting, and yesterday she was hired for 3 hrs. each day. She had thought the pay would be between $3.00 and $4.00, but was later told that she would be paid around $5.00
				Compare this to the $1.61 she had been making with her long days of baby sitting. She had cause to be happy. She has made only $1200 so far this year, so the job at the day care center will not interfere with her medical, food stamps, etc. ---B now has to worry about the tonsilectomy, but ~~would like to have it done during a school vacation~~
				so it would not interfere with her work. As part of the visit, I drove her to the store and post office and then took her home. We did considerable talking and she seemed very happy. (I hope this really works.)

PEER COUNSELOR PROGRESS NOTE

Client Name _____ Goals _Socialization_

_____

P. C. Signature ___ _____

1. Date _3-28-90_

2. Type of Contact: One-to-one _✓_ Phone____ Length of Contact _2 hrs_

   Please check every category (including Improved, Stable or Deteriorated)

3. Appearance	I	S	D	Comments: neatly dressed as usual
		✓		

4. Mood	I	S	D	Comments: Client becoming more concerned over situation
			✓	Talked about "almost wishing" she could go to rest home, w/c forgetfulness, failing vision etc. also inability to walk without cane.

5. Life Events	I	S	D	Comments: Client had just had blood taken for some kind
				of test - a Dr. Nelson but did not know why nor could Wrkr ascertain why or how this happened. Memory appears to be failing more. This visit consisted of two-hour trip through Burlington to Avon - back to Mt Vernon to see site of house she and husband

6. Coping	I	S	D	Comments: had built
			✓	client seems unable to plan or cope. Problems seem to overwhelm her. Did not even know why she had blood test - perhaps brother arranged it?

7. Progress	I	S	D	Comments: Not good, per above
			✓	

8. Change in Plan? _Yes_ — Wrkr will discuss with Supervisor - if possibly a visit with client (and Wrkr) would be appropriate. Client is very proud & doesn't want 'charity' Have never discussed cost of nursing home or possibly boarding home if available - is very low income.

PEER COUNSELING PROGRAM   171

Peer Counselor Descriptive Word List

These are descriptive words and sentences you may want to integrate into your progress notes:

> Client seems . . .
> Client appears . . .
> Client indicated . . .
> Client reports . . .
> Client ambivalent . . .
> Client demonstrated . . .
> Client guarded . . .

Descriptive Words

integrate	improve	expressed
acknowledge	guarded	discomfort
perseveres	intent	uncomfortable
support	anxiety	catastrophic
isolation	increase	acute
grief	decrease	chronic
examine	perception	incontinence
gradual	delusional	confusion
resolution	refocus	significant
indirect	fear	risk
direct	hopeful	immobile
deterioration	hopeless	incidence
depression	stressed	issue
exacerbate	reframe	reaction
generalizations	generalize	cognitive
recent	uncertain	orientation
remote	appropriate	agitated
behavior	labile	insight
limited	independent	tearfulness
marked	gross	prolonged
impairment	response	restlessness
irritable	withdrawal	prominent
pervasive	supportive	techniques
conflicts	apathy	disruptive
decline	remarkable	fixed

Key Word List to Describe Symptoms

A
aggressive
agitated
amnesic
angry
antisocial
anxious
apprehensive

B
bizarre

C
callous
catatonic
child-like
compulsive
confused

D
delinquent
delusional
dependent
depressed
disorganized
disoriented
distorted
distracted
distressed
disturbed
doubtful

E
eccentric
egocentric
elated
emotional

envious
excited
explosive
extremism
extroverted

F
fantisizes
fatigued
fearful

G
grandiose
grief

H
hallucinatory
hostile
hyperactive
hypersensitive
hypochondriacal
hysterical

I
illogical
illusional
immature
imprecise
impulsive
inappropriate
inattentive
incoherent
incompetent
indecisive
inept
inhibited

insensitive
insomnia
intolerant
introverted
irresponsible
irritable
isolated

J
jealous

L
labile

M
maladjusted
malingering
melancholic
misinterprets
moody
mute

N
negative
nervous
nonsensical

O
obsessive
overactive
oversensitive

P
panic
paranoid
perplexed
pessimistic
phobic

plastic
pressured

R
rebellious
regressive
rejected
resentful
resistive
restless
rigid

S
sad
sanguine
self-absorbed
self-centered
selfish
senile
shy
stubborn
stupor
suspicious

T
talkative
timid

U
uneasy
unemotional

V
vain
violent

W

Source: Donna Hazelton, R.N., Psychiatric Nurse, Skagit Community Mental Health Center

Sentences Which You May Use When Appropriate

Client appeared to be experiencing increased agitation . . .

The recent confrontation added to his anxiety . . .

Encouraged client to vent his frustration in verbal way . . .

Recent changes in client's life have increased her problems with sleep . . .

Client demonstrated mild confusion with an inability to concentrate for more than brief periods of time . . .

Client appears grossly lacking in judgement . . .

Client has increased social withdrawal . . .

Not oriented to time, place, or person . . .

Client experiencing obsessive thought patterns . . .

Affect is subdued, at times depressed . . .

Client conversation indicates alertness . . .

Thoughts are somewhat fleeting . . .

Client's smile is somewhat suspicious . . .

Client expresses vague thoughts regarding . . .

Client has a reoccurrence of poorly organized thoughts . . .

Client's delusional system concerns her fear of being left alone . . .

Client shows gross impairment in her ability to . . .

Client guarded, reticent and ill at ease . . .

Client affect is shallow and blunted . . .

Client's speech is coherent . . .

Client has acceptable sleep and eating patterns . . .

Client appears stable and able to maintain . . .

Treatment plan is to reduce frequency and intensity of episodes . . .

SESSION IV

The Helping Model

Session IV

Session Guide To The Trainer

As the facilitator, your job now becomes the presenter of information on counseling skills. To keep from overwhelming the trainees we use many examples and many scenarios from our own counseling experiences. Add both successful and unsuccessful examples to your collection. We use a combination of counseling theories from Gerard Egan and Allen Ivey, both in keeping with the level of paraprofessional skills we require from the Peer Counselors.

Each session focuses on dealing with the elderly client and the uniqueness of counseling the elderly client as opposed to counseling other populations.

In introducing the stages of helping, it will be wise for the facilitator to reinforce the use of empathy, paraphrasing, reflection of feelings, and summarization. Though there is never enough time to practice these skills in class, the dyad and triad exercises in the training become your most effective learning tool. The facilitator's use of a creative and interesting presentation will keep the energy high, encouraging the trainees to work on these skills outside of class.

"*The Forgotten Mother*" by Dorothy Canfield Fisher can be used for a variety of learning experiences: Group discussion around aging; learning; parenting; loss and life review. Memories can come from this story. In this story, the trainees are given an excellent example of how we are effected by early experiences, coloring the rest of our lives, yet we may not consciously recall the path to such feelings. You will want to use the story in a way that fills your group needs.

Session Materials

- Copies of *The Forgotten Mother*
- Examples of counseing situations
- Scenarios for role playing

Session IV

The Helping Model

If the only tool you have is a hammer,
you tend to see every problem as a nail.

Abraham Maslow

Today's Goal

- Introduction to the three stages of the Helping Model.
- Review Guidelines to Feedback
- Gain awareness into basic expectations for Peer Counseling

Strategy

Using group lecture and group discussion, cover specific stages of helping, lending examples to each element of the stages. Case examples are helpful when identifying the ways in which a counseling technique is actually used by a Peer Counselor.

The story "The Forgotten Mother" is used to discuss the subtle and often unconscious ways in which people develop particular beliefs and attitudes about life. Help trainees see the connection between the story and their own experiences. Continue to review the four elements of listening, reinforcing the use of them during group discussion and interactions, and role playing.

Using the trainee's statements regarding fears about counseling, model the elements of good counseling skills and feedback. Keep humor and sensitivity present. Dramatic and humorous role playing or exaggeration can be used by the facilitator to emphasize the elements of helping. During dyads, facilitator can assist trainees with specific words and reflections in order to help the process start.

Learning Objectives

- *   Clarify the building stages of counseling skills.
- *   Increase comfort in using a counseling style of communication.
- *   Reinforce the listening skills needed when working with grief.
- *   Investigate the creativity and purpose of the helping model.

Handouts and Workbook Materials

Levels the Helping Model
Guidelines for Giving Feedback
Expectations for Counselors
Requirements for Creativity
Eight tasks of Effective Helping
The Forgotten Mother - a short story

And So We Learn
The Counseling "Language" . . . Session IV

I. "Temperature Reading"

Allow 2-3 minutes for members to clarify issues from last week. Listen for cues regarding their learning level.

II. Introduction of the Helping Model

Using newsprint to list examples of the segments of each stage of counseling, help the trainees to demystify "counseling." For paraprofessional counseling the emphasis is on Stages I and II with Stage III for more advanced Peer Counseling skills. Trainees will attempt to try and intellectualize the stages. It is important that the facilitator leads the group towards the motivation and attitudes necessary for counseling and away from cognitive theory.

In working with older clients, the areas of concern are most often:
Depression
Loneliness
Loss
Grief
Poor health or diminished abilities
Financial stress

Trainees will want to know ways in which these counseling stages can "fix" clients. Time must be spent helping the trainee understand that clients may not have "fixable" problems. Their job as a peer counselor is to support the older client who is attempting to understand and adjust to the multiple changes in his or her life. With the aging mental health client, maintaining a stable level of independent living is significant progress.

III. Expectations for Counselors

A review of the requirements for creativity will help trainees to identify their client's underlying feeling in order to clarify their issues.

There are 13 counseling expectations with which the trainees will become familiar and internalize.

Review the list of expectations for counselors in group discussion.

Experiential Exercise - "Expectations Clarification"

Forming triads, instruct trainees to discuss the 13 counselor expectations within the small groups. Identify those statements that seem unclear. Have the triad create examples of three of the statements to bring back and share with the larger group.

Example - Use of analogies and metaphors

Client: An 80-year old man reports to his peer counselor that he feels he has "nothing left," that he is thinking about giving his fishing gear to his son as he can't use it any more.

Peer Counselor: You sound pretty sad when you talk about "hanging up your fishing gear," I guess you remember all the good days of catching fish and it seems to you like your "fishing days" are over.

Group Discussion

What is the relationship of the counselor/client.

What is the difference between content and emotion?

Why use metaphors?

What are the signs that you are engaged in resistance?

Key Element:

Encourage trainees to use their many natural talents when relating to their client. Creativity and flexibility will stimulate their client's view of life, as well as their own.

IV. Feedback Guidelines

Using a group discussion of the story "Forgotten Mother" as a vehicle for introducing feedback, the facilitator covers the guidelines to giving feedback by responding to statements by the group members as they discuss the story.

Example:

Trainee: "I think the story was just about a doctor who was getting old and doing some remembering; actually it reminded me of my mother.

Facilitator: I hear you saying the story started you thinking about your mother, but that the story was about remembering as we get older.

The facilitator will continue to point out feedback skills and to model feedback to the group throughout the session. Group discussion is encouraged regarding the story theme of how we learn from our parents and how this relates to our client's reminiscing.

Key Element:

We all learn, subtly, a word, a view, a lifeview, through the smallest interaction, even in this class. This point is being made over and over again.

V. Closing

Encourage and support trainees for their use and completion of homework. Remind them to write in their journal/workbook, especially regarding any feeling that may have come to them when reading *The Forgotten Mother.*

VI. Summarization

There is much cognitive materials in this session. The trainee will experience some anxiety and feel a bit overwhelmed. Many parts of the helping model are designed to give the trainee an overview of counseling techniques. All of these techniques will not necessarily be incorporated into each counseling session. When concerns about being able to "learn" arise in the group, your affirmation and therapeutic skills will need to be used. There is a lot of information for the trainees to "inject" in eight short weeks. Your validation of their work on listening skills, and understanding the concerns of aging is of great importance. The facilitator always needs to interweave the issues of the aging client into the specific counseling skill.

I hear and I forget
I see and I remember
I do and I understand

Chinese Proverb

Recommended Reading

Alpaugh, P. & M. Haney. Counseling the Older Adult, Ethel Percy Andrus Gerontology Center: University of Southern California Press, 1978.

Carkhuff, R. R. The Art of Helping, Amherst, Moss: Human Resource Development Press, Inc., 1977.

SESSION IV

Handouts & Workbook Materials

Levels of the Helping Model

STAGE I: **Initial Problem Clarification**

* Attending   focus on client, "being with client."
* Listening   verbal and nonverbal encouragement, establish trust.
* Probing   honoring self and others, encourage client to self explore.
* Understanding   empathy, working with client.

STAGE II: **Challenging Process - Finding Workable Goals**

* Summarizing   help client to clarify problem situations, "accept ownership of problems."
* Information giving   peer counseling helps client acquire information to see problem in new light.
* Confrontation   challenges peer counselor to help client look at smoke screens that keep them from knowing themselves.
* Self-Sharing   sharing your own experiences with client as a way of modeling self-disclosure.
* Immediacy   direct mutual talk about what is happening between you and the client.

STAGE III: **Action - How clients are to do what they want to do**

* Brainstorming   listing ways client has coped in the past, life review, memories, fantasies, realities.
* Support & Challenge   nonjudgemental, non-advise, non-expectations.

• Problem Solving   using peer's and client's creativity to address the problem. Assertiveness, reinforcement - celebrate the steps, the learning.

Source: Gerard Egan, <u>The Skilled Helper</u>

Creativity is . . .

* If the Requirement for Creativity is -

1) optimism and confidence - client feels:
   depressed and powerless;

2) acceptance of uncertainty - client feels:
   ambiguity and need to escape;

3) wide range of interests - client feels:
   narrowed by anxiety and pain;

4) flexibility - client feels:
   rigid;

5) verbal fluency - client feels:
   unable to express him/herself;

6) curiosity - client feels:
   fear of searching due to past hurts;

7) independence - client feels
   dependent, fights efforts to be helped (yes, but);

8) nonconformity - client feels:
   conservative, need to go with group;

9) persistence - client feels:
   ready to give up soon.

The Eight Tasks of Effective Helping

For the most part the exercises presented here are grouped around and follow the order of the eight tasks that need to be undertaken in the effective management of problem situations. These tasks are:

1. Assessment. This means helping clients find out what's going wrong and what's going right in their lives. Successful assessment helps clients identify both problems and resources. Assessment helps clients see any given problem in a wider context. Assessment goes on throughout the helping process.

2. Focusing and initial problem exploration. This means helping clients identify the particular concern or concerns they want to deal with and beginning the exploration and clarification process.

3. New perspectives. This means helping clients see themselves, their concerns, and the context of their concerns more objectively, that is, in such a way as to begin to see what they would like to do about them.

Steps 1, 2, and 3, therefore, deal with problem indentification and clarification.

4. Goal setting. This means helping clients set problem-managing goals. A goal is nothing else but what a client wants to accomplish in order to manage a problem situation or some part of it more effectively.

   A goal refers to what a client would like to do about a problem situation. The next two steps taken together consitute program development. Program development deals with how clients might go about accomplishing their goals.

5. Program possibilities. This refers to helping clients see the many different ways that any given goal can be accomplished. It also refers to helping clients identify the resources available for accomplishing goals.

6. Program choice. This refers to helping clients choose the kind of program that best fits their style, resources, and environment.

7. Program implementation. This refers to helping clients implement the programs they have chosen and helping them overcome the obstacles they encounter as they do so.

8. Evaluation. This refers to helping clients monitor their participation in programs, their accomplishments of goals, and their management of problem situations.

Source: <u>The Skilled Helper</u>, Gerard Egan

EXPECTATIONS FOR COUNSELORS

1) Clear definition of the relationship.
   Purpose of the relationship can be negotiated by those involved.

2) Your responsibility is to maneuver and be flexible.

3) Distinguish between emotions and content.
   Speak to emotion first.

4) Reframe.

5) Use analogies and metaphors.

6) Stress strengths and support.

7) Confront without anger/judgement.

8) Accept manipulation as OK.

9) Check assumptions/judgements.

10) Learn to recognize when you are engaged in resistance.

11) Learn how client processes information.

12) Set limits (see #1).

13) Know what you're working with
    - strengths   - motivation
    - weaknesses   - capacity

Source: Tamar Groffman, M.S.W., psychotherapist, Bellingham, Washington

Guidelines for Giving Feedback

1. <u>Is the receiver ready?</u>   -   Has the receiver indicated he is ready to listen and accept the feedback as it is intended? There is little point to giving feedback that won't be heard or will be misunderstood.

2. <u>Is it descriptive, not interpretive</u>   -   Feedback is a description of your perception and reactions. Interpreting meanings of another's behavior is a guessing game the other may resent. Let him share his own meanings if he's so inclined. If you want to check your perception of his meaning, be very clear that is what you are doing.

3. <u>Does it cover recent happenings?</u>   -   The closer feedback is to the time the behavior occurred, the more helpful it is. When feedback is given immediately, all know exactly what it refers to and feelings about the situation are most valid.

4. <u>Is it on changeable things?</u>   -   The value of feedback to the other is in being able to modify behavior if he wants to. Reactions to things that can't be changed are not usually helpful.

5. <u>Is it an overload?</u>   -   If you give another too much feedback (whether positive or negative) or too many things all at once, it may be more than he can deal with and lose track of all you are saying.

6. <u>Does it share something of the giver?</u> -   Giving feedback can create a sense of imbalance in the relationship. It generally helps the receiver feel more comfortable and be more active if the giver can share some of his own feelings and concerns as he gives his reactions to the other.

7. <u>Is it specific rather than general?</u>   -   Be specific by quoting and giving examples of what you are referring to.

Source: <u>The Evaluative Process in Psychiatric Occupational Therapy</u>, Barbara J. Hemphill, M.S., O.T.R., Editor, Charles B. Slack, Inc., 1982, pp. 29, 36.

Guidelines for Receiving Feedback

1. <u>Check for understanding</u>   -   Use a technique such as paraphrasing to be sure you understand the meaning of the other's reactions. Watch out for becoming argumentative or taking a lot of time giving the rationale for your behavior (being defensive), rather than working to understand the other's feedback to you

2. <u>Ask for feedback about specific things</u> -   You can help the giver provide useful reactions by asking for feedback about specific things. This indicates your areas of readiness to receive feedback and helps him be specific rather than general.

3. <u>Share your reactions to feedback</u>   -   Sharing your reactions to the feedback you have received can help the giver improve his skills at giving useful feedback. It also lets him know where he stands with you on a feeling basis so that the relationship can continue to grow. If he goes off uncertain about your reactions to his feedback, he may feel less inclined to risk sharing them with you in the future.

<u>*Questions to Enhance Feedback Process*</u>

_____ Did I enable the client to speak as freely as possible about himself without burdening him with my own values, biases, or concerns?

_____ Did the client gain some understanding of himself and his problems? Was he able to share with me how he felt and what he thought?

_____ Did I really listen to what his concerns were or did I try to program him to mine?

_____ Do I have a greater understanding of the person? Do I know what additional information I need in order to understand him better?

_____ Are the goals for treatment becoming more diffuse or more specific and clear? Are the goals my goals, the client's goals, or were the goals mutually arrived at?

_____ Did my questions and responses facilitate the client's discussion? Was I able to refocus the client's discussion when he strayed from the topic being discussed?

Source: <u>The Evaluative Process in Psychiatric Occupational Therapy</u>, Barbara J. Hemphill, M.S., O.T.R., Editor, Charles B. Slack, Inc., 1982, pp. 29, 36.

The Forgotten Mother

It was one of Dr. Burrage's sayings that neither he nor his son—his adopted son, that is—knew anything at first hand about mothers. "Dr. Wright's died at his birth. And I lost mine when I was between four and five. Can't remember her at all. Well, yes, I do have a dim picture of someone with brown hair, rather soft and light, with a lock that often fell over her forehead. I can remember how she used to brush it back with her hand. Queer, how a meaningless gesture like that should stick in a child's memory. Then there's something connected with her in a recollection I have of walking along a beam laid on the ground. You know how kids love to do that. She was there at the time, I presume."

Once, four or five years after his beloved adopted son had gone into practice with him, another faint memory of her emerged into visibility from nowhere, as things from the past do come back to people approaching old age. The two doctors had been sitting late before the fire in a sociable silence. They often ended their days by such a quiet time together. The bond between them was so close that they scarcely needed words to share each other's thoughts. The clock striking midnight aroused them from this silent communion of comradeship. "Well, son, we must get to bed," said Dr. Burrage, heaving himself up from his armchair. He added, "Odd! Just now, I seemed to be way back in the past . . . back to some time when I sat quiet like this with my mother."

"I thought you couldn't remember her," remarked Dr. Wright, winding his watch.

"Well, of course I can't. Not really," admitted the older man. "I was too young when she died to remember her."

He was repeating what people always say about children whose mothers die young; what had been said in his hearing a great many times when he was a little boy of five. "No, he won't remember her. He's too young." Especially had this been said by the handsome, energetic young woman who, when he was six, became his stepmother, and who from that time on ran the family life so competently that his father, from earning very little, made constantly a bigger and bigger income and blew his brains out in a fit of jealousy and drunken melancholia when he was forty-two. His handsome stepmother soon married again and went away to live in the Philippines. From then on Henry Burrage—but he was twenty then—had to manage by himself without any parents at all. For the few recollections of his mother, vivid at the time of her death, had long ago been blurred to nothingness by time and his stepmother.

Naturally some memories endured longer than others. Not until he had lived four or five years without her did the hawk episode fade out of his mind. There was nothing much to it anyway, and it happened when he was quite small. His mother—his own mother—had taken him to spend the day on a farm—he never knew whose, nor why. Probably it belonged to a cousin or uncle of hers. There were other children there, older than he, good-natured country children used to playing with all ages, who carried him out to a game of tag in the back yard.

He had not liked being taken away from his mother by strangers, although the strangers were only boys and girls bigger than he. A back yard that did not have his mother in it, might have—he didn't know what. The first thing he saw as he looked suspiciously around was an apple tree between the house and the barn, and he didn't like that, either. A dead limb on it pointed stiffly off towards a grove of old oaks set so thickly that he could not see what was in the darkness under them. Only a strip of plowed field lay between the yard and the darkness under the trees. It was too narrow to suit Henry. He wished his mother had come along. Without her, everything in this new world held a menace. The kind, masterful older children sent him to and fro in the game. His feet trotted docilely wherever he was told to go; but in his heart a dark pool of uneasiness brimmed slowly up towards fear. The dead branch kept pointing so.

After a time the big girl who was directing proceedings sent him to hide behind the lilac bush, next to the house. It was close to an open window. As he squeezed himself down into his hiding place he heard through the window two grown-up voices speaking in dark secret tones. The game was blind man's bluff. It was the first time he had ever played it, and he found it terribly exciting. His heart rose sickeningly into his throat every time the hooded "it" came near, groping dreadfully with those blind clutching hands. Once they grasped and shook the thin branches of the bush that were his only poor shelter. His throat drew together convulsively into a knot. When the game's center shifted to the other side of the yard, he sank down on his heels, worn out with tension, trying to get his breath through that knot. But now behind him, a man's bass voice, rumbling ominously, said,"Hand me my gun, will you, Ella? I want to have it handy if I see that hawk in the woods."

A hawk. A hawk! What was a hawk, the little city boy asked himself feverishly, that a man—big he must be to have a deep voice like that—should be so afraid of it that he must take his gun with him. He stood up to peer fearfully through the twigs of the bush over at the dark trees, hiding something so dreadful that great grown-up men were frightened of it, and covered his face in his arms. If a man was frightened of it—Henry's legs gave way under him. A hawk! What is a hawk? He whispered the evil-sounding word over to himself, crouching behind the lilac bush. Fear oozed out of the woods, as out of a cracked bottle, and, thick, clammy, black, flowed sluggishly across the field towards Henry. The other children had stopped playing, and were talking. He had forgotten them. The vague menace that had darkened the air ever since he had left his mother, grew blacker. He could feel how every repetition of the evil word drew towards him the unknown danger out from the darkness under the oak trees. Cold sweat burst from his pores, trickling down his back like ice water. Never again in all his life from that moment on to his dying hour, did Henry Burrage feel such strangling terror.

And now the older children turned and ran back to the little guest, putting out their hands, dragging him out, saying kindly, cheerfully, "Come on! We're going over to the woods to play. Come on!"

This saved the little boy's reason. For the shock pierced through the numb nightmare helplessness in which he had been crouching, frozen, silent, crazed, and awoke his instinct for self-preservation. Here was no dangerous unknown that muffled a little boy in blackness without showing anything against which he could fling himself in resistance. Here were real arms and legs and bodies he could fight. Here was good flesh and blood which he could bite and kick and scratch. They would never take him to the woods where the hawk would get him. Never. Never. He would kill every one before he would go to the woods.

He was seized and held high in the air. The grownups had run out of the house, rushing to the struggling, screaming children. The farmer, his rifle still in one hand, with the other had torn the little boy from his murderous attack. Through his own frantic sobbing, Henry could hear that everyone was loudly talking, the bewildered, frightened children protesting, "No, we were not teasing him. We weren't even anywhere near him. We had only—" the elders saying, "If he were my child, I know what I'd do!"

He heard a man's voice say, gloatingly, "You've got to punish him, Mary, this time. You've just got to whip him. If you don't, I will."

A woman cried out, "Look what he's done to poor little Ella's dress. He ought to be spanked till he can't—"

Then his mother's voice—his mother's voice! He had forgotten that he had a mother. "Give him to me Ed. Don't you touch him Aunt.

He was in her arms now, in his mother's arms, he was clutching at her with all his might, she was carrying him around to the other side of the house, away from the forked tongues of anger licking hotly around them.

She sat down on the ground in the shade of a big currant bush and let him cry and cry and cry, holding him close till—could it be true, could it be true!—he felt that if he could keep on crying only a little longer, he would have wept away the dreadfulness that had seemed the end of life. With his every sob, he could feel it going away. The muscles of his clenched hands began to loosen. The relief made him cry harder than ever.

When the last wild sob was over, he himself, not a fear-crazed maniac, just Henry, sitting on his mother's lap and feeling something smooth and soft in his hand. It was the ribbon at her throat on which his hand had been clenched so tautly that he could not, when he first tried, open his fingers. That ribbon was blue, wasn't it? Seems as though it had been blue when he saw his mother tying it before the mirror, this morning, ages ago, before they had come to this place. He opened his hand and lifted his head to look at the ribbon. His eyes were still swimming, he was still drawing long convulsive breaths that sounded like sobs. They did not feel like sobs. They felt like coming up for air where you could breathe, after having been held a long time under water. His breathing slowed down. He began to finger the crumpled blue ribbon with grimy little hands.

At this his mother smiled at him and set him down on the ground beside her. "What do you say we lay out a pretend farm?" she proposed. She cleared a space on the earth with a sweep of her hand and began to make a wall of pebbles around it. "Where do you think to road ought to go?" she asked him.

He showed her where he thought the road should be. She leaned forward to draw the line of it as he pointed, and a lock of her soft brown hair fell down over her eyes. She put it back with her hand. Henry reached for a bit of old shingle that would make a bridge. "Let's have a brook," he said. He had meant to go on to say, "I like brooks, don't you?" but his voice was so shaky he didn't try. "Yes, brooks are sort of nice," his mother answered.

They worked together, making fields and the barnyard, looking for stones small enough and flat enough to be steppingstones. The little boy's breathing and pulse gradually slowed down till they were nearly all right. His mother did not ask him—she never asked him—what had made him act so naughty. But presently he asked her something. In a trembling whisper, and keeping his head bent very low, he asked, "Mother, what is a hawk?" She told him, and added a story from her own country childhood about a brave mother hen who had fought off a hawk from her baby chicks.

He sank his head still lower. "It's not a-a-a dragon?" he breathed.

"No, oh, no," she told him quietly, "only a bird, not as big as that rooster over there." As she told him this, she sat up, and put back her hair from her forehead with her hand.

He lifted his head then and looked into her eyes, deeply into his mother's honest eyes.

They went on making a play-farm, the little boy moving pebbles here and there, his mother making a rail fence out of twigs. They scooped out a place for a pond, and put moss around the sides. He said, "I'm going to make a road go a long, long way, clear off to town."

All the while there was flowing into him the knowledge that he was safe, that there was nothing to fear, that hawk is only a bird no bigger than a rooster. He had been filled to the smallest cell of his body with terror. Now terror was gone, and into the empty little Henry that was left poured confidence and courage. Flooding rich and warm, this tide of faith in life began to circulate in his every vein and artery. It did not come from his mother. It came from his having learned what the things you are afraid of, really are. Those oak trees—they were nothing but trees. The stiff evil pointing branch—it was only a piece of dead wood. A hawk is only a bird.

The knot that had been strangling him loosened, loosened, fell away.

Presently his young mother saw that her little boy was sound asleep, so soundly asleep that he did not even wake up till they were at home again.

He never spoke of that day. Nor did his mother. During the next year he learned so many new things—trains and telephones and how to go to the grocery store alone, and how to tie his own shoelaces—that when he remembered his mistake about the hawk he was quite ashamed that he had ever been such an ignorant baby. So he forgot it.

There was no such reason for forgetting the time he walked the beam, and all his life he kept a few shreds of memory about that. About a year before his mother died, a long squared timber—perhaps left behind by the builder who had just finished a new cottage next door—lay for a day or two across the front yard of the little one-story brown house that was Henry's home. One morning when Henry's young father came out on the front porch after breakfast, a gust of the boyishness such a short time behind him blew him up on it to run lightly from one end to the other, setting his feet down on the narrow beam with nimble precision, and leaping off at the other end with a pirouette of triumph. So of course little Henry must do this also. He stepped happily up on the end, as his father had. But when he lifted one foot to put it in front of the other, he fell off. The grass was soft. He was not hurt at all, but very much surprised. He rose at once and tried it again more cautiously. Again, before he could set down his advancing foot he lost his balance and tumbled off on the grass. His father laughed good-naturedly at the clumsy child, looked at his watch, kissed his wife goodby, pulled down his vest, and went off to the factory office to work. But halfway down the street he turned and came leaping back to kiss his wife goodby again. "You look like sunshine," he told her. This was because she wore a yellow dress with ruffles, she said. He shook his head, put his hand gently on her hair, and went away again. She stood on the porch, looking after him and smiling.

Henry had been thinking hard about walking the beam. He felt that his two falls were due to his not having really put his mind on it, and with great care he stepped up once more. He fell off at once. At this he lost his temper, scrambled up to his feet, kicked the beam with all his might. It was very hard, and Henry's foot was soft. He hurt his toes dreadfully and gave a yell of rage.

"What's the matter?" asked his mother, turning her head towards him. She was still smiling although by this time Henry's father had turned the corner and was out of sight.

"I want to walk this thing the way father did," he told her, frowning and sticking his lower lip very far out.

"Well, why don't you?"

"I ca-a-an't!" he complained in a nasal whine.

"Yes, you can if you want to." She stopped smiling, and gave her attention seriously to her son's problem, and stepped down from the porch to where he stood. "You can do anything—if you want to enough to learn how," she told him.

"How do you learn things?" he asked dubiously.

"You keep trying to."

So he began to try and she to keep him trying. He was soon ready to give up, but she reminded him a good many times what fun it would be to know how to run along as his father had, so after resting and eating another piece of bread and butter, he tried some more. It went better. He took two steps without falling. His mother clapped her hands and looked proud He learned that it helped to wave his arms around as he stepped cautiously forward. His mother brought out a basket of mending and sat on the edge of the porch, watching him as he took those two steps over and over—and fell. Presently he took three before he fell. "Goody!" said his mother. "Try again."

But he was hot and tired, and sorry that he had ever begun this stupid business. What did he care about it! He turned around to his sand pile and went on with a mountain he had started there yesterday. His mother said nothing. A little anxiously, he called her attention to the bigness of the mountain he was making. She nodded and smiled pleasantly. But she did not clap her hands or look proud. "Oh, dear!" thought little Henry crossly. He went on patting and poking at his mountain, but he did not see it. "Oh, dear!" he said. Presently he went back to the beam.

"That's fine," said his mother.

But it wasn't fine at all. It wasn't a bit fun any more. It was just work. Yet somehow, it didn't seem quite so hard to do. By and by, he had taken six tottering steps before falling. And then seven, and then eight He and his mother looked at each other proudly.

After lunch and his nap, when he went out on the front porch the tiresome thing was still lying across their yard, as he felt it lying across his mother's mind. Yielding to this pressure, he went back languidly and practiced some more. His mother came out beside the beam to watch. "You're getting along well," she said. He tried harder.

"Why," said his mother, holding out her hands to show, "you've only so much more to go, to do it all."

Then it came to Henry. Before he had even once shakily teetered his way from one end to the other of the beam, he was not shaky any more. Something in his head that had been holding out against his wanting to do it, gave way. Something in his legs that had been wavering and uncertain, straightened and steadied. Henry knew how. Straight and true he trotted to the far end of the beam and jumped off. He was tired, quite tired, but happy. "Watch me!" he told his mother, and stepping up, trotted all the way back. Whatever had made him think it was hard to do?

"Well, Henry!" said his mother.

Henry knew by the way she said this that she was just as proud of him as she could be. It was not the first time his mother had been proud of him, but it was the first time he had known she was. It was glorious! His heart shone. He ran to her to hug her knees with all his might. She was a Friend, Henry's mother was, so she had quiet Quaker ways and did not squeal and call him darling and honeybunch and such things. But Henry knew what she meant.

There were no other Friends in the town where Henry's father had taken his young bride, so she had no Meetings to go to. But sometimes she and little Henry had Meeting by themselves. Once in a while of a winter afternoon, before the stove (his parents were poor as well as young and had only a stove, not a furnace), once in a while in summer, out in the side yard under the very old oak tree that overhung the tiny cottage, Henry's mother would say, "What do you say we have Meeting?"

Henry liked Meeting pretty well, although there wasn't much to it. All you did was just to sit quiet. Sometimes when he was still very small, he sat on his mother's lap. Sometimes he sat beside her and held her hand. She let him do whatever he felt like doing, so long as he was quiet. Sometimes, when they had Meeting out-of-doors, he slid down and lay on his back on the ground, looking up into the strong, crooked, rough branches of the old oak tree, and through them at the blue, blue sky. Once or twice he dozed off into a nap. Once or twice his mother prayed. Always the same prayer, "God please make my little boy strong and good." The first time, "What is 'God'?" he asked her curiously, but shyly, for a string inside him had been softly plucked by the sound of her voice when she said the work. She answered him, "When a little boy wants to do what's right, that's God in his heart."

But mostly there was no talk at all. Just a stillness, and Mother's face so quiet and calm that it made Henry feel quiet and calm to look at it.

Then she died and he began to forget her. It did not take long. He was so young, four and a half years old. And his stepmother was so devoted to him. She was the daughter and only child of the rich man who owned the factory where Father went to work in the office, so of course after she married Father he got a better job, and after that a better one yet. There was soon plenty of money, instead of too little. They moved to a new home. It was so large and his father thought the plain old furnishings just wouldn't do. So everything was bought fresh and new. There was nothing, not a chair, not a picture, nor a scarf, nor so much as a handkerchief that could remind little Henry of his mother who had died.

"You're my little boy now, honeybunch!" his pretty stepmother often told him, hugging him hard. "And I'm going to give you a . . . good . . . time!" She never said anything to him about his mother, but, bit by bit, one time or another, he overheard how she talked to other people—how she pitied him because his mother had deprived him of the toys and candy and clothes every child needs to be happy. "Think of it! He had never been to the circus! And he had never had a toy with wheels—not so much as a little express wagon! Nor any fun either. His mother was a Quaker. She didn't know how to have a good time!"

Henry's stepmother, whom he was taught to call by her pet name of Tulip—knew all about having a good time. She saw to it that Henry's father did, too. They were always dressing to go out in the evening, to dinner, to a country club dance, to a restaurant in a city forty miles away, to the theater—or perhaps for a week end in New York. Henry learned to dodge them for a few days after a New York week end because they had headaches and were cross. "I can't ever make up to my poor husband," Henry heard her say to other people, "for those pokey moldy years of his first marriage."

Once a visitor asked her, idly, "Did you ever know his first wife?"

Tulip's face darkened. "Yes, I did! That is, I met her once or twice. I remember her very well." Her voice was sharp.

"What was she like?"

"I always hated her!" cried Tulip. "She was one of those horrid women who are satisfied no matter what they have! She was always smiling. I hated her."

Another time, some years later, one evening after a good many cocktails, when talking to a man who excited her, she said she didn't care who knew that she fell dead in love with Henry the first time she saw him, a young employee in her father's office, and had nearly died of jealousy of the plain, dowdy Quakeress he was married to. "It runs in our family," she said proudly, "to have strong feelings. No Quaker blood in us!" And sure enough, by and by, her feeling for the man who excited her grew so strong that Henry's father shot himself.

But that was later, after Henry had grown up, or almost, and was in college.

Nobody had ever thought of such a thing as his going to college—Tulip because it seemed to her a hideous waste of time for anybody to bother with books; Henry because he was lazy, spoiled, and ignorant; Henry's father because he always thought just what Tulip did. As to the rest of the people who knew Henry and his father and Tulip, half of them were sure the kid would be in the reform school by the time he was old enough for college, and the other half couldn't see any more sense in book-learning than Tulip did.

Eight or nine years after her marriage, Tulip began to get tired of Henry. It was just about the time when she had finally succeeded in killing and completely burying his mother. Perhaps she knew this. Perhaps it was because he had all of a sudden stopped being a cute kid with cute ways and had grown into a gangling, clumsy, long-legged boor with the worst manners in this world. So Tulip told his father that though it simply broke her heart to be separated from the dear boy, she felt he ought to be in a good military school where he would be handled by men. Of course his father felt so too, as soon as Tulip told him to.

From that time on, Henry had no home and no mother and no father. In June he went from his prep school into a summer camp, and in September back to prep school, staying in Tulip's house only a few days in between times. The first year he was at school was one long horror to him. Badly trained, badly taught, badly spoiled as he was, nobody liked him, and he hated everybody. The school was what is called "well run," that is, run so that on the surface nothing could be seen of what was really going on in any boy's life. Setting-up exercises, cold showers, chapel, games, drill, meals—every minute of the day was spent in doing something active—left! right! left! right!—under the eye of a supervising officer, and plenty of them, one to every six boys. All that was Henry (and a good deal of him had accumulated by this time) lay festering in the dark, far beneath the school's flawless varnish.

His first summer camp began in the same way—why not, the camp being run to make extra money by three of the officer-teachers on the school faculty. But it was worse, because by this time adolescence—whatever we mean by that—had come to him. In the well-run school it meant that when those strong qualities which were to make Henry a man of power, for good or evil, came violently into life, they found him shut up in solitary confinement in a lightless cave. Like waves from an ocean immeasurably greater than Henry, they thundered along under the low rocky roof of the cavern which was now the only place the real Henry had to live in—flooding over him, lifting him off his feet, half drowning him, battering him against the sides of his prison till he was all one bruise. At the meeting where the officer-teacher-counselors of camp put their heads together about how to keep the boys in order, "Watch out for that Henry," they said. "He's got bad blood in him." So the guard set on Henry redoubled. To the right and to the left of him, wherever he was, stretched ranks of other boys, under the same discipline as he—they called it discipline—a watchful teacher-officer at each end of the row. It was a very well-run camp. His mother, quite forgotten, lay in her grave far away.

But one of the teachers liked to go fishing. One morning in July, he felt like having a day on the lake and needed a boy to help him with the other oar of the heavy lake boat. Henry, because he was big for his age and because nobody else wanted him around, was told off for this duty. After they were well out on the water, the teacher, guided by those unseen weather signs legible to fishermen, decided that he would have better luck if he fished from an island at the other end of the lake.

By the time they had landed there, the teacher had thought of a way to get rid of the disagreeable hulking fellow who would certainly make a noise if he stayed near. He said in a tone of imitation geniality, "Wouldn't you like to try your hand too? Take this rod, and go around to the cove at the other end of the island, and see how you make out with casting." He added indulgently, longing for a whole day of quiet for his own fishing, "Take your lunch along so if you have good luck you won't need to stop."

Henry, fishing rod in hand, clumped heavily on his big feet through the woods to the other end of the island. It was not more than a mile away from the fisherman-teacher, but every step of that distance took Henry into a realm where since his little boyhood he had not in a waking moment set foot, not once—into quiet, solitude, and silence. A huge weather-beaten granite rock, shaded by an age-scarred oak tree, lay like a fallen giant, half in the water of the cove, half on the beach. Henry climbed up on it and hung his feet over the edge, his huge clumsy feet that made him awkward and showed he was to be great in stature among men. He fastened the imitation fly on his line as he had seen his teacher do, and made a few casts, with no success. It was not very interesting. Presently his arm tired. Having no watchful supervising teacher near him to keep him active, he laid his rod down.

It was great, he thought, not to have anybody around to spoil his sitting and doing nothing, if he wanted to. He looked down idly at his feet. Funny how light it made a person feel not to be slogging along, left, right, left, right, hammering down hard and heavy on the earth. It must make your feet surprised to be floating, nothing but air under them. He swung them idly to and fro to feel their lightness. Then, forgetting this, he let them hand down and stared at the sunlit water, brim-brim-brimming up on the beach of the little voice where he sat, quiet and still for the first time since—he could not remember when he had ever sat so still as this. Back of him a bird dropped a sleepy summer note into the woods. After a while he slid down on the warm rock, stretched himself out and put his arms under his head. Strange, as he looked up into the strong, crooked, rough old oak branches, strange how light he began to feel, all of him, not just his feet. The rock was so strong. It bore him up as though his heavy, overgrown body that was too big for him weighted no more than that of a little tiny boy on his mother's lap.

He lay thus a long time. An hour? Two hours? Once, looking up at the arch of the sky, bent over the lake, he thought that it was as blue as a piece of blue ribbon.

He had lain thus, motionless and relaxed for most of the morning, when he shut his eyes, pinched them shut, with a shudder. He had felt surging towards him one of those frightful waves of feeling that left him battered and bruised to the bone. But this was not shut up and driven with savage force along a tortuous narrow channel deep in blackness. It had the whole universe to spread out in. It flooded over him from everywhere, from the sky, from the earth, the kind sun, the lake's calm stillness. He had been relaxed too long to stiffen himself against it, and when it reached him—soft, warm, mighty, gentle—it floated him off as light as air, up and up like a thistledown into the vast spaciousness above him where there was room for everything! Those terrific wants were only a part, a small part, of him, of living, of what was before him. There was room for them, for everything—sunny, limitless room in which life's different parts fitted together in their true proportions, made one shapely whole which a lonely big boy almost a man need not dread, need not fight, need not be ashamed of.

The knot that had been strangling him, loosened, loosened, fell away.

When he was dropped again, light as thistledown, on the strong sustaining rock, Henry, big overgrown boy though he was, rolled over on his face and began to cry. There was no one to hear him. He could cry as much as he wanted to.

When he had cried as much as he wanted to, and sat up again, he felt better—why, he could hardly believe it, he felt so much better. And, good gosh! Was he hungry! He ate his lunch to the last crumb, strolling up and down the little beach. Then he tried seriously to fish and did catch two rock bass, little fellows. After that he went in swimming, and after that he just lazed around, playing with pebbles. Some, the flat ones, he skipped across the water. The pretty rounded ones he arranged vaguely in designs, stars and diamonds and things, thinking to himself how much better everything looked when it was arranged in a pattern.

When he heard the teacher coming, crashing through the woods, he was a little ashamed of being such a kid and brushed his hand back and forth to smooth out the designs he had made.

"Well—?" asked the fisherman-teacher. He looked at the two bass, small ones. It was four o'clock. They had been fishing for eight hours. He himself had nine pounds and a half of fish. His face told Henry what he thought of Henry as a fisherman. But he has passed examinations in pedagogic theory, remembered that a teacher must give his students plenty of encouragement and always think of something positive not negative to say, so he smiled and said in a cracked, imitation-cherry voice, "Pretty good, Henry. Pre-t-t-tty good, for the first time."

But Henry didn't hate his falseness and pretense, nor want to strangle him for it, as he would yesterday. He thought to himself with sympathy, "Gosh, it must be fierce to have a job like that."

After that most of Henry's leisure time was spent in fishing. He never became very expert at it, that is, he never brought back from his long solitary days of angling any very big catches. But he continued to go. And fishing is such a right masculine sport that nobody at school, or camp, or even in Tulip's house, interfered with it. They interfered with him less anyhow after that first summer. There was less need to. "He was," they said proudly at faculty meetings, "coming out all right after all." As with so many other troublesome boys, the right school turned the trick, gave him just what he needed. He turned the corner of adolescence without disaster and became another person, a credit to their teaching. They were actually sorry to have him graduate.

When he did, he told his father and Tulip that he was going to study to be a doctor. They tried their best to dissuade him from this absurd idea. And so did everybody else who knew him. Tulip told him a thousand times, earnestly, "Now, Henry, don't be foolish! You know you'll never be able to stick it through! Don't you realize that it would take eight years! You'd simply die of boredom! You'd never have yourself a good time! Not once. Eight of the very best years of your life, when you might be having the best times, you'd be leaning over sick people and catching their diseases. Wherever in this world did you get such a crazy idea, anyhow?

She repeated this with variations a good many times. Every time, when her breath gave out and she had to stop, Henry answered her sheepishly that he guessed he could stick it out all right. But he never told her wherever in this world he got such an idea, because he did not know.

Stick it out he did for those endless eight years, during five of which he had to support himself, his father dying and leaving no money. Tulip, of course, felt no call to spend her substance on another woman's son. Twice he had to drop out and get a business job to make enough money to go on with.

He was a big, grave, rather graceless man of twenty-seven when he finally had M.D. to put after his name, and began the practice that was to bring him such rich rewards, was to bring his patients help, protection, consolation. Old Dr. Hepplewaite took him in at once as assistant—"I don't say Henry's brilliant. But there's something—perhaps something about his character—that'll be useful to him in the practice of medicine."

There certainly turned out to be, although people differed as to what its name was. Some of his patients called it dogged persistence. "Dr. Burrage just won't let go of a patient," they said, comforted when he came lumbering into the sick-room. But others insisted it was his fearlessness. "You can feel it all over Dr. Burrage—he simply doesn't know what fear is," they said. And indeed when someone once asked him, he said he didn't know but that that was so, he really couldn't ever remember being seriously afraid.

He was a very fortunate man, one of those to whom the right things happen. Good luck seemed to be with him in all his personal relations, as well as in his professional work. He did not marry one of the stylish lively, professionally-coifed society girls who fluttered around the young doctor as he began to succeed, any one of whom would have brought him money, social prestige, and influence. To their annoyance he married a quiet, brown-eyed little thing ("Not even neat! You should see her hair. It's always falling down!" they said scornfully) who brought him nothing but a heart so pure and loving that when she died young, it went on beating faithfully in the doctor's memory, making him happier than any flesh-and-blood woman he might have married to take her place.

All alone in life now, good luck . . . the greatest of good luck . . . led him to adopt the orphan who turned out such an ideal son. The quiet, undemonstrative love between the older and the younger man was so serene and steady that all who knew them saw their own paths more clearly in its light. Yet who else would have picked out that child, of all others! He had been a regular little demon, the doctor's older patients said when they told the story, as they often did. Left an orphan at four, he had been taken in by a family who did not want him—they had plenty of nice children of their own, older, and were dismayed by this passionate, bad little boy. But they were distant relations of his parents, and there seemed to be nobody else willing to give him a home. Dr. Burrage must have seen him, many's the time, as he came and went in that house, taking care of the old grandmother who was paralyzed and bedridden. And he knew of course, the way doctors know everything, that the little boy was not a welcome addition to the family. But he had never seemed to pay any attention to him till one day, stepping into the house, he found the children—the grownups too—in the midst of a frantic storm. The little fellow—the one who grew up to be Dr. Wright—was in a frightful tantrum, acting like a mad dog, screaming and kicking and scratching and biting the other children. The father rushed in just as Dr. Burrage arrived, and pulled the child away. The mother was crying and saying, "Just look what he's done to poor little Betty's face. This time he's got to be punished! If I have to do it myself he's going to be whipped till he—"

But the doctor had taken one long step forward and snatched the child into his own arms. "Leave him alone!" he said. "Don't you touch him. Leave him to me!"

No, he never claimed to have had any sort of prophetic divination about what the little boy's qualities really were. In later years, when people asked him, he always said honestly, "Why, I couldn't tell you what made me do it. I really haven't any idea. I just did."

Dorothy Canfield Fisher: *"The Forgotten Mother"*
from A Harvest of Stories
Harcourt, Bruce and Co., New York. 1950

SESSION V

Grief, Loss and Mourning in the Aging

Death

Grieving for a loved one lost?
Perhaps not lost,
Just to another life ascended
But lost, the same, unto the griever.

Grief perhaps not unbefitting
For griever cannot loved one follow;
Nor would the transit
Surely surcease sorrow.

For, if death sees the last of woe
And ends in heavenly bliss,
How close the beloved
Without shared ills and pain?

Perhaps t'were best
To hold the grief
As mark of loved one passed
And yet not forgotten.

Bill Urschel
January 30, 1991
Peer Counselor, San Juan County

SESSION V
Session Guide To The Trainer

In this session trainees begin to express their wounds and pain. For some, this will be difficult. The group will react as a microcosm of the general population's response to grief, loss, and mourning. Take time to let trainees develop an awareness of the difficulties in expressing grief and loss. A group may be very silent until the facilitator or a risking trainee begins to share losses they have experienced. Starting the group on an intellectual acknowledgement of the stages of grief helps them move more comfortably towards recognizing grief and loss in their own lives.

Review the many losses that are unrecognized and unvalued, such as loss of a pet. Globalize this to more personal losses, helping the trainees to feel the particular stages of grief. Trainees will better understand their client's loss, grief, or repressed grief through group sharing.

Discussions of spiritual issues can be difficult. The facilitator needs to guide the group towards healthy views regarding the nature of spiritual expression. Denial of the need for spiritual expression by the clients can lead to such problems as depression or the inability to experience intimacy. These sessions on grief, loss, and death are often therapeutic for the trainees. The facilitator may encourage a member who appears to be increasingly agitated or withdrawn to seek professional help to deal with their grief. This is an excellent time to demonstrate how mental health facilities are of benefit to all community members. Encouraging people to join widow's groups, support groups, or to see a psychotherapist lets the trainees know that you use and believe in mental health services as an aid to good health.

Loss is the major issue with aging!

The relaxation and breathing exercises should be attempted only if you, the facilitator, are experienced or comfortable using them.

Session V

Grief, Loss and Mourning In The Aging

To resolve your grief you must accept the fact: What was will never be again.
You will have to give yourself permission to grieve for it, if you do not, you will never
appreciate the future which may be even better or more meaningful than the past.

Elizabeth Kubler-Ross

Today's Goal

- Familiarity with the impact of losses in aging.
- Identifying personal and societal philosophies of loss, grief and death.
- Review stages of grief and mourning.

Strategy

Enlisting the experience of trainees who have had losses and have come to some resolution will add to the group's discussion. The sharing of losses, the understanding of the universal reactions to loss can create in the group a forum for experiencing their own loss and grief. Support, empathy, encouragement and non-judgement by the facilitator and group members will allow the natural healing process to take place. The intensity of multiple losses experienced by seniors and the feelings of helplessness and powerlessness to relieve the pain, can be viewed most effectively through the trainee's awareness of loss as a major issue for the elderly.

Learning Objectives

- Gain awareness of the many losses and expressions of those losses in aging.
- Increase knowledge of the stages of grief.
- Introduction to counseling a client experiencing grief.

Handouts and Workbook Materials

- The "Social Readjustment Rating Scale"and Preventive Measures.
- Stages of grief.
- On loss.
- When grief is not expressed.
- Body breathing, shoulder massage.

And Now We Remember the Losses . . . Session V

I. "Temperature Reading"

Sharing has by now become more relaxed and personal. Unresolved issues start to surface and need to be attended to during the remainder of the session.

II. Multiple Losses Due To Aging

Using group "brainstorming," list all the various types of loss people experience with the aging process. Using the following case study, have group identify this person's various losses.

Case Study

Jason is 94-years old. He is the last remaining sibling in his family. He was widowed five years ago. He and his wife had been married for twenty years. His first wife had died in her early 50's and he remarried the "love of his life" at age 74. Jason had been a successful farmer and was able to be active in the family farming business until his 70's. Jason was restricted from driving his car at age 70 due to vision problems. His eldest son, who now runs the family farm, recently lost his arm in a farm related accident and is having severe complications. One grandson and the son's wife work to keep the farm operating. Jason lives on the family homestead with his dog, Gus. He has a housekeeper come in two times a week, and his family helps with the preparation of meals several times a week. Jason's vision is deteriorating to a point to where he can no longer plant his vegetable garden and his family is urging him to leave the homestead and move in with them. Jason is financially comfortable, but must rely on his daughter-in-law to take care of his bills. Jason called his daughter-in-law to report concerns about his dog, Gus. The veterinarian found that Gus has cancerous tumors and had to be put to sleep. Jason's life-long neighbor and buddy suffers from Alzheimer's disease, and his wife feels she will soon have to place him in a nursing home. Jason cries sometimes causing his family to be uncomfortable. They tend to visit him less frequently.

Group Discussion

- List the obvious losses Jason has had in the past five years.
- What are the social losses he has had?
- List the number of roles Jason has lost.
- Discuss society's general attitude regarding strong expressions of emotions.
- Why and how is crying discouraged?
- Have you ever feared that if you start crying you'll never stop crying?
- Have you ever feared that if you ever "let go" of a strong emotion that it will "run wild"?

Some of the losses which need grieving:

Death of friend, mate, lover
Miscarriage
Parts of one's body, loss of sight, hearing, amputee
Physical changes: menopause, injury, illness
Divorce, separation
The break up of a love affair
Religious faith
Idealism or a particular belief
Dreams, anticipations
Leaving places, such as moving from farm to city
Career identity
Role as a parent; mother, father
Loss of childhood
Loss of childhood hopes, for what you never will have
Loss of a pet

Key Element -

*Grief is the emotional reaction to loss which shows itself in waves of feelings.
The process is to encourage the expression of grief while understanding that it is both universal and highly individual.*

III. Stages of Grief

From Kubler-Ross and Robert Kavanaugh we gather the various stages of the grief process. These stages are part of the natural healing process necessary in recovering from any loss. Loss is the universal stressor for the elderly. Much of the emotional content of counseling elderly clients centers around loss, related emotions and the helplessness often experienced. Teaching the trainees to review their own losses and their particular style of resolution will ready them to be comfortable with the client's manifestations of grief.

Stages of Grief: Kubler-Ross

1. Shock   2. Denial   3. Anger
4. Bargaining   5. Depression   6. Acceptance

Stages of Grief: Robert Kavanaugh

1. Shock, denial   2. Disorganization   3. Volatile emotions
4. Guilt   5. Loss and loneliness 6. Relief
           7. Reestablishment, reorganization

Experiential Exercise - "Exploring the Stages of Grief"

Forming dyads, have partners choose one of the stages of grief, create an example of that stage and role play their example.

Example -

Shock = "I can't (I won't) believe it. I think the X-ray got mixed up. I'm going to talk to more doctors."

The peer counselor is instructed to use various intervention such as active listening and reflection of feelings in order to help the "client" come to terms with this stage of grief.

Key Element -

Loss intensifies feelings of helplessness and powerlessness. Allowing for acceptance of honest, painful emotions are the keys to healing. Many trainees are widows or have unresolved grief, this group will be a part of their acceptance of their loss and can be a catalyst for emotional and spiritual growth.

IV. Grief and Mental Health Concerns

There are many ways in which people create substitutes for grief when grief is too painful or not an acceptable form of emotion.

Forms which take place when grief is not expressed:

- Depression or manic behavior = "the death of emotion."
- Introjection = takes "death" inside of oneself, living for "2" of us, take on symptoms.
- Physical Symptoms = backaches, arthritis, asthma.
- Substitution = placing the grief for the 1st person onto a 2nd person, they often catch the anger of the grief process.
- Robot-style = shuts down, vows internally never (Clint Eastwood style) to attach again, never to get close again.
- Sex = using increased sexual activity as a release, leading to promiscuity.
- Acts of violence and crime.
- Avoidance = avoids anything which would touch off the grief feelings.
- Drugs, alcohol and overwork as a way to protect themselves from feeling the grief.
- Vicarious = grieving through other people's losses.
- Wandering = out of touch with their "base," center.
- Rage = fixated on the anger stage.
- Child Abuse = the childhood griefs that are naturally experienced by children stirs up our own unresolved grief.

Group Discussion

Knowing the stages of grief, understanding it as a natural and good process and being able to share that information with your client can be extremely helpful. As we age, death and losses come closer and the client may want to talk over his fears with someone. The peer counselor offers that listening ear with similar experiences and the training that affords him the knowledge that the client's grief talk is healthy and purposeful. For some trainees the discomfort will be an issue to address,as listening to someone's fears about death may make them face their own fears around death.

Questions

- What and how do ones spiritual beliefs come into counseling when dealing with grieving clients? Or do they?

- What steps might a counselor take to help the client clarify the issues around loss?

- What about self-disclosure at this time?

For trainees, the hardest part of counseling is to deal with the many negative issues that clients present. Spend time reviewing how a peer counselor can listen for both the positive and negative comments.

Examples -

- Accentuating the negative - "Life is too hard, you're right."
- Accentuating the positive - "Things are hard for you now— could you think of some ways we could work on this?"
- Overly positive - "Oh, you're going to be OK! Don't worry." [1]

Key Element -

Practice counseling with the trainees loss and grief issues,
for this is their time of change and increased awareness into grief.

V. Closing

- Have each trainee score the "Social Readjustment Scale" at home.

- Review the handouts for next week. Be sure trainee continues the processing of this session with friends and family.

- Encourage a journal entry today.

1. Allen Ivey and Normal Gluckstern, Basic Attending Skills, p. 5, Microtraining Associates, 1974, 1982

VI. Summarization

The sessions on grief and loss, and death and dying can be very disturbing for some trainees. If the session ends on what seems a very heavy note, use a breathing or relaxation exercise to end comfortably. Reminding them of how much they have experienced and learned through their lives and how well they have lived will ease some of the heaviness of looking at aging losses.

Recommended Reading

Kubler-Ross, Elizabeth. <u>On Death and Dying</u>. New York: Macmillan Publishing Co, 1969.

SESSION V

Handouts & Workbook Materials

The Social Readjustment Rating Scale*

Life Event	Mean Value
1. Death of spouse	100
2. Divorce	73
3. Marital separation from mate	65
4. Detention in jail or other insitution	63
5. Death of a close family member	63
6. Major personal injury or illness	53
7. Marriage	50
8. Being fired at work	47
9. Marital reconciliation with mate	45
10. Retirement from work	45
11. Major change in the health or behavior of a family member	44
12. Pregnancy	40
13. Sexual difficulties	39
14. Gaining a new family member (e.g. through birth, adoption, oldster moving in, etc.)	39
15. Major business readjustment (e.g. merger, reorganization, bankruptcy, etc.)	39
16. Major change in financial state (e.g., a lot worse off or a lot better off than usual)	38
17. Death of a close friend	37
18. Changing to a different line of work	36
19. Major change in the number of arguments with spouse (e.g., either a lot more or a lot less than usual regarding child-rearing, personal habits, etc.)	35
20. Taking on a mortgage greater than $10,000 (e.g., purchasing a home, business, etc.)	
21. Foreclosure on a mortgage or loan	30
22. Major change in responsibilities at work (e.g., promotion, demotion, lateral transfer)	29
23. Son or daughter leaving home (e.g., marriage, attending college, etc.)	29
24. In-law troubles	29
25. Outstanding personal achievement	28
26. Wife beginning or ceasing work outside the home	26
27. Beginning or ceasing formal schooling	26

The Social Readjustment Rating Scale* (cont.)

Life Event	Mean Value
28. Major change in living conditions (e.g., building a new home, remodeling, deterioration of home or neighborhood	25
29. Revision of personal habits (dress, manners, associations, etc.)	24
30. Troubles with the boss	23
31. Major change in working hours or conditions	20
32. Change in residence	20
33. Changing to a new school	20
34. Major change in usual type an/or amount of recreation	19
35. Major change in church activities (e.g., a lot more or a lot less than usual)	19
36. Major change in social activities (e.g., clubs, dancing, movies, visiting, etc.)	18
37. Taking on a mortgage or loan less than $10,000 (e.g., purchasing a car, TV, freezer, etc.)	17
38. Major change in sleeping habits (a lot more or a lot less sleep, or change in part of day when asleep)	16
39. Major change in number of family get-togethers (e.g., a lot more or a lot less than usual)	15
40. Major change in eating habits (a lot more or a lot less food intake, or very different meal hours or surroundings)	15
41. Vacation	13
42. Christmas	12
43. Minor violations of the law (e.g., traffic tickets, jaywalking, disturbing the peace, etc.)	11

*From Holmes, T.H. and Rahe, R.H.: The Social Readjustment Rating Scale. Journal of Psychosomatic Research 11:213-218, 1967.

Thomas H. Holmes, M.D.
Department of Psychiatry and Behavioral Sciences
University of Washington School of Medicine
Seattle, Washington 98195

Preventive Measures

The following suggestions are for using the Social Readjustment Rating Scale for the maintenance of your health and prevention of illness:

1. Become familiar with the life events and the amount of change they require.

2. Put the Scale where you and the family can see it easily several times a day.

3. With practice you can recognize when a life event happens.

4. Think about the meaning of the event for you and try to identify some of the feelings you experience.

5. Think about the different ways you might best adjust to the event.

6. Take your time in arriving at decisions.

7. If possible, anticipate life changes and plan for them well in advance.

8. Pace yourself. It can be done even if you are in a hurry.

9. Look at the accomplishment of a task as a part of daily living and avoid looking at such an achievement as a "stopping point" or a time for letting down.

10. Remember, the more change you have, the more likely you are to get sick. Of those people with over 300 Life Change Units for the past year, almost 80% get sick in the near future; with 150 to 299 Life Change Units, about 50% get sick in the near future; and with less than 150 Life Change Units, only about 30% get sick in the near future.

So, the higher your Life Change Score, the harder you should work to stay well.

Source: Thomas H. Holmes, M.D., Professor of Psychiatry and Behavioral Sciences, Unviersity of Washington, Seattle, Washington.

RELAXATION EXERCISES

Body Breathing

Find a place with plenty of space around you and lie down. Close your eyes and find a comfortable position . . . Take some time to become aware of your body . . . Now focus your attention on your breathing . . . Notice all the details of your breathing, as the air flows effortlessly into your body and then out again . . . Feel the air as it moves into your nose or mouth and down your throat, and feel your chest and belly expand to receive this life-giving air . . .

Now imagine that you breathe into other parts of your body. Imagine that some of the air that you breathe in flows down into your pelvis, on down your legs, and into your toes. Imagine that your legs expand a little as you breathe in this air, and contract a little as you breathe out . . . Do this for a couple of minutes.

Now try breathing into your arms and fingers for a while . . . and notice how you feel as you do this . . .

Now breathe into you head and neck . . .

Now breathe again deep into your chest . . .

Shoulder Massage

I want each person to silently find someone else that they would like to give something to and stand behind that person . . . Eventually you can make this into a circle with everyone facing clockwise . . . Now sit down in a close circle and silently massage or rub the back, shoulders and neck of the person in front of you. Close your eyes and don't talk. Communicate with the person in front of you with your hands, and communicate with the person behind you with noises. Experiment with different kinds of massage and listen to the noises from this person to find out what parts he wants massaged, and what kind of massage or stroking he likes best. Make noises to tell the person behind you what kind of massage you prefer. Do this for about five minutes . . .

Without talking, turn around and face the other direction in the circle and massage the back of the person who was previously massaging you. Again, communicate forward with your hands and backward with noises for about five minutes.

Now take a few minutes to talk with the person in front of you and behind you—share your experience of massaging and being massaged. How did your massages differ, and how well could you communicate with each other, etc.?

VARIOUS ELEMENTS OF
GRIEF AND THE GRIEVING PROCESS

1. <u>SHOCK:</u>
    temporary escape from the pain and reality of loss;
    trance-like; appearance of no reaction.

2. <u>EMOTIONAL RELEASE:</u>
    crying, tears, expressions of grief

3. <u>DEPRESSION:</u>
    feeling alone, isolated, abandoned
    God may even feel unavailable

4. <u>PHYSICAL SYMPTOMS:</u>
    impact of grief on the body

5. <u>PANIC/ ANXIETY:</u>
    worrying, concerned with losing touch with reality, fearful

6. <u>GUILT:</u>
    normal feelings of "should or could have" done something to prevent
    or avoid the loss

7. <u>HOSTILITY / ANGER:</u>
    mad; why me?, resentful

8. <u>RESISTANCE TO CHANGE:</u>
    mourning focus; keeping the memories alive, not being able to
    remove personal belongings; refusal to change patterns

9. <u>HOPE:</u>
    emerges and is experienced

10. <u>RE-AFFIRM REALITY:</u>
    integrating the loss into life

Source: Lecture by Karen Kent, M.S.G., Older Adult Services, Eastside Mental Health, Seattle, WA., Geriatric Mental Health Certification Program, University of Washington, 1990

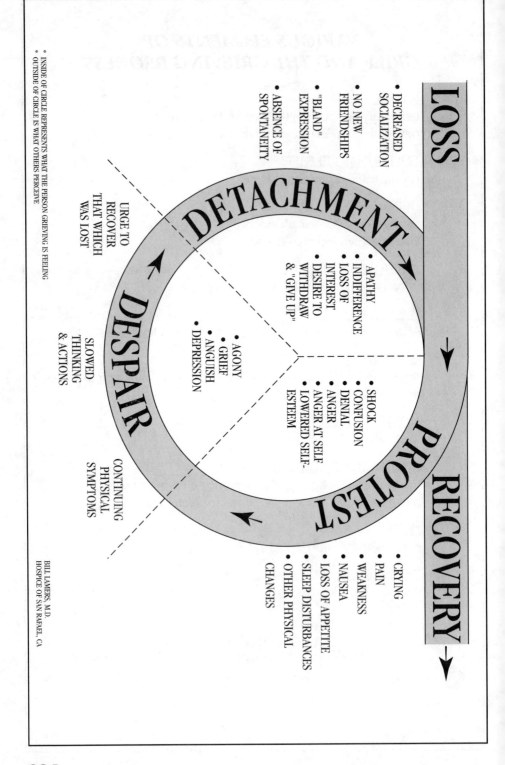

LOSS → → →

RECOVERY → → →

DETACHMENT →

PROTEST

DESPAIR

DETACHMENT
- APATHY
- INDIFFERENCE
- LOSS OF INTEREST
- DESIRE TO WITHDRAW & "GIVE UP"

Outside (LOSS):
- DECREASED SOCIALIZATION
- NO NEW FRIENDSHIPS
- "BLAND" EXPRESSION
- ABSENCE OF SPONTANEITY

PROTEST
- SHOCK
- CONFUSION
- DENIAL
- ANGER
- ANGER AT SELF
- LOWERED SELF-ESTEEM

Outside (RECOVERY):
- CRYING
- PAIN
- WEAKNESS
- NAUSEA
- LOSS OF APPETITE
- SLEEP DISTURBANCES
- OTHER PHYSICAL CHANGES

DESPAIR
- AGONY
- GRIEF
- ANGUISH
- DEPRESSION

Outside:
- URGE TO RECOVER THAT WHICH WAS LOST
- SLOWED THINKING & ACTIONS
- CONTINUING PHYSICAL SYMPTOMS

* INSIDE OF CIRCLE REPRESENTS WHAT THE PERSON GRIEVING IS FEELING
* OUTSIDE OF CIRCLE IS WHAT OTHERS PERCEIVE

BILL LAMERS, M.D.
HOSPICE OF SAN RAFAEL, CA

On Loss
(Summarized from <u>How To Survive The Loss Of A Love</u>, by Colgrove, Bloomfield & McWilliams)

loss   surviving   healing   growing

Phases of Recovery: shock/denial; anger/depression; understanding/acceptance; having all the facts/being affirmed in one's feelings/confronting the loss.

BE WITH THE PAIN, FEEL THE HURT
YOU ARE MORE THAN THE WOUND YOU ARE SUFFERING
THE PATTERN OF HEALING AND GROWTH LOOKS LIKE THIS:

ACCEPT THE HELP/COMFORT OF OTHERS   OR
RE-AFFIRM YOUR BELIEFS
WEATHERING A CRISIS: A STRONGER YOU, A DIFFERENT YOU, A
MORE EVOLVED YOU.

<u>Obvious Losses</u>
    death
    break-up
    separation
    divorce

<u>Not so Obvious</u>
    loss of job
    money
    moving
    illness (loss of health)
    changing teachers, schools
    robbery
    success (loss of striving)
    loss of cherished ideal
    loss of long-term goal

<u>Inevitable</u>
    death or separation imminent

<u>Temporary Losses</u>
    mini losses

<u>In Limbo/Doubt</u>
    not knowing what will happen next
    waiting for information,
    medical texts

<u>Losses Related to Age</u>
    childhood dreams
    puppy love
    crushes
    adolescent romances
    leaving school (drop out, graduate)
    leaving home
    changing jobs
    loss of "youth", "beauty"
    loss of hair, teeth
    loss of sexual drive (drive
    remains, ability falters)
    menopause
    retirement

Mental Health and Aging: Loss & Grief

I. Normal Grief
    A. Definition - Grief is an emotional reaction to a loss. Something of value is no longer mine.
    B. Losses - 3 major losses associated with aging are:
        • Widowhood   • Retirement   • Chronic physical disorders
        Multiple losses are more common in later life, and they often occur in a more concentrated period of time. Anticipatory grief may frequently occur.

Common losses:		
relocation	loss of youth/beauty
loss of pet	giving up driver's license
less money/prestige	role changes
decreasing independence	menopause
changes in life goals	loss of friends
families at a distance	divorce
memory	strength

    C. Emotional Reactions - Normal recovery time from a major loss is 1-2 years. The recovery is "normal" if there is a gradual healing over time. Normal emotions: shock, depression, anger, acceptance, guilt, fear, sadness
        Any of these emotions may be expressed physically.

II. Unresolved Grief
    A. Definition - Grief that doesn't go away over time. The individual doesn't heal. The most common types of unresolved grief:
        1) delayed reaction: Feelings are blocked because there is no time to grieve, no permission to express feelings, because of multiple losses occurring, etc.
        2) exaggerated reaction: Individual becomes frozen in one emotion such as denial, guilt, anger. The grief becomes chronic.
            Exaggerated grief may also be expressed by the individual assuming the traits or illnesses of the dead person or by overidealizing the person.
    B. Factors that increase the risk of an unresolved grief process within the older population:
        • unexpected, sudden death   • absence of a social support network
        • death of an adult child   • extreme dependency on the deceased
        • missing body • unresolved conflicts • lack of permission to grieve
        • avoidance of expressing emotions   • not enough time to grieve
        • assumed responsibility for the death   • loss is socially unacceptable
        • previous unresolved deaths • cumulative losses

III. <u>Strategies to Help a Grieving Person</u>

Chinese proverb:

You can't prevent the birds of sorrow from flying over your head, but you can prevent them from building a nest in your hair.

Assist the person to:

1) Acknowledge the loss
   - see the body
   - have a funeral or memorial service
   - talk repetitiously about the person, the death, the funeral, etc.
   - understand the magnitude of their loss

2) Identify and work through unresolved issues:
   - confront their thoughts on afterlife - Where is the person?
   - unfinished business with the deceased
   - if emotions delayed, relive the death
   - if emotions exaggerated, suggest therapy
   - use rituals, guided imagery, linking objects. role playing

3) Ask forgiveness:
   - for real or imagined wrongs
   - from God or the deceased

4) Differentiate between the survivor and the dead person.

5) Examine their defenses
   - alcohol, drugs, business.

6) Facilitate future movement:
   - adjusting to environment w/o person
   - discovering meaning in life for them alone

Source: Karen Kent, M.S.G., from presentation, to Geriatric Mental Health Certification Program, University of Washington, 1990.

"CRISIS":
Opportunity riding
the dangerous wind.

*The Chinese word
picture for the word "crisis" is
composed of two different symbols:
<u>danger and opportunity.</u>*

After a while you learn the subtle difference

Between holding a hand and chaining a soul,

And you learn that love doesn't mean leaning

And company doesn't mean security,

And you begin to learn that kisses aren't contracts

And presents aren't promises,

And you begin to accept your defeats

With your head up and your eyes open

With the grace of a woman, not the grief of a child,

And learn to build all your roads

On today because tomorrow's ground

Is too uncertain for plans, and futures have

A way of falling down in mid-flight.

After a while you learn that even sunshine

Burns if you get too much.

So plant your own garden and

decorate your own soul, instead of waiting

For someone to bring you flowers.

And you learn that you really can endure …

That you really are strong

And you really do have worth

And you learn and learn …

With every good-bye, you learn.

Anonymous

SESSION VI

Death, Dying & Spiritual Values

Session VI

Session Guide To The Trainer

Many trainees in your group will have suffered losses and deaths in recent years. It is often one of the reasons they are volunteering for this service. Yet, many may not have completed their grieving. Your preparation and knowledge of guiding the group through the "grieving process" will be essential for a positive outcome. This session will use your therapeutic skills, helping the trainee see the importance of personally looking at their own issues, feelings, and concerns about death. The more they are able to resolve these issues, the more they will be able to connect with their clients.

Keeping these sessions on an experiential personal level need not be without humor. Your humor and warmth can bring a sense of perspective to the subject.

If you choose to use triads or dyads to role play grief or loss, guide the trainee of each group to develop nurturing skills. A crying client can be overwhelming for the trainee to handle alone.

Experiences, stories, videos and music are tools for accessing feelings. All can have an intense impact on the trainees. Be sure trainees have made appropriate closure on the subject before they leave for the day.

Spiritual discussions must stay non-judgmental. The facilitator can intercede when "religious beliefs" become the point of focus. The purpose is to explore spiritual alternatives, to help trainees deal with death in a positive way.

Your comfort level with the expressions of grief, and in particular expressions of sadness and crying, will ease the group. It signals that tears are an appropriate healing tool.

Trainees will ask "What do I do if my client starts crying?" Help the trainees to experience how it feels to be nurtured and supported through crying. This will answer their unstated fear which is "What do I do if I start crying?" Help the trainees to see grief as an ocean with a multitudes of waves. This is an interesting and effective metaphor. With each wave, the pain is less deep and the healing period longer. However, the waves continue slightly, perhaps forever.

Dr. Lawrence Jacobs, a Seattle psychotherapist, once stated that 10 years after his father's death, he would sometimes still become tearful when he heard his father's favorite song.

On newsprint draw the wave action of grief:

LOSS
OR
DEATH

TIME LINE

SESSION VI

Death, Dying and Spiritual Values

In everything one must consider the end.

Jean de La Fontaine
(17th Century)

Today's Goal

- Increase trainees comfort level with issues of dying.
- Discover the various spiritual philosophies and their importance to aging clients.
- To validate the grief process and encourage it within group process.

Strategy

Encourage and engage trainees in the sharing of their own experiences with death, dying and grief. Create a nurturing, warm and fuzzy atmosphere in which this sharing can be healing. Use music, readings or videos on the topic to help trainees access their feelings in regards to death. The group support and acceptance will lead to clarity on how difficult it is to express grief.

Learning Objectives

- Review the basic steps of grief process.
- Personalize the issues of death and dying to gain in-depth knowledge of the process.
- Reframe death, and dying as a part of world order and spiritual sense.

Handouts and Workbook Materials

- Six days of Dying - Bateson
- Northwest Indian poem
- Scripture from Ecclesiastes
- When Someone You Love Dies
- Psychological Aspects of Dying

And We Search the Darkness . . . Session VI

I. "Temperature Reading"

Allow 2-3 minutes for each member to clarify issues from last week.

Key Element -

> *These questions on grief and death require processing. Your temperature reading time needs to be sensitive to the individual issues this topic accesses within the group.*

II. Death and Dying Review

Use poetry, music or video to bring the discussion of death and dying to a more personal level. This will help the trainees access some of their experiences with death and dying. You may want to bring in a speaker from Hospices or a member of the clergy with a "sensitive ear" to the grief process or a staff member who's expertise is in dealing with grieving clients.

The element of spiritual concerns are part of the senior's grief. Be sure the speaker or the facilitator is clear about respecting this as a valued issue in death work. The facilitator can guide the group with encouragements regarding the difficulties of discussing death and dying. Kubler-Ross states that the one most important gift to give a dying person is your deepest, authentic presence. Because of the issues this brings up for the Peer Counselors, we must first help them to deal with their own mortality. Many clients will want and need to talk about their dying. The peer counselor will need to be comfortable with this in order to be present for the client. The client's spiritual beliefs are essential to their grief talk. Christian, Jewish, Moslem, Buddhist, Hindu, Atheist, agnostic or a combination of these spiritual forms may be expressed. A trainee must be encouraged to respect the client's spiritual belief system.

> *Because of the issues this brings up for the Peer Counselors, we must first help them to deal with their own mortality.*

Questions for Group Discussion

- Name the stages of grief and state how a Peer Counselor might support the client at various stages of grieving.
- When a client repeats the story of her husband's dying many times, what might she be telling the Peer Counselor?
- How might the Peer Counselor help the client move through the denial stage of grief?

Experiential Exercise: "Writing Your Epitaph"

Form small groups of 3-4 trainees. Be sure each group is supplied with a tissue box and writing materials. Instruct each group to spend 15-20 minutes together, with each member preparing a fantasy of their funeral, ceremoney and/or epitaph. Have each member of the small group verbally share that fantasy with the group. Encourage them to visualize what it would be like. The facilitator needs to be sensitive to the responses of tears, anger, denial and humor. These feelings can be validated when the groups rejoin the larger group.

Key Element -

Acceptance of the emotional release experienced by the group members
– shared tears – is evidence of <u>Being Present.</u> Tears heal the wounds of grief.

III. Discovering Spiritual Philosophies

How an aging, dying client expresses their philosophy of death is highly individual and a personal matter. Therefore, dealing with death must always be in accord with the desires and within the timeframe of that individual. A trainee too eager to "fix" a client's grieving, or one who is unfinished in their own grief process, can be counter-therapeutic. The facilitator can help the trainees see the power of honoring the client's grieving process by honoring the trainee's struggles with death and/or spiritual philosophies.

Case Study:

A 72-year old trainee from one of our classes was in great need of proselytizing his Christian beliefs about death and the "hereafter" during the group sessions on loss, grief, death and dying. As a life long bachelor, his faith had carried him through much loneliness, adding to his rather rigid life/death view. He consistently denied his grief, by quoting scriptural references, and emphatically stating his spiritual stance. The group graciously accepted his point of view and encouraged him to express his feelings about his losses. He steadfastly held to his denial.

Several sessions later another trainee, a 75-year old woman who had been widowed less than a year, was recalling for the group, the death of her husband. This was her story:

Emma and her husband had been married for some 50 years. They had both immigrated from Finland and learned to speak English, but throughout their marriage, when they wanted to show each other intimacy and special caring, they would speak to each other in their native language. Emma recalled how her husband loved to hear her sing the old church songs of his youth. His death was preceded by a massive stroke, which left him semi-comatose and unable to speak. Shortly before his death

Emma visited him at the hospital. She washed and combed his hair, tenderly cleaning his body. She then took his head in her arms, gently rocking him and sang to him, in Finnish, old church hymns. Emma's husband died the next day without regaining consciousness.

Emma cried as she shared her loss and grief. The group also cried. The group then, in total awe, watched as the rigid denial slipped away from our bachelor trainee. He covered his face with his hands, sobbing long, soft tears.

This group cartharsis accessed some of their unfinished grief. It illuminated the healing qualities of sharing honest, painful emotions, as no lecture or discussion could have accomplished.

Key Element -

> *This group may be the place where trainees start to process their own grief.*
> *These are seniors – they have experienced numerous losses. The energy and*
> *closeness is intensified by this sharing.*

Group Discussion

Depending on the level of intimacy in the group, this session may end with out verbalization. With silence, hand holding, and hugs trainees can experience the comfort of knowing they are not alone. This group can be their support system and a place to consider life changes, just as they can be that support system to their clients.

IV. Closing

Review handouts for next week.
Announce any speakers for next week.
Encourage feedback, if appropriate at this time.
Let the energy of the group dictate the closing of this session.

V. Summarization

The power of this subject needs to be acknowledged by the facilitator in order to validate the feelings of the group. Spiritual, cultural, and philosophical questions arise in this session, giving the courage to look at death and its connection to life. As a life developmental stage, seniors face the end of life daily. These sessions will diminish some of the fear of death and resistance to grieve. *Death is the last adaptation one must make in life.*

> *Friendship doubles our joy and divides our grief.*
> Anonymous

Recommended Reading

Anderson, Robert. *I Never Sang For My Father.*
New York: J. B. Lippincott & Sons, 1973.

Pincus, Lily. *Death & The Family.*
New York: Vintage Books, 1974.

SESSION VI

Handouts & Workbook Materials

DEATH, DYING AND SPIRITUAL VALUES

To everything there is a season,

And a time for every activity under heaven;

> *a time to be born and a time to die,*
>
> *a time to plant and a time to uproot,*
>
> *a time to kill and a time to heal,*
>
> *a time to tear down and a time to build,*
>
> *a time to weep and a time to laugh,*
>
> *a time to mourn and a time to dance,*
>
> *a time to scatter stones and a time to gather them,*
>
> *a time to embrace and a time to refrain from embracing,*
>
> *a time to search and a time to give up,*
>
> *a time to keep and a time to throw away,*
>
> *a time to tear and a time to mend,*
>
> *a time to be silent and a time to speak,*
>
> *a time to love and a time to hate,*
>
> *a time for war and a time for peace.*

Ecclesiastes 3:1-8

How Do You React
When Someone You Love Dies?

Because grief can be so painful, and seem overwhelming, it frightens us. Many people worry if they are grieving in the "right" way, and wonder if the feelings they have are normal. Most people who suffer a loss experience one or more of the following:

Feel tightness in the throat or heaviness in the chest

Have an empty feeling in their stomach and lose their appetite

Feel guilty at times and angry at others

Feel restless and look for activity but find it difficult to concentrate

Feel as though the loss isn't real, that it didn't actually happen

Sense the loved one's presence, like finding themselves expecting the person to walk in the door at the usual time, hearing their voice, or seeing their face.

Wander aimlessly and forget and don't finish things they've started to do around the house.

Have difficulty sleeping, and dream of their loved one frequently

Experience an intense preoccupation with the life of the deceased

Feel guilty or angry over things that happened or didn't happen in the relationship with the deceased

Feel intensely angry at the loved one for leaving them

Assume mannerisms or traits of their loved one

Feel as though they need to take care of other people who seem uncomfortable around them, by politely not talking about the feelings of loss

Need to tell and retell and remember things about the loved one and the experience of their death

Feel their mood changes over the slightest things

Cry at unexpected times

These are all natural and normal grief responses. It's important to cry and talk with people when you need to.

Source: Karen Kent, M.S.G., Psychological Aspects of Dying, from presentation, to Geriatric Mental Health Certification Program, University of Washington, 1990.

Psychological Aspects of Dying

"Dying is not hard. It is living until you die that is hard."
Kubler-Ross

1. What are the fears

    A.   Physical Concerns
            1.Pain
            2. Loss of control of bodily functions
            3. Sedation
            4. Body image

    B   Psychological Concerns
            1. Dependency on Others
            2. Isolation
            3. Dying alone
            4. Unfinished business
            5. Meaning of life/death

II Strategies for Helping

    A.   Work through your own death issues
    B   Encourage the grieving process
    C.   Assist them to complete business
    D.   Include them in decision-making
    E.   Let them die their own way
    F.   Positive body image
    G.   Touch
    H.   Maintain hope but truthfulness
    I   Retain dignity
    J.   Learn from the dying person

Source: adapted from presentation by Robin Westby, M.S.W., psychotheraptist, Geriatric Services, Everett, WA.

SIX DAYS OF DYING
By Mary Catherine Bateson

reprinted for lecture at Antioch University, Seattle, WA 1980

IN 1978 GREGORY NEARLY DIED OF LUNG CANCER. Part of his recovery was Catherine traveling from Iran to help with his book, <u>Mind and Nature: A Necessary Unity</u>.

Catherine Bateson, the only child of Gregory Bateson and Margaret Mead, is an anthropologist presently at Amherst College, Massachusetts. In Gregory Bateson's <u>Steps to an Ecology of Mind</u> (1975, Ballantine) there is a collection of "metalogues," semi-fictional conversations between father and daughter inspired by real dialogues they had when Catherine was a child. Some other family members present in this account are: Gregory's wife Lois, whom he met while working on his "Double Bind" theory of schizophrenia and creativity at the VA Hospital in Palo Alto, California during the 1950's; Nora, Lois and Gregory's daughter, now 12; John, Gregory's son by his second marriage; and Eric, Lois's son by prior marriage. In addition to Catherine's own considerable work, she has collaborated frequently with her father. She authored <u>Our Own Metaphor</u> (1972, Knopf) which is an account of a conference organized by Gregory; she helped with his most recent book, <u>Mind and Nature: A Necessary Unity</u> (1979, Bantam): and she is completing her part of co-authorship with Gregory on a forthcoming book, <u>Angels Feat</u>. Also she is literary executor for both her father and Margret Mead. It is clear the metalogue never stopped.

* * * * * * *

Just as the intimacies of childbirth and early mothering have gradually been restored, first with natural childbirth and rooming in and most recently with childbirth in the home, so there is a growing effort to meet death more intimately and simply. The logical end of this development is that people die at home or in an environment as close to home as possible. The depressions which used to afflict mothers after childbirth are probably related to interruptions in the early intimacy between mother and child, which plays a biological role in the establishment of parental love and care. Similarly, the shadows of guilt and anger which so often complicate grief may also be related to interruptions in the process of caring, and they may be lightened by the experience of sending someone we love with our own hands, so that much that seems externally repellent and painful is transmuted by tenderness.

Death is surely more variable than birth. Where experiences are difficult to predict or compare, the specific is more useful than vague generalization. This is an account of the period from the 2nd to the 7th of July of 1980, the period in which I experienced the death of my father, Gregory Bateson. I can only describe events as I perceived them: other members of the family or close friends may find my perceptions bizarrely at odds with their own. Nevertheless, I think all of us agreed that the fact that we were with my father at the guesthouse of San Francisco Zen Center where he spent his last days and was laid out after death, gave us the privilege of a rare and blessed participation. We felt that we gained a new understanding of some of the things that my father taught, and also of the teachings of Zen Buddhism. Trying to make experience explicit in words is not typical of Zen, but it was something my father cared about. Lois Bateson, his wife, commented that Gregory had been a teacher all his life and that he continued to teach in the manner of his death. The privilege we experienced can only partly be shared. Still, the attempt at description may be helpful, for it is at moments of birth and death that it is easy to become timid and to be cowed into an acceptance of standard institutional forms.

My father's illness began in mid-spring and I came to California to be near him in June, arriving one day before he was hospitalized.While he was in the hospital I had to be away for about a week, to keep a previous commitment, and I returned to San Francisco on July 2 to find that he was out of the hospital and being cared for at Zen Center where I too went to stay. Two days before I had left, we had been talking with some sense of realism, about where he might be able to convalesce, but even as I departed that had come to seem unrealistic. Lois felt the gradual change in the quality of the nurses' care as, with implicit triage, they shifted from effort of healing to courtesy to the dying. Towards the end of the week, Lois made the decision to discontinue intravenous feeding - he was eating and drinking little and then to bring him to Zen Center and nurse him there, knowing that he would probably die there.

Gregory had entered the hospital June 10th because of respiratory crisis that proved to be pneumonia and an unexplained pain in his side.Everyone assumed that the pain was related to the lung cancer he had had in 1978 which was expected to be terminal and then went into remission. He himself felt that the pain might be a local nervous disorder related to his earlier surgery, and went back to a term used by his old friend the neurophysiologist and systems theorist, Warren McCulloch's, who had described how a group of nerves, regenerating after surgery, might get into a self-reinforcing cycle of resonating pain, but McCulloch's term, cousalgia, proved to be unacceptable in current parlance and was treated as fantasy in the context of cancer. The pain had driven him to his bed in late May where pneumonia had followed in lungs long handicapped by emphysema and the cancer episode. He had been living at Esalen Institute in Big Sur since the cancer and friends there came and went with counsels spun from different epistemologies, the multiple holisms of an unfocused new age. He had dutifully done a session of imaging and was told that perhaps indeed he did not want to live. He had by his bedside an array of megadoses of various vitamins and microdoses of homeopathic medicines, wheat grass juice available in any quantities he would accept it, and at the same time he was told that he was too preoccupied with the physical and should be concerned with the spiritual, this being available in various traditional and syncretic forms.

When we left Esalen, heading for San Francisco in a VW van with a supply of emergency oxygen, we had two possible destinations, either UC Hospital or Zen Center. I do not believe Gregory was making a choice between "holistic" and "establishment" medicine, but a choice between multiplicity and integrity. He maintained a profound scepticism towards both the premises of the medical profession and the Buddhist epistemology, but certainty is scarce and there is a kind of relief to be found in a system that expresses the disciplined working out of a set of premises, whatever these may be. Furthermore, he wanted to be in a place where he could have more information about what was happening and where his own curiosity would be allowed to play a role, his own vitality nurtured by knowledge rather than by hope.

When we arrived at UC Hospital and got the diagnosis of pneumonia, everyone concurred that pneumonia was something that establishment medicine knew how to handle and that is made sense to stay there. Gregory was deeply tired and in need of an impersonal, matter-of-fact environment, and for several days he wanted few visitors and as much new information about his condition as non-intrusive diagnostic procedures would provide. X-rays showed no growth or spread of cancer and provided no explanation for the pain. At that point, after working carefully on the details of a will, Gregory and his doctor decided that relief from pain was what he needed most, and he had several days relatively frequent and large doses of morphine. When Lois demanded a recess in which he could be fully conscious and able to discuss other treatment possibilities after these days, he remained somewhat blurred and disorientated and the pain was a dull ache rather than an agonizing burning sensation. He was terribly weakened, partly by vomiting caused by some of his medication. He spoke of going home and came lurching out of bed in the middle of the night, asking for scissors to cut the I.V. and oxygen tubes. Much of his talk was metaphorical and so discounted by nurses who made cheerful and soothing noises, but he remained very much himself, relating in clearly different ways to different people, compliant but skeptical. Our initial optimism in this period was a response to the decrease in pain and the improvement in pneumonia, but it was premised on a recovery of strength and will to live which did not occur.

During the last week in the hospital, there was a reoccurrence of the pneumonia, necessitating another round of antibiotics, and finally an explanation of the pain, when an eruption around his side provided the identification of Herpes zoster (shingles). This form of herpes is a virus which attacks the nervous system, causing acute unilateral pain, especially in the elderly, and eventually a skin eruption. It is almost impossible to diagnose before the rash, and in Gregory's case the location of the pain on one side of his body was all too easy to connect with cancer. No one dies of shingles, but the pain may continue indefinitely; it does seem reasonable to say that Gregory died by withdrawals from unexplained pain, and that explanation came too late to save him.

The six days of the title are the three days from my return to the moment when his breathing ceased, approximately at noon on July 4, followed by the three days until his cremation. Thus, not all of the punctuation from the natural process of death, but it serves to frame a period instead of focusing in a single moment. During those six days we were at San Francisco Zen Center, with most of the family and a few close friends sharing in the nursing and the Zen Community providing practical help and a context of content tranquility.

On the morning of July 2, Gregory asked his son to kill him. The asking was not a fully conscious request for practical steps - he suggested getting a stick and hitting him over the head with it, as if a brutal overstatement to achieve the opposite of euphemism - but it was a demanding paternal honesty. When I arrived, Lois suggested that John and her son Eric and I meet with Michael, Gregory's friend and physician, hoping that we would accept as a group what she had already accepted in the decision to leave the hospital. Michael talked about the fact that there were serious aggressive forms of treatment that could be taken to keep Gregory alive, and about his sense, having observed Gregory during the earlier crisis and in the intervening period that Gregory had been turning toward death and that such interventions would be inappropriate and ultimately futile. All of us felt that mentally at least Gregory's withdrawal was probably irreversible, whatever the mechanism involved and that his wishes should be respected as far as they could be.

What this meant was giving up the pressure on him to suffer those things that might prolong his life, setting up for a few minutes, respiratory therapy or an oxygen tube at his nostrils, another spoonful of custard, another sip of broth - while making each of these available if in any way he indicated he wanted them, or doing anything else we could to make him more comfortable. The more deeply one rejects the separation of mind and body, the more difficult it is to treat the processes of diseases and death as mechanical and alien to the self. Even as one gives up the image of an eternal enemy, of death personified as the Grim Reaper or reified in the name of a killing disease, the problem which lives in most people's unconscious becomes conscious, the feeling that the death of those we love is a betrayal. We tend to feel that someone who is dying has an implicit obligation to stay alive: to accept treatment, to make an unflagging effort and, indeed, to think thoughts that would support the effort at life rather than the drift towards death, not because doing so is comforting but because it may be a real factor in what happens.

We went back into the room where a hospital bed had been brought for Gregory, and we shared some sherry and stilton cheese. Gregory accepted a mouthful of each. We sat in a half-circle open around his bed and a student and friend of Gregory's, Steve, played the violin, while Lois accompanied him with chords on the tambur and those who could harmonize their voices, weaving a wandering chant in the darkening room for what seemed a very long time. During the music Gregory, half dozing brushed the tube that was supplying oxygen away from his nostrils, and each of us, I suppose struggled with the impulse to get up and replace it. Some of us were crying quietly. The music was gentle mourning, uniting the various terms to which each of us had come in acceptance of his death into a single covenant. When the music ended we sat for a while, listening to his labored, drowning breathing. After a time, lights were lit, Gregory stirred himself to eat and drink a little more, a few mouthfuls, the night watches were shared out and one of the Zen students entering the room restored the oxygen tube. After that it was put back or offered several times, but eventually each time he rejected it.

Within the rhythm of our day, one of a small group was always with him: Lois, or Kathleen, a friend and a nurse who had come with the family from Esalen, or I, or John and Eric, or Robert, the Zen priest who manages the guest house. Each evening different Zen students, some of them friends and others unnamed, would come and sit in the room also, erect and immobile unless they were needed, for Baker Roshi, in touch every day by telephone from across the country, wanted the students to approach the suchness of dying and to give their quiet support to Gregory and to us. He instructed them to deepen their empathy by breathing in unison with Gregory, supporting and sharing. Those of us staying in the house slept at different hours and slipped out briefly to join in meditations in the Zendo or to chant or to join in the Eucharist at a convent around the corner. Others came and went. We felt that for Gregory the process of dying proceeded gradually but without even a clear distinction between sleeping and waking.

On July 3 Gregory spoke occasionally, making gestures of affection and recognition, but much of what he said was blurred and unintelligible. He also spoke to others. He seemed to see around the bed and once or twice asked whether a particular person was indeed present or only a dream. It was often necessary to move his big ungainly body for he had become almost completely incontinent. This more than anything was reminiscent of the care of an infant, but moving him to clean or change pads or to guard against bedsores became especially difficult on that day because although he was not able to help at all, there was a sort of recalcitrance in his body against these indignities. He gave an impression of deep concentration.

Jerry Brown came in on the evening of the 3rd and Gregory recognized him and stretched out his hand to greet him, calling him by name! As Jerry left and we settled down for the night, Gregory's labored breathing had slowed to the point where sometimes the interval between breaths left room for a momentary doubt of whether another breath would follow. We shared the certainty that less than a day remained. Gregory was dying as people die in books, gradually sinking towards death in a self-reinforcing process. Intravenous feeding and continuous oxygen could drag that process out., interfering with the choice of mind and body not to sustain life, and another counter attack might have been possible on the pneumonia which we could hear in Gregory's breathing. But pneumonia has long been called the "old man's friend" I never thought of my father as an old man until he was dying.

During the late night and the morning hours of the 4th July each of us had time alone with him. He still smiled and responded to a hand clasp or would draw a hand to his lips. Touching seemed important, and the hospital bed enforced an isolation that had to be bridged. I found I wanted to give him the sound of a voice, so I read aloud the final chapters of the Book of Job. I held up a flower from one of the vases, not as something sweet and pretty but as a symbol of the order of truth to which he had been most true, the grace and intricacies of mental phenomena underlying the patters of the biological world, and wondered whether a flower could still invoke that allegiance as, for someone else, a lifted cross could invoke a whole life lived in the Christian context. He would have been able to call the flower by name.

By mid morning he was unable to drink, and we put tiny amounts of water in his dry mouth to give some moisture, afraid that he would choke on any more, unable to swallow. His breathing was laborious and slow. Lois noticed a pattern of blotches on his chest which at first we thought was a further eruption of the herpes and then realized it was a result of a change in circulation.

A short time later, Roger, a friend from Esalen, saw the pupils of his eyes dilate as his mind encountered the dark. So we gathered around the bed, some six of us who had been caring for him most closely, hardly breathing ourselves as we waited from breath to breath, the time stretching beyond the possible, and yet again and again followed by a gasping, reflective inhalation, and then again the lengthening pause. I kept praying that he would be free from each next compulsive effort, let go, rest, and then after a time no further breath followed, we stood still, slowly relaxing with the faintest sighs, barely able to return to a flow of time not shaped by that breathing. Lois reached forward, after her office, and gently closed his eyes.

We did not at that time pause to mourn but slowly found our way into the expression of continuing care. After Lois, and my turn, I reached out and began to straighten his arms, then folding his hands. Someone lowered the bed to the flat and dropped the sides. I thought briefly of those cultures in which the bodies of loved ones are transmuted at the moment of death into something impure, polluting those who touch them. During my lifetime few Americans have tended their dead, just as few have tended their dying, and we had to grope our way, following cues from other times or other cultures. For Lois the available model was the Balinese one, in which the bodies of men are washed by men and those of women by women, but for me the model was the Western one where women have received the newly born and the newly dead into their care.

In the end we all worked together, removing the soiled pads, cleaning away the final traces of excrement, lifting and turning and washing each limb, shifting from side to side this beloved body from which all tension and recalcitrance were drained so that he suffered our care with curious innocence. The blotches on his skin faded.

Roshi had instructed that all traces of the sick room be removed, and Gregory was lifted and carried to the double bed at the other side of the room, dressed in a bathrobe and covered with the sheet and spread. He was still a little too long for any bed. With half a dozen Zen folk joining in the hospital bed and table were dismantled and carried out, the linens and the clothes and basin we had used to wash him with were removed. Consulting each other in muted voices, we bound a kerchief around his chin, experimenting with the angle until we were able to close his mouth, collecting and composing ourselves even as Gregory's body and the room were made serene in composure. As the work was completed, Robert surveyed the scene and then went and straightened the folds of the bed cover so they fell in sculptured order to the floor. Then he set up a small altar, a table with an incense burner at the foot of the bed, and said that now he would show us how to offer incense to Gregory: bow (the bow whose name is "asking"), touch a few grains of incense to the third eye in the center of the forehead, place them on the burning charcoal, add a few more grains, bow. It seemed to me well to perform an act which was both alien and completely formal, combining affection and courtesy with total estrangement. From that time, incense burned constantly in the room, and two or more of the Zen folk sat and watched. Gregory was not a Buddhist, but Zen mindfulness and decorum were for him an affirmation of the intricate order of mind. We sat for a while, and soon I went and slept in another room of the guest house.

When I woke up and returned to my father's bedside it was late afternoon. His body was cold now when I touched his hands, and the tracery of red blood vessels in his cheeks drained of color. Someone had removed the kerchief and combed his hair. As his body had settled gradually into the rigor of death, his face a gentle, just slightly mischievous smile, and with the wisdom of mothers who refuse to believe that their infants first smiles are caused by gas, we felt we could recognize the carrying over of irony into peace. As he had weakened and had been able to express less and less, the final attribute distilled from the others was sweetness, so this was the natural form into which his features settled, unfalsified by cosmetics and skillful artices of morticians who teach the dead to lie to the living about what they meet at journey's end.

Downstairs we drank sherry and ate the stilton cheese that Gregory loved with other members of the immediate circle who had not been present at noon, in undefined shared sacrament. Through the next two nights and two days, a new pattern developed an echo of the rhythm of Gregory's last days. The Zen students came and went, keeping their virgil and we also took turns being by Gregory's side, watching the continuing changes as death increasingly and more deeply asserted itself. The window was kept open to the cool San Francisco weather, and in the morning he seemed to me a thousand miles more distant, his skin pale as was, his hand still and very cold. As a child I believed that the dead became such strangers immediately, not realizing that there is a maturation in death. Having offered incense once, I found I preferred to enter the room informally and sit close by his side, touching his hand in greeting and farewell.

Our Buddhist guides told of their belief that the soul lingers near the body for up to three days before it finally departs, so that cremation should not occur for three days and the body should be attended, especially during the first two days, and they encouraged us and other visitors to read out loud or to address Gregory. At the same time, all of us had limited experience and we were shy of the physical complications of keeping a body for long period of time, so the decision was made to send the body to the crematorium on the 6th. That morning the Zen students withdrew, leaving the watch with Gregory to the family. My sister Nora and I went in together, sitting for a time on either side of the big bed as she explored the quality of death, feeling his hands, asking about the mechanism of rigor, wondering at the absence of the familiar bulk. Reb, on of the Zen teachers, spoke of him as being like a beached whale, but at the end he was strangely diminished. Then the Neptune Society van came, and Gregory was wrapped in a sheet that someone had carefully ironed that morning, strapped to a stretcher, and finally his face was covered with a dark green wrapper. The Zen Guest House is an old and gracious building, with stairs wide enough for one to make a final departure on a stretcher or in a coffin, and probably Gregory was not the first person to leave it so.

Baker Roshi's advice was to stay as close to the process as possible, following Gregory step by step through the concrete reality, so on the 7th the family went to the crematorium with a small group of Zen monks who had also been close to Gregory. We took various things to send with him into the fire: a volume of Blake's poetry, flowers and sweet smelling herbs, individual roses. We gave him a small crab that Eric and John had gone out with a flashlight to capture the night before in memory of the way he had taken each of us to study tide pools and the way he had taken a crab with him year after year to his opening classes at the Sna Francisco Art Institute, to open his students' eyes to the "fearful symmetrics" of organic life. Nora brought a bagel because he had once quipped at Esalen that the hole in a bagel would be reincarnated in a donut. There were incense and the ashes of incense from Zen Center.

We went into the backstage of the crematorium where the great ovens are, a disheveled and unkept region of noisy machinery. His body was on a plank on a wheeled stretcher, and when the covering was turned back we could see that rigor had passed and his mouth had fallen open, his head fallen sideways. His body seemed gray and abandoned as if finally life had fully receded. We piled our gifts within the shroud and offered incense, and as the Zen folk chanted in Sanskrit we each whispered whatever other prayers we felt the moment needed. Reb, the Zen priest officiating, whispered in his ear before the oven door was closed. None of us felt any longer the need or desire to touch him.

Reb showed Lois the button to start the oven as in another age she would have set the flame to pyre of fragrant woods. And then he suggested that we go outside to where the smoke of the crematorium was escaping into the bright sky.

The Relevance of 1854
A Speech by Chief Seattle

There was a time when our people covered the land as the waves of a wind-ruffled sea cover its shell paved floor, but that time long since passed away with the greatness of tribes that are now but a mournful memory. I will not dwell on nor mourn over our untimely decay, nor reproach the paleface brothers with hastening it, as we too may have been somewhat to blame.

Youth is impulsive. When our young men grow angry at some real or imaginary wrong, and disfigure their faces with black paint, it denotes that their hearts are black, and that they are often are cruel and relentless, and our old men and old women are unable to restrain them. Thus it have ever been. Thus it was when the white man first began to push our forefathers further westward. But let us hope that the hostilities between us may never return. We would have everything to lose and nothing to gain. Revenge by young men is considered gain, even at the cost of their own lives, but old men who stay at home at times of war, and mothers who have sons to lose, know better.

Our good father of Washington – for I presume he is now our father as well as yours, since King George moved his boundaries further north – our great and good father, I say, sends word that if we do as he desires he will protect us. His brave warriors will be to us a bristling wall of strength, and his wonderful ships of war will fill our harbors so that our ancient enemies far to the northward – the Haidas and the Taimpsians, will cease to frighten our women, children and old men. Then in reality will he be our father and we his children.

But can that ever be? Your God is not our God! Your God loves your people and hates mine. He folds his strong protecting arm lovingly about his paleface and leads him by the hand as a father leads his infant son – but he has forsaken his red children – if they really are his. Your God makes your people wax strong every day. Soon they will fill all the land. Our people are ebbing away like a rapidly receding tide that will never return. The white man's God cannot love our people or He would protect them. They seem to be orphans who can look nowhere for help. How then can we be brothers? How can your God become our God and renew our prosperity and awaken in us dreams of returning greatness? If we have a commonly heavenly father, He must be partial – for He came to His paleface children. We never saw Him. He gave you laws but had no word for His red children whose teeming multitudes once filled this vast continent as stars fill the firmament. No; we are two distinct races with separate origins and separate destinies. There is little in common between us.

To us the ashes of our ancestors are sacred and their resting places is hallowed ground. You wander far from the graves of your ancestors and seemingly without regret. Your religion was written upon tables of stone by the iron finger of your God so that you could not forget. The Red Man could never comprehend nor remember it. Our religion is the traditions of our ancestors – the dreams of our old men, given to them in the solemn hours of the night by the Great Spirit; and the visions of our sachems, and is written in the hearts of our people.

Your dead cease to love you and the land of their nativity as soon as they pass the portals of the tomb and wander way beyond the stars. They are soon forgotten and never return. Our dead never forget the beautiful world that gave them being. They still love its verdant valleys,it murmuring rivers, its magnificent mountains, sequestered vales and verdant lined lakes and bays, and ever yearn in tender, fond affection over the lonely-hearted living, and often return from the Happy Hunting Ground to visit, guide, console and comfort them.

Day and night cannot dwell together. The Red Man has ever fled the approach of the White Man, as the morning mist flees before the morning sun.

It matters little where we pass the remnant of our days. They will not be many. The Indians' night promises to be dark. Not a single star of hope hovers above his horizon. Sad-voiced winds moan in the distance. Grim faces seem to be on the Red Man's trail and wherever he goes he will hear the approaching footsteps of his fall destroyer and prepare stolidly to meet his doom, as does the wounded doe that hears approaching the steps of the hunter.

A few more moons. A few more winters – and not one of the descendants of the mighty hosts that once moved over this broad land or lived in happy homes, protected by the Great Spirit, will remain to mourn over the graves of a people – once more powerful and hopeful than yours. But why should I mourn at the untimely fate of my people? Tribe follows tribe, and nation follows nation, like the waves of the sea. It is the order of nature and regret is useless. Your time of decay may be distant, but it will surely come, for even the White Man whose God walked and talked with him as friend with friend, cannot be exempt from the common destiny. We may be brothers after all. We will see.

We will ponder your proposition and when we decide we will let you know. But should we accept it, I here and now make this condition that we will not be denied the privilege without molestation of visiting at any time the tombs of our ancestors, friends and children. Every part of this soil is sacred in the estimation of my people. Every hillside, every valley, every plain and grove, has been hallowed by some sad or happy event in the days long vanished. Even the rocks, which seem to be dumb and dead as they swelter in the sun along the silent shore, thrill with memories of stirring events connected with lives of my people, and the very dust upon which you now stand responds more lovingly to their footsteps than to yours, because it is rich with the blood of our ancestors and our bare feet are conscious of the sympathetic touch. Our departed braves, fond mothers, glad happy-hearted maidens, and even the little children who lived here and rejoiced here for a brief season, will love these somber solitudes and at eventide they greet shadowy returning spirits. And when the last Red Man shall have perished, and the memory of my tribe shall have become a myth among the White Men, these shores will swarm with the invisible dead of my tribe, and when your children's children think themselves alone in the field, the store, the shop, upon the highway, or in the silence of the pathless woods, they will not be alone. In all the earth there is no place dedicated to solitude. At night when the streets of your cities and villages are silent and you think them deserted, they will throng with the returning hosts that once filled them and still love this beautiful land. The White Man will never be alone.

Let him be just and deal kindly with my people, for the dead are not powerless. Dead, did I say? There is no death, only a change of worlds.

Do not stand at my grave
and weep.
I am not there. I do not sleep.

I am a thousand winds that blow.
I am the diamond glint on snow.

I am the sunlight on ripened grain.
I am the gentle autumn rain.

When you wake in the morning hush
I am the swift, uplifting rush
of quiet birds in circling flight.
I am the soft starlight at night.

Do not stand at my grave
and weep.
I am not there. I do not sleep.

Anonymous from
Northwest Indian News

Mental Health
Problems of Aging

SESSION VII

Session Guide To The Trainer

If you bring in special staff to present on mental illness subjects, be sure they understand the Peer Counseling Program. Overwhelming the trainees with technical terms is not only frightening, it is boring. Trainees want to know about various mental illnesses. They need information relating to the symptoms and signs, and how these relate to aging. Although many trainees are sophisticated, educated people, they are still somewhat fearful of mental illness. Your job is to reduce that fear by presenting the facts and demystifying mental illness. Many seniors react negatively to the word "crazy." As mental health professionals, it is good to spend some time explaining to the trainees "our career colloquialisms."

Our presenters divide their subjects into categories such as:
1) Psychotic disorders
2) Depression, Dementia and Anxiety
3) Personality disorders
4) Medication review

All categories are discussed in terms of the older adult diagnosis and treatment.

A significant number of trainees may have family members who suffer from mental illness. In one of our groups (15 members), two were parents of adult schizophrenics, one was the parent of an adult with bi-polar illness, two were parents of young adults who had suicided, and one was the parent of an adult who was developmentally disabled. Sharing their experiences and pain were an essential part of the presentation on mental illness. The parent's acknowledgment of their grief, guilt, anger added to education of the group. A positive outcome was a discussion of the progress made in chronic mental illness issues over the past 15 years. Video tapes or movie clips work well to bring about updated information.

A significant number of trainees may have family members who suffer from mental illness.

Session Materials

* Library books on mental illness and aging
* D.S.M. - IIIR   * P.D.R.
* Newsprint   * Charts
* Generations Journal on Mental Illness and Aging, Spring,1988
• Video tapes: "Titticutt Follies," "Rainman," "Losing It All."

Session VII
Mental Health Problems of Aging

God, grant me the grace to accept with serenity the things that cannot be changed, courage to change the things that should be changed and wisdom to distinguish the one from the other.

Reinhold Niekuhr

Today's Goal

* Familiarity with mental illness and its relationship to aging.
* Dispel fear and myths of mental illness.
* Introduction of symptoms and behavior signs of specific mental illnesses.

Strategy

Lecture presentation on major mental illness and its degree of disability in the aging population. This can be presented in factual, clinical format (DSM III R) without overwhelming the trainees. Examples of each disorder will help give a clearer view of what the trainee might encounter with an aging client. A knowledgeable presentation on medications and how they assist in the treatment of the elderly who suffer severe or chronic mental illness will dispel misconception of "drugs" and also dispel fears regarding such issues as overdose and institutionalization.

Present the trainees with the handout list and, on newsprint flip chart, list major categories of mental disorders. Help trainees by group discussion, to view mental illness as only "part" of the client's life, not as consuming and therefore a hopeless, helpless condition. Dispel fear of "crazy" behaviors with information and your own experience in working with mental illness.

Learning Objectives

* Increase knowledge of mental illness; assist in increasing factual definitions
* Reframe mental illness as a part of the client's problem, not as the client themself
* Create a positive, hopeful approach to treating mental illness.

Handouts and Workbook Materials

* Diagnostic Criteria Lists
* Mental Status Examination
* Geriatric Depression Scale & Key
* Chart for Depression, O.B.S., and Grief

• Depression in Older Adults
• Glossary of Mental Health Terms
• Dementia Handouts

Does Age Make A Difference? . . . Session VII

I. "Temperature Reading"

Allow 2-3 minutes for each member to clarify issues from last week.

II. Introduction To The Vocabulary of Mental Illness

Introducing the language of mental illness begins with the facilitator going over handout and case studies. Follow the outline to cover the major disorders, their treatments and their medications. Trainees may have many questions regarding mental illness, violence, hospitalization and medications. Group facilitator will need to give clear, concise, factual information.

III. Psychiatric Disorders

Overview:

A. *Organic Mental Disorders*
Types, causes, assessment, treatment, and how to communicate with confused clients.

B. *Depression (Affective disorders)*
Causes and assessment, treatment and working with depressed clients.

C. *Paranoid Behavior*
Causes, assessment, working with paranoid/suspicious clients.

D. *Psychotic Disorders*
Types, assessment, treatment and working with persons with psychotic symptoms.

E. *Anxiety Disorders*
Panic, phobias, generalized anxiety, how to work with anxious clients.

F. *Suicide*
Assessing the threat, how to work with someone who is suicidal., peer counselor's fear and other reactions to suicidal clients, other people's reactions to a suicide.

IV. Personality Disorders

Overview:

A review of personality disorders (DSM III R), looking at long-term personality patterns.

A. *Borderline Personality*
Peer Counselor's anxiety in working with such a client.

B Anger
Reasons, Peer Counselor's reactions to anger, working with this type client.

C Independence and Dependence
Personality types, fostering self-esteem, Peer Counselor's reactions to being either depended on or not needed.

D. Aggression and Combativeness
Assessing the environment and the concerns working with the combative client.

E. Institutionalization
Effects of institutional environment on behavior.

F. Sexuality
Sex and aging, sexual acting out, sex in nursing homes, the need for intimacy.

G Families and the Elderly
How families help elderly relatives, family systems (interactions among family members), family interactions with nursing home staff, working with family members.

H. Sleep Patterns and Aging
Normal changes, assessing sleep problems, when to intervene.

V. Psychiatric Treatment Issues

Overview:

A. Environmental Change, Behavioral Approaches

B. Individual Psychotherapy
Behavioral and cognitive approaches, relaxation techniques, biofeedback and pain management, brief and intensive psychotherapy, paradoxical approaches, life review and reminiscence.

C Psychotropic Medications
Used for agitation, anxiety, depression, psychosis.

D. Crisis Intervention
Assessing the crisis, working with people in crisis, how to use professionals.

E. Medications Effecting Cognitive and Emotional Functioning.

F. Counseling Skills: Regarding All Mental Disorders
Communication in a helping relationship, empathy, caring without over involvement.

Group Discussion

- What is the major concept of mental illness by the elderly?
- What is the fear?
- Why are the elderly resistant to mental health intervention?
- How can Peer Counselors assist mental health professionals in dispelling the fear?
- What are your fears regarding mental illness?

Key Element -

Keep trainees "on track" and from becoming overwhelmed by limiting information to an overview. If there is group interest for more in-depth study this can be accomplished in a Continuing Education Workshop specific to the issues such as depression, dementia, anxiety, etc.

Experiential Exercise - "Comforting Depression"

Trainees form triads to practice counseling with depressed clients. Have trainees practice and explore issues of unresolved grief, and focus on improving problem solving skills. The trainees will also practice progress note writing in this exercise. Focus should be on the ability to identify symptoms of depression as opposed to the "blues." Allow each member of the triad 5 minutes to role play the client. Again, in role play, life issues are the most reliable for learning experiences (15 minute exercise.)

- Return to large group for clarification and discussion.
- In what ways did you deal with your client's depression?
- How did you feel when your client did not respond to you?
- In what way did you find yourself wanting to give advise or minimize their complaints?
- What was your treatment plan (immediate, as opposed to long-term) for your client?

VI. Working with Mental Illness

Many trainees will want to know how to work successfully with their elderly client suffering from a chronic mental disorder. They will hope you have a "magic" formula for dealing with clients with mental illness. They may be frustrated to learn that there are limited cures. The most effective treatment is the establishment of empathy, trust, rapport, understanding and encouragement. Allow time and discussion for this to make sense to the trainee.

Help trainees to remember that all behavior is purposeful. It is our job to try and understand what the client is telling us through their behavior.

The dispelling of the myths and fears which accompany the treatment of the mental illness will be the facilitator's greatest task in this session.

Group Discussion

- Of what value are medications?
- What are some of the problems related to medications?
- Name alternative treatment modalities used by mental health professionals:
    - Stress Management
    - Biofeedback
    - Activities - exercise
    - Massage
    - Life Review
    - Group Therapy - Geriatric Day Treatment
    - Electroconvulsive Therapy
    - Nutrition
    - In-home Therapy
    - Peer Counselors
    - Family Support
    - Family Therapy
    - Alcohol Treatment
    - Multidisciplinary Teams

Key Element

The uniqueness of the peer counselor is their ability to work with a client without the stigma that is associated with the client seeing a mental health professional. This helps to allay the fear of the elderly that they will be seen as "crazy."

VII. Closing

Housekeeping duties may include a discussion regarding the end of the course. It may also include a discussion regarding the trainee's fears about not being ready.

Placement of clients will begin at this time. The facilitator needs to review the strengths and weaknesses of the peer counselor to make appropriate placements.

VIII. Summarization

As this session ends, be sure to take time to reinforce the idea this training is only a beginning in the learning process. They will continue to be learn in supervision and continuing education.

Begin to look at the group termination process and be ready to answer concerns in terms of how we will be moving to a different format, yet remain a "group." This can be a metaphor for the many unresolved closures peer counselors have experienced. Attempt to create a complete and healthy closure.

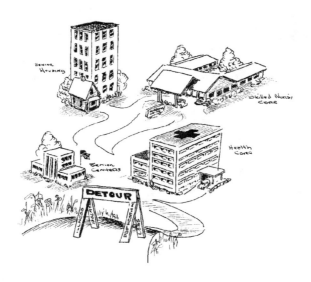

Recommended Reading

Bumagin, Victoria, and Kathryn Hern, *Aging is a Family Affair,* New York, Thomas A. Crowell, 1979.

Scarf, Maggie, *Unfinished Business,* New York, Random House.

Torrey Fuller R., *Surviving Schizophrenia*, New York, N.Y., Harper and Row, 1983.

SESSION VII

Handouts & Workbook Materials

Glossary of Mental Health Terms

acting out:
doing things not ordinarily done or tolerated; for example, undressing and coming out into the hall, yelling, hitting another patient, throwing things.

acute:
having a sudden onset, quickly becomes worse, of a short time.

Acute Brain Syndrome:
also known as delirium, is a reversible disease if caught in time before too many brain cells die or become damaged.

Affect:
an emotion that can be seen or observed when it is being felt. Different from mood. (i.e., euphoria, anger, sadness, blunted and flat, labile). Affect relates to mood as weather relates to climate.

agitated:
excessive motion when feeling inner tension, can't sit still, pacing, wrings hands, pulls at clothes, restless.

Alzheimer's Disease:
affects way brain works, damage occurs when cells are lost and nerve endings damaged, causes general deterioration of mental ability.

antidepressant medication:
used to help individual return to more normal emotional state, often improves sleep, appetite, feeling of well-being. Some common names: Elavil, Doxepin, Tofranil, Norpramine.

anxiety:
apprehension, tension or uneasiness coming from expectations of threat or danger, can be fear of or belief of having disease, which is hypochondriasis.

atrophy:
to waste away, deteriorate.

attention span:
the ability to sustain focus on one task or activity.

blocking:
interruption of a train of speech before a thought or idea has been completed.

brain syndrome:
a group of signs or symptoms that happen together in the brain.

cerebrovascular insufficiency:a blood flow to brain in impaired.

chronic:
continuing for a long time.

Chronic Brain Syndrome: long term group of symptoms that happen together in brain.

cognitive deficits: unable to perceive or understand things around them, or to remember ideas.

compulsive: repeats behavior that supposedly will make or prevent something from happening, feels that they must do this.

confabulation: fabrication of facts or events in response to question about situations or events that are not recalled due to memory impairment.

coping behavior: what people do to try to deal successfully with their lives.

delirium: unclear state of consciousness, usually quick onset, usually only lasts briefly.

delusion: a false personal belief based on incorrect ideas about what is reality.

dementia: loss of intellectual ability so that it interferes with the way a person operates, personality and behavior changes, consciousness is clear.

depression: feelings ranging from disappointment to hopelessness, helplessness, severe depressions cause changes in eating, sleeping, ability to enjoy oneself, weight gain/loss, pulling away from family, friends, not taking care of self.

differential diagnosis: to separate as unlike another diagnosis.

disorder: ailment of body or mind.

disoriented: confusion about person (self or others), place (where they are), and time (day, date, time on clock).

empathy: a current understanding of an individual patient's feelings, gained by "borrowing" that patient's feelings in order to understand them, sensing the patient's world as if it were your own, never losing the "AS IF".

feelings: emotions, emotional experiences (see affect and mood).

functional (brain):   work done by brain, ideas, calculations, emotions, etc.

hallucination: something which is real to individual and is perceived by their senses, but does not exist as they think it does, something seen, heard, felt, etc.

hypochondriasis: unrealistic explanations of physical signs or sensations as being abnormal, leads to being preoccupied with fear or belief of having disease.

illusion: a misperception of a real external stimulus, i.e., seeing a tray cart and the patient sees it as a load of wood going by his door, or you walk in the door and the patient says, "Hi, Sally", but your name is Marnie.

labile: may change moods very quickly for no reason, i.e., may cry and then start laughing when there has been no change in the conversation, may look very sad then suddenly start laughing or be laughing and suddenly start crying.

manic: overexcitement, hyperactive, "can't slow down", thinks everything's great, may be very irritable, usually thoughts and speech very rapid, jumps around on subjects, usually sleeps considerably less, can be dangerous state for health.

Mental Status Examinations: tests given, usually by talking, to determine person's awareness and ability to think clearly and in ways needed to function.

metabolic activity of brain: chemical changes and care in brain cells aided by continuous blood flow.

mood: an overall, lasting emotion that effects way we see the world, i.e., anger, depression, apathy, fear, etc.

neurological examinations: (EEG, CAT scan) medical tests using highly technical machines to determine how brain is working.

neurosis (neurotic):   symptoms which cause distress or conflict in coping ability.

obsessive: persistent ideas, thoughts or urges keep coming back without person wanting them to.

oriented:	aware of person, place and time.
paranoid:	believes or suspects they are being harrassed, persecuted or unfairly treated.
Parkinson's Disease:	group of symptoms of nerve problems which shows itself as problems with movement (slow, stooped posture, small shuffling steps, tremors in advanced stages).
pathologic:	causes disease.
personality:	deeply ingrained patterns of behavior, including way we relate to, understand and think about world around us and ourselves.
phobia:	persistent, irrational fear of an object, activity or situation causing desire to avoid.
psychosocial:	relates to mental/emotional and contact with other people (society).
psychosomatic (disorders):	ailments which actually originate in the mind which cause real or imaginary physical effects.
psychomotor functioning:	how person moves or acts according to how they feel.
psychotic:	ideas about reality are very incorrect, delusion and hallucinations.
schizophrenic:	has psychotic symptoms, deteriorates from previous ability to function, begins before age 45, episodes lasting at least 6 months are termed "chronic.".
suicidal ideation:	thoughts of death and wanting to harm (kill) oneself.
syndrome:	group of symptoms that occur together.
withdrawn:	pulls away emotionally, avoids friends, family.

AFFECT

An immediately expressed and observed emotion. A feeling state becomes an affect when it is observable, for example, as overall demeanor or tone and modulation of voice. Affect is to be distinguished from mood, which refers to a pervasive and sustained emotion. Affect is to mood as weather is to climate. Common examples of affect are euphoria, anger, and sadness.

A range of affect may be described as broad (normal), restricted (constricted), blunted, or flat. What is considered the normal range of the expression of affect varies considerably, both within and among different cultures. The normal expression of affect involves variability in facial expression, pitch of voice, and the use of hand and body movements. Restricted affect is characterized by a clear reduction in the expressive range and intensity of affects. Blunted affect is marked by a severe reduction in the intensity of affective expression. In a flat affect there is a lack of signs of affective expression; the voice may be monotonous and the face, immobile.

Affect is inappropriate when it is clearly discordant with the content of the person's speech or ideation. Example: A patient smiled and laughed while discussing demons who were persecuting him. An affect should not be termed inappropriate however, when it is inappropriate merely to the situation, such as laughing when told that a relative has died; in such instances it would be more apt to refer to inappropriate behavior.

Affect is labile when it is characterized by repeated, rapid, and abrupt shifts. Examples: An elderly man is tearful one moment and combative the next; a young woman is observed by her friends to be friendly, gregarious, and happy one moment and angry and abusive the next, without readily apparent reason.

Source: compiled by Martha Day, M.S.W., past Coordinator of SCMHC Peer Counseling Program.

Mental Status Examination

Appearance and Behavior
Does patient appear (dress and behavior) normal or unusual? look depressed, manic, suspicious, frightened, hostile, etc.

Orientation
To time, place and person

Memory
Does patient remember events/dates for long ago (years?) and recent? Can he/she remember 3 objects in 3 minutes?

Speech
Is speech organized, coherent, pressured, slow, low volume, loud, or delusional? Does patient hallucinate?

Affect
Is patient anxious, depressed, hostile?

Cognition
Is patient able to think as clearly as a normal person with same level of education? Have patient count to ten (10) and backwards. Simple calculations.

Abstraction
Have patient tell similarities and differences of objects such as orange and banana.

Judgement
Does patient know what is appropriate behavior in certain circumstances?

Normal vs. Abnormal Behavior

Before we can begin any discussion of mental illness in older adults, we must first explain the difference between normal and abnormal behavior.

Normal behavior is characterized by a number of positive approaches to life, such as:

- Possessing a positive attitude toward self
- Having goals in regard to growth and development.
- Possessing a feeling of separateness
- Perceiving reality accurately
- Feeling competent in relation to the environment.
- Experiencing positive interpersonal relationships.

Abnormal behavior, on the other hand, contains elements of:

- Personal suffering.
- Inability to adapt to change or to "fit in" with standard behavior.
- Irrational behavior.
- Inability to comprehend.
- Loss of control.
- Unpredictability.
- Disregard for societal morals and standards.
- Feelings of discontent and unhappiness.

The National Institute of Mental Health states that the severely mentally ill person is one who suffers from a chronic or relatively permanent mental illness. This illness is one that disrupts the ability to successfully manage activities of daily living. This may have resulted in hospitalization or institutionalization at some point in life.

Source: Chums & Choices Project, Ohio Department of Mental Health

Psychosocial Disorders

Affective Disorder

Depressive Disorder
Low energy, poor or exaggerated appetitie, disrupted sleep pattern, dysphoric mood, sense of hopelessness, possible suicidal ideation.

Bipolar Affective Disorder
Manic - generally high energy, increased activity, pressured, intrusive speech, decreased need for sleep, grandiose ideas, impaired judgement.

Thought Disorder

Major disturbances in thinking and judgement as well as mood and behavior. Can include delusional ideation and/or hallucinations. Present with schizophrenic, paranoid and atypical psychotic disorders. Can be present with Depressive or Bipolar Disorders.

Delusions
False and firmly held beliefs not susceptible to modification or correction by logical persuasion. For example, paranoid, depressing, grandiose and erotic delusions.

Hallucinations
Spontaneous, unwilled sense perceptions which can be experienced through any of the five senses. Auditory and visual perceptions tend to be most commonly experienced.

Anxiety or Panic Disorder

Repeated, prolonged episodes of immobilizing symptoms of fear, overdependence, disorganization and inability to follow through with generally non-threatening behaviors. Somatic symptoms including rapid heart rate, excessive perspiration and gastrointestinal distress are common.

Personality Disorders

Characterized by deeply ingrained, inflexible, maladaptive personality traits which cause major disruptions in relationships, employment, follow-through with care needs as well as all other aspects of life experience. Borderline disorder tends to be most difficult to manage. Includes: Borderline; Passive-Aggressive; Dependent; Narcissistic; Histrionic; Institutional.

Source: Diagnostic and Statistical Manual of Mental Disorders, DSM III R, 3rd Edition Revised, published by the American Psychiatric Association, Washington, D.C., 1987.

Manifestions of Mental Disorder

The following manifestations of mental disorder may be observed in the elderly who fall within acute dysfunctional, prolonged dysfunctional, and disturbed functioning categories. Generally, these elderly persons would meet state mental health priority definitions.

Underlining indicates some symptoms which are often overlooked as indicators of mental disorder in elderly persons and are often attributed erroneously to the natural consequences of aging. Any one of the underlined symptoms alone would not justify a DSM III diagnosis of mental disorder. However, when such symptoms are combined with level of functioning criteria and the indicators of acute mental illness, chronic mental illness, and serious disturbance defined in RCW and WAC, the elderly individual may be diagnosed as having a mental disorder.

Disturbance of sleep cycle - insomnia and/or daytime drowsiness
Memory impairment
Disorientation
Deterioration in judgment
Difficulty with abstract thinking, such as numbers
Changes from usual behavior typical for that person
Rambling, incoherent speech
Multiple somatic complaints
Poor appetite or significant weight loss
Feelings of worthlessness, self-reproach, or excessive guilt
Recurrent thoughts of death
Withdrawing from usual level of activity
Apathy, loss of interest
Fatigue, loss of energy

Agitation, hyperactivity, such as pacing, rocking restlessness
Personality change
Delusions
Suspiciousness, paranoid thinking
Disturbance of mood - manic or withdrawn behavior
Hallucinations
Wandering
Irritability
Emotional lability - weeping or inappropriate laughter
Pressured talking
Distractibility
Flight of ideas, loose associations, illogical thinking
Bizarre behavior

Unrealistic preoccupation with the idea of having a serious disease, or unrealistic interpretations of physical signs or sensations as abnormal

Anxiety as indicated by motor tension, autonomic hyperactivity or apprehensiveness

Panic attacks

Phobias

Obsessive thoughts

Compulsive behaviors which interfere with daily functioning

Blunted affect

Suicidal ideation or attempts

As noted above, the underlined symptoms, when noticed in an elderly person, are particularly likely to be attributed to the effects of aging or to the effects of the various physical ailments and illnesses which are frequently experienced by elderly. It is important, however, to recognize that they may also be symptomatic of depression, dementia, or other physical or mental illnesses.

Disgnostic Criteria for
Depression

<u>Affective</u>
<u>Facets</u>

- sadness, discouragement
- crying
- anxiety, panic attacks
- brooding
- paranoid

- irritability
- states they feel sad, blue, depressed, low, nothing is fun, down in the dumps

<u>Social and</u>
<u>Interpersonal</u>
<u>Facets</u>

- withdrawal from usual activities
- hallucinations (short duration)
- inability to express pleasure
- feelings of worthlessness
- self reproach for minor failings

- unreasonable fears
- delusions of poverty
- decreased sex drive
- critical of self and others
- passive

<u>Somatic,</u>
<u>Psychomotor</u>
<u>Facets</u>

- increased or decreased body movement
- difficulty getting to sleep, staying awake, waking early
- decreased or sometimes increased appetite
- fatigue
- can't concentrate, think or make decisions
- slowed speech, pauses before answering, decreased amount of speech, low monotonous speech

- pacing, wringing hands,
- tachycardia pulling or rubbing hair, body, clothing
- weight loss or sometimes gain
- preoccupation with physical health, especially fear of cancer
- thoughts of death
- suicide or suicide attempt
- constipation

Source: adapted from <u>Diagnostic and Statistical Manual</u>
<u>of Mental Disorders III R</u>, 1990.

Geriatric Depression Scale

Name _____ Date _____ Date of Birth _____

CIRCLE THE BEST ANSWER FOR HOW YOU FELT OVER THE PAST WEEK

1. ARE YOU BASICALLY SATISFIED WITH YOUR LIFE?   YES NO
2. HAVE YOU DROPPED MANY OF YOUR ACTIVITIES   YES NO
    AND INVESTMENTS?
3. DO YOU FEEL THAT YOUR LIFE IS EMPTY?   YES NO

4. DO YOU OFTEN GET BORED?   YES NO
5. ARE HOPEFUL ABOUT THE FUTURE?   YES NO
6. BOTHERED BY THOUGHTS YOU CAN'T GET OUT OF YOUR HEAD?   YES NO

7   ARE YOU IN GOOD SPIRITS MOST OF THE TIME?   YES NO
8. ARE YOU AFRAID THAT SOMETHING BAD IS GOING   YES NO
    TO HAPPEN TO YOU?
9. DO YOU FEEL HAPPY MOST OF THE TIME?   YES NO

10. DO YOU OFTEN FEEL HELPLESS?   YES NO
11. DO YOU OFTEN GET RESTLESS AND FIDGETY?   YES NO
12. DO YOU PREFER TO STAY AT HOME, RATHER THAN
    GOING OUT AND DOING NEW THINGS?   YES NO

13. DO YOU FREQUENTLY WORRY ABOUT THE FUTURE?   YES NO
14. DO YOU FEEL YOU HAVE MORE PROBLEMS WITH   YES NO
    MEMORY THAN MOST?
15. DO YOU THINK IT IS WONDERFUL TO BE ALIVE NOW?   YES NO

16. DO YOU OFTEN FEEL DOWNHEARTED AND BLUE?   YES NO
17. DO YOU FEEL PRETTY WORTHLESS THE WAY YOU ARE NOW?   YES NO
18. DO YOU WORRY A LOT ABOUT THE FUTURE?   YES NO

19. DO YOU FIND LIFE VERY EXCITING?   YES NO
20. IS IT HARD FOR YOU TO GET STARTED ON NEW PROJECTS?   YES NO
21. DO YOU FEEL FULL OF ENERGY?   YES NO

22. DO YOU FEEL THAT YOUR SITUATION IS HOPELESS?   YES NO
23. DO YOU THINK THAT MOST PEOPLE ARE BETTER OFF   YES NO
    THAN YOU ARE?
24. DO YOU FREQUENTLY GET UPSET OVER LITTLE THINGS?   YES NO

25. DO YOU FREQUENTLY FEEL LIKE CRYING?   YES NO
26. DO YOU HAVE TROUBLE CONCENTRATING?   YES NO
27. DO YOU ENJOY GETTING UP IN THE MORNING?   YES NO

28. DO YOU PREFER TO AVOID SOCIAL GATHERINGS?   YES NO
29 IS IT EASY FOR YOU TO MAKE DECISIONS?   YES NO
30. IS YOUR MIND AS CLEAR AS IT USED TO BE?   YES NO

Source: T.L. Brink

Scoring Key: Geriatric Depression Scale

1. Are you basically satisfied with your life?
2. Have you dropped many of your activities and interests?
3. Do you feel that your life is empty?
4. Do you often get bored?
5. Are you hopeful about the future?
6. Are you bothered by thoughts you can't get out of your head?
7. Are you in good spirits most of the time?
8. Are you afraid that something bad is going to happen to you?
10. Do you often feel helpless?
11. Do you often get restless and fidgety?
12. Do you prefer to stay home at night, rather than go out and do new things?
13. Do you frequently worry about the future?
14. Do you feel you have more problems with memory than most?
15. Do you think it is wonderful to be alive now?
16. Do you often feel downhearted and blue?
17. Do you feel pretty worthless the way you are now?
18. Do you worry a lot about the past?
19. Do you find life very exciting?
20. Is it hard for you to get started on new projects?
21. Do you feel full of energy?
22. Do you feel that your situation is hopeless?
23. Do you think that most people are better off than you are?
24. Do you frequently get upset over little things?
25. Do you frequently feel like crying?
26. Do you have trouble concentrating?
27. Do you enjoy getting up in the morning?
28. Do you prefer to avoid social gatherings?
29. Is it easy for you to make decisions?
30. Is your mind as clear as it used to be?

Administration: These items may be administered in oral or written format. If the latter is used, it is important that the answer sheet have printed YES/NO after each question, and the subject is instructed to circle the better response. If administered orally, the examiner may have to repeat the question in order to get a response that is more clearly a yes or no. The GDS loses validity as dementia increases. The GDS seems to work well with other age groups.

Scoring:
Count 1 point for each depressive answer.

0 – 10 normal
11 – 20 mild depression
21 – 30 moderate or severe depression

Common Signs and Symptoms of Depression

Behavioral Changes
Crying, tearfulness, inability to cry
Social withdrawal
Psychomotor retardation
Agitation
Hallucinations
Suicide Attempt
Reduced sexual activity or interest
Disinterest in pleasurable activities
Decline in talking

Emotional Changes
Sadness
Guilt
Anxiety
Anger
Daily mood variation
Paranoia
Hopelessness
Loss of pleasure in life
Decline in productivity

Cognitive Changes
Negative self-concept/ feeling inadequate
Negative view of the world/pessimism
Negative expectations for the future
Self-blame
Self-criticism
Indecisiveness
Helplessness
Hopelessness
Worthlessness
Delusions (of guilt, sin, worthlessness)
Suicidal thoughts
Decline in attention/concentration

Physical Changes
Sleep disturbance
Eating disturbance
Constipation
Menstrual irregularity
Impotence / frigidity
Weight loss
Weakness
Low energy or chronic fatigue
Pain, unexplained origin
Diminished sexual "drive"
Vague physical complaints

Source: Gerontology Studies, University of Washington, Seattle, WA., 1989.

Guidelines for Treatment of Depression

Assess physical health and nutrition

Assess medications

Consider use of anti-depressant medication

Explore issues of loss/unresolved grief

Provide one-to-one contact

Structure time and increase activity level

Balance focus on   a) dealing with depression, and
                     b) positive conversation and/or activity

Mobilize support network

Increase social interactions

Focus on improving self-concept with positive thoughts

Promote realistic expectations of self and of life

Improve decision making and problem solving skills

Increase perception of control/effectiveness

Encourage appropriate expression of anger

Explore suicidal ideation/intent

Explore sources of stress

Increase self-awareness - self-esteem - self-reliance

Don't   Minimize complaints

        Discount reasons for depression

        Give advice - "You should's"

        Have or encourage unrealistic expectations for improvement/change

        Ignore physical complaints

        Avoid discussion of suicide.

	DEPRESSION	ORGANIC BRAIN SYNDROME	GRIEF
APPEARANCE	Usually unkept (person takes less interest in grooming, i.e., bathing, clean clothes, combing hair, shaving for men, makeup for women). Sad face.	Often unkempt, sign of self-care habit deterioration.	Nothing remarkable.
BEHAVIOR	Generalized slowing of movement and speech, poor eye contact, may be agitated (especially the aged), may be tearful.	Variable: May be restless and/or irritable. May wander. Apprehensive or frightened for no reason.	Crying: sad face. May show mildly slowed speech and movement.
FEELING (Affect & Mood)	Sad, despondent, guilty, anxious, may talk about feeling worthless, guilty and helpless.	Variable: May be hostile, anxious or depressed. May cycle frequently.	Despondent, sad, angry, guilty.
HALLUCINATIONS	Usually none.	Variable: usually visual.	None usually.
DELUSIONS	Usually none	Usually none: may misperceive a a real event and get is all blown out of shape.	None usually.
THINKING	May be confused, usually worse in the morning. Poor concentration. May have short attention span, memory and/or orientation impairment and/or slow thought flow.	Confusion usually spotty. Clear intervals mixed with confused periods. Usually worse in the late afternoons (sundown syndrome). Judgement impaired. May have impaired level of consciousness JAMCO - Judgment, Affect, Memory, Confusion, Orientation.	May express loss frequently and intensely appropriately.
PHYSICAL	Sleep disturbance (early wakening most common), constipation, loss of appetite, fatigue, headaches, hypersensitive to sound, dizziness.	May be restless and sleep fitfully.	Usually none. May have term sleep disturbance and loss of appetite.
PRECIPITATION EVENTS APPARENT	Can be precipitated by loss of love object or important factor for self-esteem or just a function of age.	Medical illness / Abnormal aging, i.e., arteriosclerosis, strokes, athrosclerosis, cardiac failure.	Loss of love object recently (2-3 months previous), of health. Loss of job.

Source: Reprint from Summer Institute on Aging, University of Washington, Seattle, WA

Depression in Older Adults

1. Differentiate between feeling temporarily low and clinical depression.

2. Distribution of complaints in depressed 60+ individuals:
   A. Minimal or no complaints   73%
   B. Statements re: feeling sad, blue, etc. 19%
   C. Symptomatic concerns   4%
   D. Anxiety   1%
   E. Other   3%

3. Reasons for depression:
   A. Loss of role (occupation, family role, community role)
   B Loss of support
   C Health issues

4. Challenges in the provision of treatment
   A. A large segment of the elderly who are depressed identify their problems as medical in nature.
   B. Preconceptions about mental health treatment:
      1. "I'm not crazy"
      2. It costs too much
      3. What if somebody finds out?

5. Behavioral/ Emotional changes common in depressed clients:
   A. Changes in appetite
   B. Changes in sleep patterns
   C. Psychomotor agitation or retardation
   D. Fatigue
   E. Difficulty concentrating
   F. Thoughts of death
   G. All of the above can also be symptoms of other medical problems.

6. Dealing with depressed clients:
   A. Be a good listener
      1. Work to build trust and rapport
      2. Help the client to understand the difference between needing support and being "crazy"
      3. Encourage the client to get a physical exam and make sure the physician is aware of the concerns about depression.
         a. physical problems that can cause or contribute to depression

       b.   Thyroid problems

       c.   Medications (Valium, Librium, Xanax, Halcion, Hypertensive agents).

       d.   Vitamin B-12 deficiency

       e.   Chronic pain

4. Encourage client to talk about their feelings and problems
5. Be firm in recommendations re: follow up treatment
6. Be alert to suicidal ideation

B. Assessing potential for suicide:
1. Elderly people have the highest rate of completed suicides for any age group other than teenagers.
2. Ratio of suicide attempts to completed suicides:
   a. 20:1 when age is less than 40
   b. 4:1 when age is over 60
   c. White males over 70 have a completed suicide rate twice as high as any other group.

3. Indicators of high suicide risk:
   a. Widowed or otherwise alone
   b. Poor health
   c. Drug / alcohol addiction
   d. Verbal threats
   e. Previous history
   f. Poor communication skills

C. Suggestions for dealing with high risk clients:
1. Ask specific questions about suicide:
   a. Is the client thinking about hurting himself/herself?
   b. Does he/she have a specific plan as to how this would be done?
   c. Is this plan highly lethal?
   d. Are these means available to the client?

2. Work toward getting a short term no-suicide agreement with immediate follow up by a professional.
   a. Emergency appointment at mental health center?
   b. Review voluntary/ involuntary emergencysystems

3. Seek out support and advice with situations where you feel over your head.

Diagnostic Criteria for
Dementia

Cognitive
- forget names, phone numbers, directions, conversations, events for the day.
- forget to return to or complete a task
- difficulty learning new information
- need statements repeated
- write many notes
- hesitancy in responding
- make up stories

Loss of Judgement
- spend large amounts of money
- buy unusual or inappropriate items
- inappropriate clothing, dirty clothing, body odors
- coarse language, inappropriate jokes (sexual comments or behaviors)
- ignore rules of conduct
- angry or irritable outbursts
- lack of concern for others
- self-centered

Disorganized Thinking
- difficulty with new or unusual tasks
- avoidance of complex tasks and situations
- can't sort out important and unimportant details
- difficulty generalizing, reasoning logically, or forming new concepts
- unable to communicate
- uses long phrases with little meaning
- difficulty naming objects, recalling places
- uses vague words or phrases

Personality
- apathetic
- listless
- dependent on others
- suspicious or paranoid of others
- neat or meticulous person becomes untidy
- withdrawn
- fearful
- decreased social life
- outbursts of temper

Social Interpersonal
- confused about time, place, persons
- can't perform or carry out physical activities in spite of adequate ability
- difficulty in writing, working with hands, walking
- disturbed sleep patterns and wandering
- changes in appetite
- irritability, stubborness
- depressions
- excessive reactions to stresses
- lack of spontaneity
- can't identify objects in spite of good senses
- difficulty understanding written information, yet can read it
- delusions or hallunications
- incontinence
- repetitive movements
- changes in appetite
- seizures or convulsions
- shaking, trembling
- anxiety
- jealousy
- rapid emotional changes
- delirium

Source: adapted from Diagnostic and Statistical Manual of Mental Disorders, DSM III R, and Edward L. Zuckerman, Ph.D., The Clinician's Thesaurus, 3 Wishes Press, 1991, Pittsburg, PA

Dementia

Group of illnesses / disease which affect the brain.
Begin mid-late adulthood.
Results of various diseases are the same, no matter which disease.

>dimentia umbrella term
>- Alzheimer's most commonly known.
>
>All cause decline in function of brain until death.
>- Usually 8 -10 years after disease began.
>- Sometimes rapid, some more gradual.

Symptoms/Signs

Usual progression:

Loss of Recent Memory
- events   - details
- sometimes brought out by other temporary illness, flu
- normal reserves not there - disease

Loss of Judgment / Social ability
- Ability to take in information and respond appropriately
- Familiar social situations ok at first, new ones problem.
- Communication skills at first seemingly o.k.
- Listen for content, meaning

Loss of Abstract Thinking
- Sorting out information, important from non-important
- Mathematics
- Repetitive words and phrases to communicate

Change in Emotions Seen and Expressed
- May be down in responsiveness, apathetic, flattened affect, inflection, expression
- May be up in responsiveness
- Change in personality - Change of personal care habits
- up sexually   - humor   - paranoia
- up irritability - striking out

Eventual Loss of Long-Term Memory
- Habits   - People
- Ability to talk about past events

Eventual Loss of Communication Skills
- Increasing apathy, non-responsiveness

Decreasing Physical Activity
- May see up rigidity in muscles
- May need to be fed
- Painful Cramping (especially at night)
- Eventually bedbound
- May have seizures

Incontinence

Substantial Weight Loss

Unconsciousness

Death
- Usually associated with pnemonia or infection.

Dieases Producing Primary Dementia

Distinguishing Types of Dementia
- Can be important to client, family doctor
- Some can be treated and cured
- Some have genetic risk

Three Groups of Dementia

1. Primary Undifferentiated
2. Primary Differentiated
3. Secondary

1. Primary Undifferentiated Dementia

- Disease directly affects brain tissue
- Alzheimer's
- Pick's
- Other rare diseases

*Alzheimer's

20 to 30% in mid-eighties

Named after German M.D. who identified and described in 1906
or 1907

He saw changes in brain tissue under microscope.

Neuron cells tangled, formed plaques

Occur most hippocampus

Generally age onset when recent memory problems recognized.

Earlier onset generally more sever the illness, shorter course.

* Pick's

Different tissue damage

* Normal Pressure HypdroCephalus

  Problems with fluid in brain being circulated or improper function.
  May occur after injury or infection.
  More rapid progression
  Strong disturbance standing, walking or incontinence or both
          - This comes early in illness
  Injury and gait helps diagnosis and treatment
  Injury type can be helped by surgery (Shunt)

2.   Primary Differentiated Dementia

  ### * Huntington's
  Involving withering movements
  Age 40 to 50 onset

  ### * Creutzfeldt - Jakob
  Infection due to virus
  Rapid course - months

  ### * Other Rare Forms
  Form of palsy
  Paralysis of the eye movement
  Wilson's
  Begins with liver disease

3.   Secondary Dementia

  ### * Depression
  Symptoms between dementia to depression can be similar
  Dementia usually involves depression at some point
  Often present in early stages of dementia.
  Drugs can minimize or complicate
  Treat for depression anyway
  Different daily rhythm

  ### * Vascular Disease
  History of symptoms important to diagnosis
  Affects arteries bringing blood to brain
  Stroke: interruption of blood to brain causing damage
  Abrupt onset, damage to one side of body if large artery
  Sometimes small arteries can cause gradual deterioration
  Often involves abrupt worsening with gradual partial recovery

TREATABLE FORMS
hypertension
diabetes
inflamed arteries

Delirium

Infection: pneumonia   respiratory
                     urinary   abscesses
<u>Also:</u>   hormone imbalance (thyroid)

Drug effects
Sedatives - alcohol; others
Withdrawal
Tolerance decreases with age

Alcohol
Long term brain damage

<u>Management</u>

Be aware of what limitations of cognitive abilities might be.
       - Don't <u>over-estimate</u>
Matter-of-fact, plain conversation
       - Give only "this or that" choices
       - Don't ask open ended questions
Mental tasks beyond their ability causes anxiety and up diability
       - <u>Reduce Anxiety</u>
       - watch for agitation
Stick to familiar and routine
Avoid fatigue
       - Frequent rest

Source: Lecture materials from Summer Institute on Aging, University of Washington, Seattle, WA.., and adaptations by Ronna Loerch, R.N., M.A.

Intervention - Dementia

Social Skills - Early Stages
- Ability to make casual comments, general conversation.
  Based upon long-term habits, skiils.
- Important to reinforce these as long as possible. Allows self-esteem
  and dignity to be maintained especially in social situations.
- Build on attempts at conversation. Ask general questions.
  Make general responses indicating some understanding.
- DO NOT point our errors or memory deficits.
- Keep conversation brief.
  Maximize their feelings of successful, positive exchange.
- DO NOT ask them to lead activities or do tasks which may
  embarrass or take beyond abilities.
- Stimulate more common memory themes, not recent events.

Depression with Dementia (other than meds)
- Look for activities or situations which they respond positively to.
- Don't force participation; encourage but respect feelings
  associated with shorter attention, disability.
- Give some one-on-one attention when possible.
  Recognize feelings, no cheer-up talks.
  Try written if not verbal. "Start the motion".
  Use their words. "Yes" or "No".
- Give them short, concrete tasks they can do, or brief
  assisting of other person.

Communication
- Introduce self - don't ask if they remember you.
- Use short sentences, familiar words.
- Speak slowly, clearly, but relaxed.
- Give one direction or question at a time.
- Minimize confusion and distraction.
- Watch for restlessness, stop and say "Later…:" "Another time".
- Give verbal cues if necessary.
- Reassure.
- Help along.
- Positive directions.
- Decrease abstractions; "hop in" car, etc.
- Repeat their last words if necessary.
- Assume more understanding.
- Let them know you are not understanding if necessary.

Source: Gentle Care, resources. Ronna Loerch, R.N., M.A.

Suggestions for Helping People With Dementia

The following are suggestions for helping people with dementia to function at their maximum capacity:.

Environmental Aspects

1. Provide a calm, quiet environment - hectic, noisy surroundings tend to increase confusion.
2. Establish and maintain a set routine - prepare ahead of time for a change.
3. Provide an environment with contrast, color coded areas and memory "props."
4. Provide visual cues using picture symbols as well as words.
5. Always be alert for potential hazards such as furniture legs sticking out, throw rugs, scalding hot water, etc.
6. Providing adequate lighting is essential to compensate for reduced vision.

Methodology

1. Treat people as respected, dignifed adults.
2. Talk distinctly and directly to the person.
3. Correct person tactfully when he rambles in speech and actions.
4. Explain or demonstrate each new procedure one step at a time- before asking a person to do it.
5. Ask for only one response at a time.
6. Allow person adequate time to respond.
7. Guide person by giving clear directions.
8. Give praise and recognition for positive responses immediately.
9. Teach alert person to use reality orientation props and information.
10. Give person choices when possible, and don't offer a choice when there actually is none.
11. Give a clear, simple response to any questions and requests.
12. Expect the person to understand and comply by your voice tone, attitude, eye contact and touch.
13. Promote self-care within the person's known limitations and his possible assets.
14. Show your interest and sincerity to people.
15. Show kindness and politeness while being matter-of-fact.

16. Respect people's privacy.
17. Use slow and deliberate motions.
18. Change physical environment to meet person's needs.
19. Ask permission to use first names. Use your name and their name frequently.
20. Give a clear message when ending a conversation… don't just drift away.

Organic Brain Syndromes

Delirium
Fluctuating clouded state of consciousness with difficulty sustaining attention to internal and external stimuli; sensory misperception and disordered stream of thought. This disorder is usually of brief duration.

Dementia
A loss of intellectual abilities of sufficient severity to interfere with social and occupational functioning. The deficit includes memory, judgment, abstract thought, and ability to concentrate. Changes in personality also occur such as increased irritableness. All of these symptoms are not caused by clouding of consciousness and are of longterm duration. The severity, prognosis and number and kinds of symptoms have to do with cause of dementia.

A. Alzheimer's Disease - A type of dementia characterized by gradual progressing mental and physical deterioration. Symptoms can start in middle age. The cause is not known at present.

B. Multi-Infarct Dementia - a type of dementia caused by the malfunctioning of the cerebro-vascular system so that the brain is at some level deprived of its blood supply. This causes a stepwise deterioration with a patchy distribution of deficits.

Depression / Pseudo-dementia
A mood disorder characterized by disturbance in sleep and eating patterns; loss of interest or pleasure in all life events, somatic complaints, inability to concentrate, feelings of sadness, helplessness, hopelessness, irritableness, psychomotor agitation or slowing, and loss of energy and motivation.

Source: Lecture from Doris Weaver, Good Samaritan Hospital, Puyallup, WA.

Diagnostic Criteria for
Anxiety

<u>Psychomotor</u>
- tremors
- dizziness
- blurred vision
- difficulty swallowing
- nausea
- hiccups
- tics
- headache
- tingling of the skin
- indigestion
- abdominal bloating
- changes in sleep pattern

<u>Somatic/</u>
<u>Physical</u>
<u>Facets</u>
- shortness of breath
- fast heart rate, pounding
- weight gain
- neck, back pain
- dry mouth
- chest pain
- lightheadedness
- weakness, fatigue
- sleep disturbances

<u>Emotional/</u>
<u>Affective</u>
<u>Functioning</u>
- apprehensive
- nervousness
- agitated
- dependency
- tearfulness
- panicky
- withdrawal
- can't make decisions

<u>Interpersonal</u>
<u>Facets</u>
- blame others
- constant complaining, bitterness
- poor relationships with others

Source: <u>Diagnostic & Statistical Manual of Mental Disorders, DSM III R,</u> American
Psychiatric Association, Washington, D.C., 1987

Diagnostic Criteria for
Mania

Cognitive/
Behavioral/
Affective
Facets

- increase in activity
- physical restlessness, pacing, fidgeting
- talk more, talk more loudly
- delusions of grandeur, special relationships with God or mission for CIA
- sleep less, but still seem alert
- when talking, jump from topic to topic, talk a mile a minute
- buying sprees
- gambling
- sexual indiscretions
- may harm self
- irritable, angry
- too busy to eat
- aggressive reactions when questioned about grandiose and unrealistic ideas
- Flights of ideas, raving thoughts

Diagnostic Criteria for
Delusional (Paranoia) Disorder

Behavioral
Manifestations

- suspicions, lack of trust
- exaggerated jealousy
- anger, argumentativeness, sometimes violence
- anxiety
- social isolation
- hypervigilant
- stilted, formal, or extremely intense social interactions
- letter writing complaining about various injustices
- legal actions against others
- severe problems in partnership relations
- auditory hallucinations
- love from a distance

Source: Diagnostic & Statistical Manual of Mental Disorders, DSM III R, American Psychiatric Association, Washington, D.C., 1987

Diagnostic Criteria for
Schizophrenia

Cognitive or
Thought
Disorder
Facets

- decreased ability to link ideas together in a meaningful way (loose association)
- decreased ability to imagine the "merely possible" (concrete thinking)
- ideas of reference
- magical thinking
- poverty of content of speech
- delusions (commonly of persecution or of reference)
- changes in quantity and quality of speech
- hallucinations (auditory most common)

Affective
Symptoms

- immobile face
- monotonous voice
- expressions inappropriate, discordant
- sudden or unpredictable changes in emotions

Psychomotor
Behaviors

- unusual or inappropriate body movements, such as pacing or rocking
- unusual facial movements
- decrease in reaction to stimuli
- decrease in spontaneious body movements

Residual
Symptoms

- withdrawal, isolation
- lack of motivation
- decreased interest
- inability to complete a task
- poor hygiene
- affect - flat, blunted, inappropriate
- inability to relate to others

Source: Diagnostic & Statistical Manual of Mental Disorders, DSM III R, American Psychiatric Association, Washington, D.C., 1987

Subtle Characteristics of Psychosis

- Impaired and/or poor judgment
- Lack of insight
- Poor interpersonal skills
- Poor self-esteem/ self care
- Poor organizational skills
- Poor concentration
- Limited or non-existent work skills / history
- Distorted self and other image
- Inappropriate affect
- Emotional constriction
- Poor problem-solving ability
- Lack of empathy
- Self absorption
- Need for external structure and direction / limited ability to be self-directed
- Limited motivation
- Fatiguability
- Dependence
- Low tolerance of frustration
- Extreme vulnerability to stress/ change
- Limited ability to generalize thinking, learning
- Psychomotor disturbance
- Diminished ability to experience pleasure
- Short attention span, limited interest

Source: Eleanor Thomson,, M.S.W., Director of Adult Support Services, Skagit Community Mental Health, 1989

A Brief Review of Chronic Mental Illnesses

A. Schizophrenia
B. Bi-polar disorder
C. Depression (can have psychotic symptoms)
D. Symptoms (review attached sheet for subtle characteristics)
    1. Hallucinations: False sensory perceptions
        a. Can involve any or all of the senses
            1. Auditory (most common)
            2. Visual
            3. Tactile
            4. Smell (not common)
            5. Taste (not common)
    2. Delusions: A false belief system
        1. Paranoid versus non-paranoid
E. Dealing with hallucinations/delusions
    1. Assess according to the impact on functioning rather than the content.
    2. Do not use aggressive confrontation unless the client is at risk for engaging in some negative behavior that would harm himself or others.
    3. Medications:
        a. Is the client taking his or her medications as prescribed?
        b. If not, why not? Is there anything that the peer counselor / therapist / physician can do to address these concerns?
        c. If the client is not taking the medications do they need a medication evaluation by his or her psychiatrist?

Source: Eleanor Thomson,, M.S.W., Director of Adult Support Services, Skagit Community Mental Health.

Medications

1. Several different types are used with those with mental illnesses: Neuroleptics (major tranquilizers), Anti-depressants, minor tranquilizers, Lithium Carbonate.

   A. Neuroleptics/Major tranquilizers:
      1. Examples: Haldol, Navane, Melleril, Stellazine, Loxitane, Trilafon, Thorazine
      2. Thorazine was the first to be devleoped (1952). Allowed patients to have much more freedom and eventually deinstitutionalization.
      3. Work by blocking transmission of Dopamine in the nervous system.
      4. Uses:
         a. Can reduce confusion, unclear thoughts.
         b. Reduces anxiety and tension
         c. Reduces intensity of psychotic symptoms
            1. Schizophrenia
            2. Manic episodes
            3. Agitation (low doses)
      5. Side effects:
         a. Studies indicate that 40% to 90% of people receiving neuroleptics have side effects. These will usually become evident quickly after the ct. starts medications.
         b. Types of side effects:
            1. Involuntary tongue movements / trouble swallowing.
            2. Akathesia
            3. Eye rolling
            4. Pseudo-Parkinsonism
               a. shuffling gait
               b. tremors
               c. muscle stiffness
               d. drooling
            5. Catatonia
         c. What to do:
            1. See if client has side effect medication. Examples include Cogentin, Benedryl, Artane, Kemadrin and Symmetryl.
            2. Make sure that the doctor. is aware of the problem. You can talk to the client, his or her family or the client's case manager.
   D. Lithium Carbonate:
      1. Used in the treatment of Bi-polar disorders (used to be called manic-depressive illness).
      2. Can be very effective but there is a risk that the blood level will become too high and the client will suffer from Lithium toxicity.
      3. Symptoms of Lithium toxicity:
         a. nausea

b. vomiting
   c. weakness
   d. tremors
   e. diarrhea
   g. gas
4. Lithium toxicity can result in permanent kidney damage. If you see the symptoms listed above exhibited in a person taking Lithium, particularly those who might not be taking their medications correctly, seek medical help at once.

Source: Eleanor Thomson,, M.S.W., Director of Adult SupportServices, Skagit Community Mental Health, 1989 and Donna Hazelton, R.N., Psychiatric Nurse, Skagit Community Mental Health, 1990.

Some Helpful Hints for Communicating with the Person with Cognitive Impairment

1. Call the person by name. Expect that they will respond back to you.

2. Because persons with cognitive impairments have a short attention span, expect to have to repeat ideas.

3. Use short sentences with simple ideas.

4. Use pictures, poetry and music to reach a person. Often old hymns, prayers and Bible verses come through when other things do not.

5. Always approach a person from the front and explain who you are and why you have come. Use a calm tone of voice.

6. Make sure that hearing aids are in and working, that you talk to a person's good ear. Also make sure that person has his/her glasses on if he/she needs them. Check to make sure that a person's glasses are clean.

7. Stand where a person can see you and read lips if need be. Don't stand where the light will turn you into a shadow.

8. Use a gentle orientation to reality. If they don't agree with you, don't argue.

9. Use touch. Remember that non-verbal communication comes through even when cognitive ability is gone.

10. Make an attempt to talk to the person . . . NOT AROUND THEM. Be on their eye level as much as possible.

11. Remember that it is the ILLNESS that makes persons forget. They are not on purpose attempting to make life difficult for you.

Source: Marty Richards, ACSW

Clinical Cases:
Guidelines for Their Evaluation

1. a)   What are the presenting problems?
   b)   Who is voicing the complaint?

2. What is the history of the difficulty?

3. What data is available from the mental status examination?

4. a)   What is client's emotional status?
   b)   What is "emotional status" of support system?

5. a)   What useful information is lacking?
   b)   How would you go about obtaining this information?

6. What are likely candidates for a differential diagnosis?

7. What resources are available for the client in the following areas?
   1. social support   2. professional   3. community

8. a)   What are the client's needs?
   b)   Are these needs consistent with family/caregiver resources?

9. a)   What interventions will you recommend?
   b)   What are your treatment goals?

10. How will you know if you have succeeded in your professional role?

Workshop: Psychological Treatment of the Elderly: Special Topics Faculty: Alan R. Breen, Ph.D.

Global Assessment of Functioning Scale (GAF Scale)

Consider psychological, social, and occupational functioning on a hyothetical continuum of mental health-illness. Do not include impairment in functioning due to physical (or environmental) limitations. See p. 20 for instructions on how to use this scale.

<u>Note:</u> Use intermediate codes when appropriate, e.g., 45, 68, 72.

Code

90 81	Absent or minimal symptoms (e.g., mild anxiety before an exam), good functioning in all areas, interested and involved in a wide range of activities, socially effective, generally satisfied with life, no more than everyday problems or concerns (e.g., an occasional argument with family members).
80 71	If symptoms are present, they are transient and expectable reactions to pschological stressors (e.g., difficulty concentrating after family argument); no more than slight impairment in social, occupational, or school functioning (e.g., temporarily falling behind in school work).
70 61	Some mild symptoms (e.g., depressed mood and mild insomnia) OR some difficulty in social, ocupational, or school functioning (e.g., occasional truancy, or theft within the household), but generally functioning pretty well, has some meaningful interpersonal relationships.
60 51	Moderate symptoms (e.g., flat affect and circumstantial speech, occasional panic attacks) OR moderate difficulty in social, occupationa, or school functioning (e.g., few friends, conflicts with co-workers).
50 41	Serious symptoms (e.g., suicidal ideation, severe obsessional rituals, frequent shoplifting) OR any serious impairment in social, occupational, or school functioning (e.g., no friends, unable to keep a job).

40   Some impairment in reality testing or communication (e.g., speech is at times illogical, obscure, or irrelevant) OR major impairment in several areas, such as work or school, family relations, judgement, thinking, or mood (e.g., depressed man avoids friends, neglects family, and is unable to work; child frequently beats up younger children, is defiant at home, and is

31   failing at school).

30   Behavior is considerably influenced by delusions or hallucinations OR serious impairment in communication or judgement (eg., sometimes incoherent, acts grossly inappropriately, suicidal preoccupation) OR inability to function in almost all areas (eg.,

21   stays in bed all day; no job, home, or friends).

20   Some danger of hurting self or others (e.g., suicide attempts without clear expectation of death, frequently violent, manic excitement) OR occasionally fails to maintain minimal personal hygiene (e.g., smears feces) OR gross impairment in communi-

11   cation (e.g., largely incoherent or mute).

10   Persistent danger of severely hurting self or others (e.g., recurrent violence) OR persistent ability to maintain minimal personal hygiene OR serious suicidal act with clear expectation of

1   death.

0   Inadequate information.

Source: _Diagnostic & Statistical Manual of Mental Disorders, DSM III R,_ American Psychiatric Association, Washington, D.C., 1987

SESSION VIII

Synthesis of Peer Counseling

Session VIII
Session Guide To The Trainer

You and your class have developed and grown together. They will have gone through several transitions becoming each other's "change agents."

Saying "goodbye" is as essential as was saying "hello." So, again, your therapeutic skills will be used to help the group come to a healthy closure. Your group has learned and are ready to be peer counselors Reinforcing the counseling process in this last session needs to be up-beat and positive . . . for they are scared! Expressing your feelings about the class's skill level, about their potential as peer counselors, and about the end of this training class will encourage them to think, talk, and feel what this ending means to them.

This training has been about change and transitions. What the senior trainees have gathered and reviewed about their own life, their own patterns of response is the learning. The group discussions may include sharing these changes. The acknowledgement of their patterns and choices will help them respond differently in order to find greater happiness and health.

We use a final Case Study to give the peer counselors documentable proof of their knowledge about aging, mental illness and case management.

Ending can be seen as a beginning, with hugs and tears and hope. Group members may have developed significant friendships within these eight weeks. We know this bonding and these friendships are what keeps your peer counselors connected to this work.

Share in it—encourage it—delight in it. It is the stuff of good mental health and of good aging for these seniors . . . and for all of us.

> *"Who are you?" said the Caterpillar.*
> *"I - I hardly know, Sir, just at present," Alice replied rather shyly,*
> *"At least I know who I was when I got up this morning,*
> *but I think I must have been changed several times since then."*
>   Lewis Carroll
>   Alice's Adventure in Wonderland

Session Materials

- Newsprint flip charts
- Felt tip markers
- Tissue boxes
- Final paper forms
- Information on Graduation Celebration

Session VIII

Synthesis of Peer Counseling

"No one knows what he is able to do until he tries."
Publious Syrus
CA 50 B.C.

Today's Goal

- To bring together the counseling skills and develop initial meeting strategies.
- Encourage and explore the trainee's readiness to begin peer counseling with a client.
- Effective closure, making this a creative point at which to begin a new experience.

Strategy

Much time needs to be spent with the process of beginnings and endings, and how that relates to the client/counselor relationship. Review the aspects of counseling, allowing trainees to share evidence of their learning. Validate trainees with the reassurances that they have the skills they need to do peer counseling. The anxiety they feel is also a part of the excitement of starting a new phase—as a peer counselor.

Encourage the sharing of their first meeting with their client and the case manager/therapist.

Learning Objectives

- Clarify initial meeting issues; establish expectations of time, schedule, and client response.
- Review basic counseling skills for 1st meeting.
- Review the philosophy and purpose of peer counseling.

Handouts and Workbook Materials

- Activities That You Can Share
- Document of Volunteer Commitment
- Take home final assignment
- Personal Evaluations
- Case Example

And We Begin by Doing . . . Session VIII

I. "Temperature Reading"

Allow time for peer counselors to discuss how this training has affected them. Encourage group to identify ways in which they have used this training in their own lives. Share reflections counselors might have had over the past eight weeks. Your awareness and acknowledgements of the connection between the ending of this training and other losses or closures experienced by the trainees will make this a healthy process.

II. Review of Counseling Skills and Communication Skills for First Session with Client

Explore in group discussion, the importance of the first meeting with the client. All trainees will be anxious to do peer counseling "right." Review the philosophy of this training:

1) What is your role?
2) How do you connect with your client?
3) What is the nature of the relationship?
4) How do you bring meaning and enrichment to your time with the client?

The value of <u>being present</u> becomes more evident with the development of the client/counselor relationship. This takes time to establish with the elderly client. It is a slow, progressive building of trust, as many clients are reluctant to risk trusting anyone. *Encourage the trainees to remember that the client will talk if the counselor will just listen.*

Cues for the First Meeting

- Acknowledge your anxiety, fear, nervousness.

- Keep the initial meeting short—1/2 hour or less.

- Establish your role—you are a peer counselor who works with their case manager or therapist and you are there to "talk with" or visit.

- Establish a schedule that fits with their needs.
  "I am wondering if it would be all right with you if I came to visit you every Monday morning?"

- Leave your name and when you will be back with the client. Marking your name on their calendar, on the day of your next meeting, helps the client to remember.

- You are your client's model and a mirror to their world.

- Know the limits of your skills and abilities.

Group Discussion
- Share with the group your worst fear of meeting with your client.

- What, for you, will be the most difficult?

- What are you feeling right now, when you visualize that first or second meeting?

- What are your expectations of these first couple of sessions?

- How do we, as counselors, mirror our client's world? How does this support the client?

Experiential Exercise - "First Meeting"
Form dyads and role play the first meeting with your client. Spend 10 minutes each, being the client and then the counselor. Practice "small talk" and Cues for the first meeting. Rejoin the larger group to share your experience as both client and counselor.

Key Element -

The peer counselor expectations and eagerness to "do it right" creates additional anxiety. Instill the belief that they have everything they need, to be effective counselors, except actual experience. Help them focus on the areas of counseling with which they feel comfortable.

III. Synthesis of the Eight Sessions

Over the last eight weeks, the peer counselors have grown and become a unit. They will be more self-aware and more self-confident. As with all groups, they will have developed a spectrum of attitudes, skills and abilities. Each is unique, yet all are alike. This is also the dynamics in the client/counselor relationship.

In order to bring together a reflection of the learning that has transpired over the eight weeks, the facilitator may present a Case Study to help trainees document their learning in the following areas:

Assessment of client's needs.

Appropriate counseling interactions.

Development of treatment plan, including case management.

Case Study

Anna is a chronically mentally ill woman of 83 who was turned out of our local state hospital over fifteen years ago. She suffers from paranoid delusions and evidences obsessive compulsive behaviors by washing all of her towels in her "Maytag" every day. She lives alone in a rented house and manages to stay out of trouble, most of the time. She has recently requested the help of someone who might take her shopping. Anna does not speak of her family directly, but hints that as a child she was abused, physically, by her father. She spends her day watching T.V. and checking out her neighbor through her window. There is some evidence that she is experiencing pain when she walks, but she is fearful of going to the doctor.

Issues to Be Resolved

Can this woman continue to live independently?

To what degree is her chronic mental illness connected with her aging problems?

How are they connected?

What kinds of case management would help her?

Physically, is she deteriorating?

To what degree does her isolation contribute to her paranoia? Or does it?

What are her grief issues?

Experiential Exercise - "Synthesis of Learning"

Form groups of 5-6 members. Instruct each small group to list on newsprint:

Case Study client's needs, possible diagnosis and situational status of events.

Specific intervention (Case Management) to answer those specific needs.

Specific counseling technique that might be used.

Treatment Plan and specific peer counselor participation.

Small groups then rejoin the larger group with each group choosing one member to present a staffing of the Case Study. Gather as many options as you can, to really understand the complex issues in counseling the older mental health client.

Key Element -

Knowing all you can about the client reduces anxieties. With aging clients, this may take many sessions to gather. Don't hurry!

IV. Termination of the Training Group

As in the beginning, the training process itself is the model for the client/counselor relationship. Termination is also a part of that relationship. Allow the last hour for the expressions, thoughts and feelings that come up in this last session.

Healthy closures help the peer counselors become aware of how clients have handled the many "closures" in their lives. Encourage trainees to be active in the ending experience. Encourage them to use their newly found awareness and risk taking to make a complete closure with this part of their peer counseling experience.

Group Discussion

Allow time for the stages involved in termination to be explored by the group.

Denial:
"Are we still going to see each other?"   "Nothing really changes."

Resistance:
"I'm not ready to do peer counseling, can I come to the next training classes?"

Feedback:
What part of the training was most helpful for you?
What did you like the best?   What did you like the least?

From the Facilitator to the Peer Counselors

Take this opportunity to discover what you really want out of this experience. It is a time of transition and being able to identify what you want often turns out to be more complicated than you can imagine.

- I want to be a good peer counselor.
- I want to commit myself to nine months of service.
- I want to be without stress in my volunteer work.
- I want someone to help me make decisions regarding my work as a peer counselor.

Since endings are "dyings", in one sense, the "grief" and ambivalence of trainees is understandable. The next phase of their lives (peer counseling) is taking shape. This is an opportunity to do something different with their time, something that expresses the peer counselor's abilities in a significant way.

Key Element -

End this discussion on a positive note, recognizing the many paradoxical feelings of the future peer counselors.

V. Closing

- Encourage and receive any feedback about the training.
- Be sure each peer counselor has been assigned a client, or will be assigned a client in the next week.
- Set date for 1st Supervision Session.
- Make sure everyone has Progress Notes to fill out for their sessions with their client.
- Explain the Final Paper assignment.
- Discuss the Graduation Celebration.

VI. Summarization

As we end this training, we are truly just beginning. In the words of the English novelist, John Galsworthy, "The beginnings . . . of all human undertakings are untidy." Our beginnings as peer counselors seem "untidy"—so much is left uncovered, there is so much more to know!

Genuine beginnings depend upon the integration of past experiences and new inner reconnections and awareness.

What we call the beginning is often the end.
And to make an end is to make a beginning.
The end is where we start from.

T.S. Elliott

Recommended Reading

Brides, William, *Transitions.* Addison - Wesley Publishing Co., 1980.

Session VIII

Handouts & Workbook Materials

Case Example for Case Management

This client was referred to the geriatric outreach program for case management from a friend of the clients who currently lives in the Seattle areas. She had not seen the client for several years until recently when she made a visit to see the client at her home. She had many concerns about the clients welfare and she herself was not able to do anything for her because of the distance between them

This client is a 72-year old woman who lives alone in a 22-foot travel trailer. The trailer has no running water. Water is supplied by a stream and must be hauled by the client daily for cooking and bathing. There is no indoor bathroom. There is electricity which supplies the only source of heat - a small portable heater.

The client shares this remote piece of property - five acres - with her son and his wife and two teenage children, they live in a mobile home about 100 yards from the client's. They have a telephone, but the client does not.

The client moved here to the area five years ago from Montana, to be closer to the friend and family members.

The client's income is below poverty.

The friend indicates that she does not think that the client has been to see a doctor since she moved here. She also felt that the client seemed confused about her finances and other important matters. She thought the client was having memory problems. She was concerned about the possibility of neglect by the client's family.

Activities That You Can Share

Talking about daily events that have occurred in both your lives.
Reading aloud from a favorite novel.
Writing letters.
Sharing skills, such as sewing and woodworking.
Talking about the "Good Old Days."
Listening to a favorite record or tape.
Putting a puzzle together.
Tending a garden or cultivating house plants
Playing games such as checkers or dominoes.
Looking at pictures or slides of other countries.
Washing and styling hair; applying make up, polishing nails.
Mending clothes
Taking walks outside.
Sitting quietly together; enjoying each other's company.

Remember it's not the activities that are important,
but their effect on the loneliness and isolation of your client.

Guide for Peer Counselors

Ways You Can Help

Listening
giving a person time to talk.

Understanding
saying that we understand what it is like to feel sad or angry or afraid.

Praising
acknowledging what a person has done or is doing that shows strength.

Encouraging
recognizing a person's strengths and suggesting that these strengths can help with this problem too.

Reassuring
saying that others have experienced the same, " You are not alone."

Caring
showing that we care by non-verbal expressions of interest and concern as well as by words.

Giving information

Peer Counseling Project

Take-Home Final

Please write a paragraph about what the Peer Counseling Training has meant to you or about how it has gone for you. Sign it and bring it to the last regular class day.

Personal Evaluation of Peer Counseling Class

Edeath Linderman 19 Nov. 1989

To be a part of this class group was a most significant experience for me. My interest and appreciation deepened with each succeeding class session I formed friendships that will continue long after the class had ended and I am working in the community.

I especially liked the manner in which the handouts (later to be incorporated into a Peer Counseling Handbook) were dovetailed into the information given us by mental health professionals from clinics in Skagit and Whatcom counties.

The afternoon sessions gave us ample opportunity for "hands on" experiences, beginning with the group interview prior to our acceptance into the class. We divided into small groups and were given five minutes to learn the names and interests of another class member. When we regrouped we reported to the whole class on our experience.

Our first session emphasized that complete confidentiality is essential. What was said in the confines of the classroom remained there. This allowed all of us the freedom to express ourselves with complete candor and honesty.

We were first introduced to peer counseling through role-playing. Later we progressed to real life experience. We gradually learned the terminology appropriate for use in peer-counseling situations. Speakers gave us valuable information on case management, record keeping and available community resources.

While I recognize my limitations, I feel I can approach my first client with confidence that I have learned the skills which will enable me to listen carefully and, hopefully, to help him.

I give credit for my new-found confidence in large measure to the skillfull guidance provided by peer counseling coordinator, Betty Rogers.

Sincerely,

Edeath Linderman

Nov. 21, 1989

Hi Betty:

The other day, while listening to someone speaking, I caught myself thinking about what to say next, and not really listening to what the other person was saying.

You know, it was a great pleasure to catch myself that way. Finally, a good lesson had been learned.

The important thing the course of instruction on Senior Peer Counseling has revealed, is what a poor listener a person can be.

Most of us go through life without realizing the necessity of good communication, or learning its requirements.

Yes, I was in sales for many years, and worked with people, but about things, such as cars or real estate. Counseling will give me a first opportunity to work with people, and about people (no longer about things).

Thank you, Betty, for putting up with me during those long days. Your patience was surely tested.

Our sincere gratitude for your good work on our behalf.

Thank you also, for the excellent coffee and the goodies you always thought of bringing for us.

Sincerely,

Larry Lymburner

Peer Counselor Project

For the past eight years, I have been taking college courses questing for knowledge and getting stimulating information in many subjects, namely, political science, art history, geology, poetry, short story writings, etc. All the while, however, I was refusing to look at my aging body, my changing face, and physical degeneration. I feared growing old and adding this loss to other losses sustained in a lifetime.

When I was asked why I was moving to Anacortes, to a community where I have no friends or relatives, the answer was positive that I had always planned to grow old in a quiet community, in harmony with nature, away from the crowds of people, noises, with a new home I liked in pleasant surroundings there was something still missing. I needed to use my mind on something besides television, books and meaningless conversation. Because I have always volunteered, I answered the Mental Health ad in the Anacortes paper.

How can I express what I think about the Peer Counselor Program? It opened my mind and I looked inward and backward. I talked about experiences in my life that I do not discuss. I compared these experiences to those around me and they were the same. I have learned a lot. The aging fear is less burdensome. I believe that my life's lessons can be used to benefit someone else who is dealing with problems greater than those I have faced, or perhaps the same.

I congratulate all of you for the calibre of people who staff your department and who work in this field. There cannot be a finer, more motivating teacher than Betty Rogers. Because of her, each class day was fun, filled with new ideas and mind-opening material. We grew to know each other, to become fond of each other in a caring, nurturing way, and to truly love our teacher. I know that each one of us went away feeling privileged to be a part of this learning experience.

I am not religious, but God bless all of you.

Vesta E. Lavin

PART V

Program Assessment and Research Evaluation

BENEFITS OF THE PROGRAM
Program Assessment and Research Evaluation

For the past eight years (since 1986) the Skagit Community Mental Health Center has operated a Geriatric Peer Counseling Program to serve mentally ill older adults. This program utilizes the skills and talents of senior volunteers who provide home-based services to Mental Health Center clients in a four-county rural area (Skagit, Whatcom, Island and San Juan Counties of Northwest, Washington). Volunteers receive extensive training, and work under the close supervision of Agency mental health professionals. Annually, through an active group of 60 geriatric peer counselors, this program serves approximately 150 mentally ill elderly, and delivers over 5,000 hours of face-to-face client service.

Experience suggests there are a number of important benefits from this program. Mental health clients receive extensive treatment and support services provided by

peer counselors. Peer counselors find satisfaction from a role in the community that is both demanding and rewarding. Agency professionals working in the geriatric program benefit from their association with healthy older people. The Mental Health Center extends mental health services to a significantly greater number of clients, and the community benefits from an increased level of mental health functioning among an important segment of its population, as well as greater awareness of the problem.

The overriding goals of the Geriatric Peer Counseling Program were to develop an ongoing system of recruiting, training and utilizing seniors in the provision of direct mental health service. Thus, from its initiation, an important aspect of this project has been its close collaboration with other community service providers. Initially, a project advisory committee was formed which included representation from County government, the Area Agency on Aging, Senior Information and Referral, and other programs working with elderly clients. This group supported project activity in staff selection, volunteer recruitment, and the development of the initial training curriculum.

It was initially decided that the program's one staff position would not deliver direct service, but rather recruit and train competent peer counselor volunteers who would be supervised by other Agency geriatric specialists. Thus, this approach is designed for agencies that have existing geriatric services and where supervision, case assignment, and direct treatment can be managed by mental health professionals.

Volunteers were recruited through newspaper articles featuring Agency geriatric programs and outlining the role of the peer counselors. The first class of volunteers to undergo pre-placement training consisted of 12 women and one man. In seven years the Agency has carried out 21 recruiting campaigns within a four-county area and received applications from 250 older men and women.

Applicants are screened by the Peer Counselor Program coordinator and other geriatric services staff. When possible, the program employs a group interview process involving three or four potential volunteers at one time. Upon occasion, a second interview is necessary. This model works well in identifying volunteers who are perhaps not suited for this direct service program. The few applicants in this latter category have been generally directed to other volunteer opportunities more in line with their talents and personalities.

Intensive Volunteer Training

The extensive (50 hour) initial training program for all peer counselors was developed and implemented by the program coordinator. A number of other Agency staff, including geriatric mental health specialists, the Center director, and psychiatrist all play a role in training peer counselors. Trainees receive five credit hours from Skagit Valley College on completion of the 50 hour training program. Units covered include self-awareness and communication, helping and counseling skills, case management and case recording. and community resources. A variety of published training materials, as well as locally generated information is utilized. A small number (less than 5%) of initial recruits fail to complete the basic training course.

In addition to initial training, ongoing education is an important part of this program. In each quarter, a one-day workshop is held, where the Agency provides training specifically designed to meet the needs of the volunteer peer counselors. Peer counselors have attended a variety of training experiences and have been active participants in the Summer Aging workshops at the University of Washington. In order to retain qualified volunteers, this type of program must give as well as receive. Comments from volunteers continue to reinforce the importance of provision of training to increase skills in delivering client services as well as in providing information to volunteers that will help them with their own issues related to aging.

Clients Seen Through the Peer Counseling Program

Peer counselors work effectively with a wide variety of geriatric clients. The project serves a depressed widow living in her own home, who has recently lost her sight through macular degeneration. A peer counselor works with a mentally ill man of 75 who was placed in a nursing home, but who benefits from participation in a daily day-treatment program. The project sees a woman in the early stages of dementia who can benefit from socialization and safety checks. A peer counselor supports a married couple where the husband is moving into the middle stages of Alzheimer's disease.

Volunteers try to help the long-term mentally ill remain in their own homes for as long as possible. For over two years, peer counselors worked intensively with a chronically mentally ill woman who was engaged in a series of confrontations with neighbors. This woman lived on an isolated rural island. At one point, due to trespassing charges, she was jailed overnight at the age of 82. Due to her paranoia, as well as the stigma associated with mental health treatment, she would not allow Agency professionals in her home, but would see peer counselors. A team of peer counselors worked successfully with this woman, providing client advocacy, coordination of services, and emotional support for over two years. This woman could not have remained at home during this time without this intensive and closely supervised peer counselor care.

Peer counselors are not assigned to acute cases when violence or suicide is an emergent possibility, or when demented clients can no longer keep up the semblance of maintaining a responding relationship. In order to protect all concerned, peer counselors are not matched with clients until a mental health professional has completed an initial evaluation involving the client's history, diagnosis, and treatment plan. As can be noted in the above illustrations, close collaboration between professional staff and the volunteers is a necessity.

Historical Program Data

During the period, 1986 - 1991, a total of 225 peer counselors were trained and placed in a variety of settings. Volunteers varied in terms of their pattern of commitment. Some worked with a single geriatric client for one to two years; other worked with multiple clients, perhaps in a nursing home. Others worked as a peer counselor for a time, became inactive for atime once their client no longer required them and then later reactivated with another client.

Table 1 presents data on the volume and type of placements existing for each year of the project 1986-1991. Table 2 presents data on the volume of clients (by type of setting) who were served by a peer counselor for each year 1986 -1991. A total of 400 clients received some peer counseling support over the time period 1986-1991.

Table 1
Volume & Types of Placements Each Year 1986-1991

	1986	1987	1988	1989	1990	1991
Geriatric Outreach	8	16	24	35	40	47
Nursing Homes	2	9	10	8	8	5
Geriatric Day Treatment/Care	4	2	3	1	1	2
Sr. Services Center & Outreach	1	6	5	5	6	4
Program Development/Support	-	3	4	1	1	2
Alzheimer's Support Group	-	-	-	-	-	2
Total	15	36	38	50	56	62

Table 2
Number of Clients Served Each Year 1986 - 1991

	1986	1987	1988	1989	1990	1991
Outreach	12	32	45	37	50	60
Nursing Homes	5	20	22	9	9	10
Geriatric Day Treatment/Care	23	30	57	50	50	54
Alzheimer's Support Group	-	-	-	10	10	20
Totals	40	82	124	108	119	144

Evaluation Study

In August 1990, an evaluation was completed on the previous two years of the project. The evaluation focused on determining whether and to what degree the program had met its operational objectives during this time and on assessing what were the benefits of the program to geriatric clients, to peer volunteers and to the geriatric mental health system within each county.

The operational objectives for these two year were to:

1. Expand the peer counseling system from Skagit County to involve Whatcom, San Juan and Island County through:
   - recruiting and training more peer counselor volunteers in each county
   - establishing and supporting a mental health system infrastructure to place and supervise peer counselors with geriatric clients
   - establishing a four-county support and continuing education system for peer counselors.
2. Develop and disseminate program manuals describing the peer counseling program; how to set it up and containing curriculum materials.
3. Provide consultation and support to mental health organizations desiring to implement a geriatric peer counseling program through professional presentations, training workshops and one-on-one consultation.
4. Evaluate the program and assess its benefits to clients, volunteers and the mental health system.

1. Achievement of Operational Objectives

The program met most of its operational objectives. The peer counseling program was extended to the other three counties. An additional 52 peer counselors were recruited and trained, 16 from Skagit County, 23 from Whatcom County, 4 from San Juan and 9 from Island. Thus as of June 1991, (and accounting for attrition) the program had 61 peer counselors operating in the four-county areas.

Services were extended to l66 new geriatric clients during these two years; 42 in Skagit County, 16 in Whatcom County, 6 in San Juan County and 5 in Island. As of

June 1991, a total of 69 clients who had been served in the four counties, in direct 1:1 service.

The program was successful in establishing a clinical supervision system for the peer counselors within the geriatric mental health system for each county.

A centralized peer counseling coordination and continuing education training structure was firmly established in Skagit County to serve all peer counselors in the four-county area. Monthly support meetings were held in each county.

A program manual and peer counselor training curriculum guide was written and published. Considerable consultation was provided to other organizations interested in implementing similar type programs.

2.   Benefits To Peer Counselor Volunteers

A biographic profile was compiled on 49 of 52 volunteers trained as peer counselors over the 1989 - 1991 evaluation study period. The majority (79.6%) of the peer counselors were woman, average age 65.00 years, with 23% below sixty years of age and 25% over seventy years of age. (One volunteer was 87 years of age). Sixty percent of the peer counselors were married. Also, the educational backgrounds of these volunteer peer counselors was quite high, with more than 78% having advanced post-secondary education (college, university or vocational education).

These elderly volunteers expressed all sorts of reasons for wanting to become a peer counselor. The majority expressed a desire to help someone. Some said they simply liked to keep busy and this was something interesting to do. Others referred to needs in themselves that they were trying to meet by helping others. Some said they had a debt to society and wanted to repay it.

Questionnaires were sent to 31 peer counselors to ask them about their experiences as peer counselors. Responses were received from 17 persons - a response rate of 55%. Respondents consisted of 15 women and 2 men; ages ranged from 49 to 73 years of age.

All of these peer counselors participated in peer counselor training. Thirteen (76.5%) said the training definitely prepared them for the job of being a peer counselor; 4 (23%) said it somewhat prepared them. Comments were made that the training provided them with the basics from which the "hands-on" learning could proceed.

When asked what they had learned during the training, most of the pper counselors made reference to learning to listen and to helping the client to better cope and to solve their own problems. There was also mention of skill training in how to manage different kinds of situations with difficult clients (e.g., suicide, illness, neglect, grief, etc.) Many also referred to learning things that were very beneficial to their own mental health.

The peer counselors responding to the questionnaire described many problems among their clients but a common theme was loneliness, depression, frustration, and badly needing to talk to someone. Much of what the peer counselors described they do was spending time with the client, keeping them company, taking them places, and talking to them.

When asked if they were helping the client, 10 (58.8%) said definitely, 5 (29.4%) said somewhat, and 2 (11.8%) didn't respond to the question. The peer counselors say their clients respond to them, look forward to their visits, and trust them.

All peer counselors with active clients received clinical supervision on their client in the form of a once a month meeting with other peer counselors and a mental health professional. Thirteen respondents (76.5%) said the clinical supervision was very useful, 2 (11.8%) said it was somewhat useful, and two (11.8%) said they were not getting supervision because they didn't currently have an active client.

When asked what additional clinical supervision they would like to have, most of the respondents indicated they were satisfied with what they had. A few, however, said they could use some one-on-one time with a mental health specialist on occasion in order to better deal with particularly difficult situations.

Once a month the peer counselors within each county got together for peer support meetings - to chat and socialize, to hear speakers and to talk about their own issues if they wanted These meetings were coordinated by the overall Project Coordinator. When asked if the peer support meetings were useful, 12 (70.6%) said "very useful", 3 (17.6%) said "somewhat useful", and 2 persons (11.8%) didn't respond.

Peer counselors were asked if the program had benefited them personally in any way. Fourteen (82.4%) said the program had definitely benefitted them, 1 (5.9%) said it had somewhat benefitted them, and 2 persons (11.8%) didn't respond to the question. Comments often referred to feeling more useful, doing something worthwhile, learning new things, and making a new friend.

A recent (1992) focus group with 30 peer counselors revealed the following list of knowledges, skills and attitudes or feelings they had learned as a result of their experiences as a peer counselor (see Table 3).

Table 3
Skills, Knowledge and Changed Attitudes
Learned by Geriatric Peer Counselors

Skills	Knowledges	Attitudes
• to listen	• the resources to hlep	• more tolerance
• communication skills	• knowledge of self needs	• increased empathy
• more tolerance	• knowledge of clients	• to be comfortable with silence
• ability to respect	• knowledge of people needs	• growing within self
• how to elicit	• the aging process	• receiving love
• to be more realistic	• clarifying and correcting myths	• more comfortable with feelings
• more understanding	• counseling techniques	• being more sympathetic
• sharing skills	• tools	• increased self-awareness
• how to be sensitive	• agencies to help	• more appreciative
• how to listen for the real issues	• things to do	• to be more creative
• how to analyze own thoughts and what we say	• how to deal with medicare and insurance	• increased willingness to be teachable
• how to organize	• how to deal with hospitals and doctors	• coping with emergencies (strength)
• how to deal with bureaucracy		

- how to deal with family members
- teaching family members to be more helpful
- encouraging client independence
- patience
- how to role model/overcoming barriers
- how to establish trust
- humor

- how to deal with financial problems
- how to respond to emergencies

3. Benefits to the Geriatric Clients

During the evaluation period May 1989 - April 1990, 66 (sixty-six) geriatric clients were engaged in a one-on-one relationship. In addition, another 117 geriatric clients were being served by seven peer counselors in groups. These groups included seniors in nursing homes, geriatric day treatment, Alzheimer's Support Groups, Senior Services Centers, etc.

Biographic information was available on 31 of the 66 geriatric clients (from the past two years) and on 20 old clients from the 1988 - 1989 years. Most of them were female (76.6%). Average age was 75.5 years; with 17% being under 64 years of age, 12% between 65-69 years of age, 7% between 70-74 years of age, 36% between 75-79 years of age and 38% being clients over 80 years of age.

Approximately 23% of the clients were married; over 43% were widowed. Forty-four percent of these clients were living alone, 28% with a spouse or partner, 15% with a relative and 12% with other adults. Sixty-five percent were living in a private home, 23% in an apartment or condominium. Only 13% were living in a nursing home facility.

For the majority of these clients (68%), social security was the primary source of income.

Approximately 35% of these geriatric clients had various physical disabilities or handicaps; 11% had visual handicaps and 19% had various other physical health problems. However, what was more significant was the mental health status of these individuals.

The data on the mental health conditions affecting these geriatric clients was summarized as follows:

- 22% had previous psychiatric treatment
- 28% suffered from chronic depression
- 69% suffered from some level (degree) of depression
- 24% experienced minor levels of anxiety
- 25% experienced acute-to-chronic anxiety
- 35.5% had a minor problem in relationships with children
- 29% had a minor problem in relationships with friends
- 6.5% had chronic problems in relationships with friends
- 12% had reported being a victim of spousal abuse (this is likely to be under reported due to the stigma)
- 27% had minor financial problems

- 18% had acute-to-chronic financial problems
- 8% had chronic mental handicaps
- 20% had some level of mental handicaps
- 32% had chronic mental illness
- 61% had some degree of mental illness
- 14% had some degree of prescription drug misuse
- 64% had some type of chronic illness
- 71% made frequent visits to their doctors for various physical/mental ailments
- 58% had poor eating habits; 10% having a chronic problem
- 32% (N=11) were in grieving due to the death of a spouse
- 8% (N=4) were in grieving due to the death of a son/daughter

Problems or conditions not readily apparent or minimal among many (if any) of these geriatric clients were as follows:
- history of poor employer relationships
- being a victim of elder abuse
- frequent household moves
- weight problems
- alcohol abuse problems

4. The Peer Counseling Relationships

Information on 31 of the peer counseling relationships studied during the 1989 - 1991 evaluation study period indicated that the typical pattern of contact (87% of all cases) was once per week.

Reasons/purpose of peer counseling contact for half or more of the cases were listed as follows (the percentage of cases listing the reason as a primary or secondary purpose is noted).
- companionship (primary 90%; secondary 3%)
- counseling (primary 65%; secondary 3%)
- shared interests (primary 55%; secondary 23%)
- transportation to appointments (primary 19%; secondary 26%)
- crisis control (primary 68%; secondary 32%)
- health monitoring (primary 48%; secondary 36%)

Case supervisors evaluated the degree of trust between the geriatric client and the peer counselor to be good-excellent in 20 of the cases (69%); average in eight cases (28%); and poor-fair in one case (4%).

Quality of compatibility and communication was evaluated by the case supervisors as good-excellent for 21 cases (81%); average for 3 cases (12%); and poor-fair for two cases (8%).

Of 31 peer/client relationships begun during the evaluation study period, 16 (51.6%) were still ongoing; 6 ongoing for an average of 16 months; 10 ongoing for about one year. Of the 14 closed cases, most had closed within 4-5 months. It would seem that once the peer counseling relationships got past the first few months, they tended to last for a long time.

Since 1986, reason for closure was available on 35 cases. Reasons for closure included:

- client improved (20.0%)
- client moved to a nursing home (17.1%)
- client died (14.3%)
- client request (8.6%)
- client unable to maintain relationship (8.6%)
- counselor request (5.7%)
- counselor moved away (5.7%)
- client moved away (5.7%)
- unknown (14.3%)

5. Agency Perception of Program Benefits

As part of the evaluation study, questionnaires were sent to the directors and mental health or geriatric service case managers of all the agencies that supervised peer counselors, as well as to a few agencies that interacted with the program or referred clients.

Eight agency professional stated the program primarily operated in support of and as an additional service to geriatric clients who had mental health problems. The peer counselors addressed the social needs of a client that the mental health specialist had insufficient time to do. Three professionals felt that in a few limited cases, the peer counselor acted a s a substitute for mental health services, especially when the primary causes of a client's problems or symptoms were social isolation and depression.

Six (75%) of the eight professionals said they were very satisfied with the program's recruitment, coordination and support of the peer counselors; two (25%) said they were somewhat satisfied. There was lots of praise for the expertise and commitment of the program coordinator. The two who expressed some concerns about the program made reference only to inadequate screening of volunteer applicants in a couple of cases.

All but one professional felt the program definitely provided a cost savings to Mental Health agencies. Greater and better service was extended to the elderly mentally ill population at a cost considerably less than the cost of hiring professional staff. The program was not free, since coordination, support and training were provided to the peer counselors; but this cost was relatively low compared to the benefits.

All of the professionals who responded to the questionnaire stated they definitely would like to maintain a Geriatric Peer Counseling Program attached to their agency.

PART VI

Additional Resource Materials

PART VI

Additional Resource Materials

Factors Affecting Memory

Listed below are some of the factors which affect memory function as we grow older. There is a complex interplay among these factors.

1. Depression
   Depression often increases complaints about memory functioning, and sometimes may affect memory functioning itself.

2. Boredom
   People without adequate stimulation in their lives will often have more troublewith their memory. If little is expected of us, we have little to remember.

3. Stress and Anxiety
   Stress caused by any source may impair memory function. The more severe the stress, the greater the impairment. Excessive concern about memory functioning can be a self-fulfilling prophecy.

4. Type of Housing
   People housed in custodial care institutions with little to do, or segregated from people in other ages, may show signs of poor memory.

5. Attitude and Motivation
   If a person thinks or expects their memory to be poor, and believes they cannot improve it, then this belief will likely become true in their experience. Without motivation to remember, a poor memory will result.

6. Personality, Thinking and Adapting Style, Learning Disorders
   Who a person is, and how a person has learned to think and adapt to the world affects how they learn and what they remember.

7. General Health
   Poor health can become a major distraction upsetting memory function. Low energy can mean little recall.

8. Nutrition
   A healthy, balanced diet and adequate fluid intake aids both general health and memory.

9. Medication and Chemicals
   A variety of over-the-counter, prescription drugs and alcohol and illegal drugs affect concentration, alertness and, therefore, memory.

10. Intelligence
Innate ability can take many forms. Some of us may be smart mechanically, others intellectually, a few of us in many ways.

11. Life Experience
Those individuals with many years of formal schooling may be better at remembering what they read. Accountants are likely to recall numbers easily. A lifelong baseball fan could probably give you a list of the best hitters over the last 25 years. And because the stored recollections of a long life well lived can be substantial, it may take longer to recall something for older people.

12. Knowledge and Use of Memory Strategies
People who can efficiently encode, store and retrieve information, and people who use these techniques, have an advantage over people lacking such skills.

13. Medical Conditions and Diseases
Korsakoff's syndrome, strokes, Alzheimer's Disease are examples of conditions which result in memory impairment.

14. Biologically Programmed Factors
Some of us are better able to learn in the morning, others at night. Our internal clock or circadian rhythms have an affect on memory ability.

15. Perceptions and Prejudices, Stereotypes
What we remember is affected by how we see the world. Our own or others' age, sex, race, education, social status, class, nationality, political beliefs, religious practices, physical appearance, or influence, all can bias what we record and how we record it.

16. Exercise
Our physical, rational, emotional and spiritual selves create a whole. Getting physically healthy helps us in other ways and can improve our memory.

17. Reaction Time
Slows down with age.

Source: James DeLong, Senior Services of Seattle/King County, 1988

Memory Flexibility Game

A warm-up exercise

Instructions: Work with a partner. Partner A reads List One aloud to Partner B very slowly. Partner B finds a memory to go with each item, savors it and nods for next item. (Do not discuss as you go along!) Then, Partner B reads List Two very slowly to Partner A. When you are through, talk about different ways you experienced your each memory.

List 1
A new clothing item when you were a child
Freshly baked bread
Clouds
A person you saw yesterday
Your toothbrush
Kate Smith's voice

List 2
Today's breakfast
A favorite toy
Your first day at school
A summer storm
4th of July
A song

Source: James DeLong, Senior Services of Seattle/King County, 1988

Remembering Names

STOP	ASSOCIATE
LOOK	LINK
LISTEN	PICTURE

WRITE

Example:

STOP: I want to know this person. Concentrate.

LOOK: This is an interesting face. Observe. Distinguishing features?

LISTEN: Listen to the name. Repeat the name. Ask if your pronunciation is correct; ask for spelling if necessary.

ASSOCIATION: Can you associate this name with anything? Is is a name of something? Can you make up substitute name or rhyme to associate with it?

LINK: Link the sound of the name (association) with the face.

PICTURE: Visualize this link. See it on the person's face.

WRITE: Keep a list of names you are trying to remember. Practice picturing the association.

Source: James DeLong, Senior Services of Seattle/King County, 1988

Overcoming Absentmindedness

- Observe, concentrate, do things consciously.
- Avoid and eliminate distractions.
- Develop habits and routines and stick to them.
  A place for everything and everything in its place.
- Particularly when under stress, slow down and concentrate.
- Do only one thing at a time. Finish each task before moving on.
- Use a timer or alarm clock top remind you of tasks.
- Write down tasks and chores.
- Use relaxation techniques and free association to retrieve stubborn thoughts.
- Plan your day each morning, review at noon. At the end of the day, begin to formulate tomorrow's plan.
- Use visualizations and associations to remember; Example, Picture yourself going on the day's outing. What items are you carrying, will you need?
- Count the number of items you take with you; Be sure to bring the same number home.
- Give a trusted neighbor an extra key to your home.
- To remember to take things with you, leave them by the front door.
- As you leave anywhere, look back to be sure you are not leaving an thing.
- When you park your car in a big lot, tie a balloon to the antenna to locate it.

Source: James DeLong, Senior Services of Seattle/King County, 1988

Memory

Definition: The faculty of retaining and recalling learned information.

Three Types of Memory

1. SENSORY - Information taken in through the senses. Translated to neural (nerve impulses), and transmitted to the brain. Selected by our attention.
ENCODING transforms sensory info into a code which can be understood in short term memory.
2. SHORT TERM MEMORY - Capacity is seven digit (+ or - 2). Time limit for holding info is 20 to 30 seconds. Info must be actively rehearsed to remain in short term memory. Distraction severely upsets short term memory. Information is either forgotten or passed to . . .
3. LONG TERM MEMORY - Unlimited capacity. Each rehearsal transfers some information from short to long term memory. Five to seven repetitions may firmly root information in the long term memory.

Remembering what you read

1. Take notes / make outlines - organize. Simplify to reinforce reading material.
2. Underline key words.
3. Annotate in margins.
4. Chain method - cue words.
5. Reduce interference and distractions.
6. Timing - morning/evening person. Not when fatigued before bed. Read, sleep, recall.
7. Spacing - For integrated recall, read over 3 days instead of 1 day.
8. Tell someone what you read - repetition.
9. Interest = concentration.
10. Review strengthens memory.
11. Better health = better memory. Eat nourishing meals. Improve physical fitness. Use stress management techniques. Get rest. Build friendships. Involve self in your community affairs.

Memory by Association

We learn and remember everything that is new to us only by connecting it with something we already know.

Many of these associations have been unconscious - we don't know why we remember things: *** It is to our advantage to form our associations consciously and to form our connections in a way which will be most easily remembered.

Three Ways of Forming Associations

A. Based on Logic and Reason, Matter of Fact, Intellect
    1. Similar sounds - (Rack-Back, Memory-Memphis)
    2. Synonyms - (words with similar meanings)
    3. Whole and part
    4. Groups of "things" (Books, magazines, printed material)
    5. Cause and effect (If "this," then "that")
    6. Matching pairs - (ham and eggs, hat and coat)

B. Based on Imagination
    1. Not bound by logic.
    2. Where logic doesn't work - imagination fills the gap.
    3. Imagination can be developed.

C. Based on Emotion
    1. What you care most about is most easily remembered
    2. Group things according to likes-dislikes, etc.

Source: James DeLong, Senior Services of Seattle/King County, 1988.

Strategies for Memory Improvement

A. Encoding - Converting information to a form the mind can remember .
- Get information clearly. Ask a person to repeat or spell their name, ask a person to speak up. Use adequate lighting for written material.
- If you find yourself thinking "I can't remember this" and feeling discouraged, you won't remember it! Develop a positive attitude toward your memory. This includes forgiving yourself when you do forget, and patting yourself on the back when you remember. Notice your successes!
- Reduce or eliminate distractions when you are learning something new.
- Whenever possible,plan to learn new information at a time of day when you are mentally alert.
- Practice and use note taking skills.
- Notice contextual cues.
- Use memory techniques and cues:
  - * Method of loci   * Homes
- Use imagery to help you learn.
- Avoid medications which affect concentration.
- Be interested in what you are learning. This leads to concentration.
- Combine visual, auditory, and sensory learning whenever possible.

B. Storage
- To deepen the storage of information, review the information over a number of days. Each evening review the names of people you met.
- Write down names of people you meet, appointments you make.
- Memory works through association, or connecting information with something we already know. Associations may be formed by intellect, imagination, or emotion.
- Whenever possible, classify and organize information as you learn it. Examples of ways information may be classified:
  - Similarity of sound - memory and Memphis.
  - Whole and part - book and pages.
  - Things of the same species - printed matter, edible plants.
  - Cause and effect - knowledge follows study.
  - Law of contrast - oldest and youngest, biggest and smallest.
  - Law of similarity.
  - Matching pairs - pen and paper, ham and eggs.
  - Law of propinquity or nearness - nearness of time, place, or some other relationship of any object in memory recalls other objects that were connected with it in a previous experience.

C. Retrieval: Recovery information from storage.
- By associating a person's name with their face, each time you see them their face will be the cue that calls to mind their name.
- If you can't remember a person's name, silently go through the alphabet, reviewing names starting with each letter.

Diagnostic Criteria for
Alcohol Abuse and Dependence

<u>Central</u> <u>Nervous</u> <u>System</u> <u>Symptoms</u>	• incoherent speech • aggressive behavior • agitation • tremors, shakes • convulsions • impaired coordination and reflex action • hangover • lethargy • restlessness
<u>Impact</u> <u>on</u> <u>Health</u>	• blackouts • bruises or burns in unusual places • sleep disturbance • incontinence • malnutrition • impaired judgement • fear, paranoia • mania • delirium • memory loss, confusion • daily drinking
<u>Social/</u> <u>Interpersonal</u> <u>Impact</u>	• accidents • financial problems • interpersonal relationship problems • problems on the job • problems with the law

Source: <u>Enrichment Materials</u>, University of Victoria, B.C., Canada and <u>Diagnostic and Statistical Manual of Mental Disorders, DSM III R</u>, 3rd Edition Revised, published by the American Psychiatric Association, Washington, D.C., 1987.

Aging and Alcohol Abuse

Alcohol abuse among older men and women is a more serious problem than people generally realize. Until recently, older problem drinkers tended to be ignored by both health professionals and the general public. The neglect occurred for several reasons: our elderly population was small and few were identified as alcoholics; chronic problem drinkers (those who abused alcohol off and on for most of their lives) often died before old age; and, because they are often retired or have fewer social contacts, older people have often been able to hide drinking problems.

Some families may unthinkingly "encourage" drinking in older family members if they have the attitude that drinking should be tolerated because older people have only a limited time left and therefore should be allowed to "enjoy" themselves.

As more people learn that alcohol problems can be successfully treated at any age, more are willing to seek help to stop drinking.

Physical effects of Alcohol

Alcohol slows down brain activity. It impairs mental alertness; judgement, physical coordination; and reaction time - increasing the risk of falls and accidents.

Over time, heavy drinking can cause permanent damage to the brain and the central nervous system, as well as to the liver, heart, kidneys and stomach.

Alcohol can affect the body in unusual ways, making certain medical problems difficult to diagnose. For example, the effects of alcohol on the cardiovascular system (the heart and blood vessels) can mask pain, which may otherwise serve as a warning sign of heart attack. Alcoholism can also produce symptoms similar to those of dementia - forgetfulness, reduced attention, confusion. If incorrectly identified, such symptoms may lead to unnecessary institutionalization.

Alcohol, itself a drug, mixes unfavorably with many other drugs, including those sold by prescription and those bought over-the-counter. In addition, use of presrciption drugs may intensify the older person's reaction to alcohol, leading to more rapid intoxication. Alcohol can dangerously slow down performance skills, (driving, walking, etc.) impair judgement, and reduce alertness when taken with drugs such as:

- Minor tranquilizers: Valium (diazepam). Librium (chloradiazepoxide), Miltown (meprobamate), and others.
- Major tranquilizers: Thorazine (chlorpromazine), Mellaril (thioridazine), and others.
- Barbiturates: Luminal (phenobarbital), and others.
- Pain killers: Darvon (propoxyphene), Demoral (meperidine), and others.

- Antihistamines (both prescription and over-the-counter forms found in cold remedies.)

Use of alcohol can cause other drugs to be metabolized more rapidly producing exaggerated responses. Such drugs include: anticonvulsants (Dilantin), anticoagulants (Coumadin), and antidiabetes drugs (Orinase).

In some people, aspirin can cause bleeding in the stomach and intestines. Alcohol also irritates the stomach and can aggravate this bleeding. The combination of alcohol and diuretics can reduce blood pressure in some individuals, producing dizziness.

Anyone who drinks - even moderately - should check with a doctor or pharmacist about possible drug interactions.

Who Becomes a Problem Drinker?

In old age, problem drinkers seem to be one of two types. The first are chronic abusers, those who have used alcohol heavily throughout life. Although most chronic abusers die by middle age, some survive into old age. Approximately two-thrids of older alcoholics are in this group.

The second type begins excessive drinking late in life, often in response to "situational" factors - retirement, lowered income, declining health, and the deaths of friends and loved ones. In these cases, alcohol is first used for temporary relief but later becomes a problem.

Detecting Drinking Problems

Not everyone who drinks regularly or heavily is an alcohol abuser, but the following symptoms frequently indicate a problem:
- Drinking to calm nerves, forget worries, or reduce depression
- Loss of interest in food
- Gulping drinks and drinking too fast
- Lying about drinking habits
- Drinking alone with increased frequency
- Injuring oneself, or someone else, while intoxicated
- Getting drunk often (more than three or four times in the past year)
- Needing to drink increasing amounts of alcohol to get the desired effect
- Frequently acting irritable, resentful, or unreasonable during non-drinking periods.
- Experiencing medical, social or financial problems that are caused by drinking.

Getting Help

Older problem drinkers and alcoholics have an unusually good chance for recovery because they tend to stay with treatment programs for the duration.

Getting help can begin with a family doctor or member of the clergy, through a local health department or social services agency, or with one of the following organizations:

Alcoholics Anonymous (AA) is a voluntary fellowship of alcoholics whose purpose is to help themselves and each other get - and stay - sober. For information about their programs, call your local chapter or write to the national office at P.O. Box 459, Grand Central Station, New York, NY 10163. They can also send you a free pamphlet on alcoholism and older people entitled *Time to Start Lviing*.

National Clearing House for Alcohol Information is a federal information service that answers public inquiries, distributes written materials, and conducts literature searches. For information, write to P.O. Box 2345, Rockville, MD 20852.

National Council on Alcoholism distributes literature and can refer you to treatment services in your area. Call your local office (if listed in the telephone book or write to the national headquarters at 733 3rd Ave., New York, NY 10017.

Reprinted from National Council on Alcoholism, September 1987.

Alcohol/Drugs and the Elderly

1. Older persons who have drinking problems are likely to have health problems that complicate their situations.

2. Elderly persons represent an increasing proportion of our population. In 1976, 10% of our population was age 65 or older. By 1990, 15% of our population will be 65 or older.

3. The older alcohol/drug abuser is not as likely to appear in treatment statistics as younger alcoholics.

4. Of patients in treatment programs, very few came as a result of medical intervention or through efforts of lawyers, chaplains and psychologists.

5. Physiological changes due to aging may account for a decreased alcohol consumption among the elderly. The ratio of body water increases with age. Alcohol is almost completely soluble in water, but not fat, so the same amount of alcohol intake by older people results in higher alcohol concentrations in the blood and the brain.

6. Diagnostic problems constitute one of the greatest barriers to treatment of alcoholic older persons. What is perceived as senility or frailty due to old age may be alcoholism or drug abuse.

7. There is a lack of community facilities and treatment know-how for alcohol/drug problems specific to the elderly. Lack of financial resources or insurance benefits prohibits available services to the aging alcoholic.

8. Older substance abusers are often regarded as poor treatment risks. Programs and agencies often concentrate shrinking resources on younger populations who can be "rehabilitated."

9. An older person may be taking over-the-counter or prescription drugs which can produce harmful results taken with even a small amount of alcohol.

10. Older adults make up 11% of our population, yet use 25% of all prescription and over-the-counter drugs.

11. Alcoholism is not just a disease but a cry for help indicating an inability to cope with the loneliness, depression, hopelessness, illness and other factors of normal aging in our society.

12. Of the 100 drugs prescribed most often to the older adult, more than half can interact adversely with alcohol.

13. Excessive use of alcohol can hasten the degeneration of the aging body and bring on premature senility through mental deterioration.

14. There are at least two groups of older alcoholics: 1. Those reacting to one or more stresses of aging, and 2. Those who have had a long history of alcohol abuse and continue drinking to excess.

15. As many as 20% of our 75+ age group are taking 6 or more medications.

16. 20% of our aging people share medications with someone else.

17. While alcohol is tempting and acceptable, we must get rid of the myths that drinking is one of the few pleasures left for the elderly to enjoy.

18. Our current elderly population grew up in an era when alcoholic beverages were not considered drugs and alcoholism was not considered a treatable illness.

19. Elderly persons may be more susceptible to the effects of alcohol than young persons. Tolerance may begin sooner and adverse behavioral reactions common.

20. Alcoholism among the elderly often can be successfully treated, if it is recognized and appropriate measures utilized. Geriatric programs and alcoholism programs must collaborate in managing the elderly alcohol/drug abuser in the community, in treatment, or in the institution.

Sources
1. Alcohol and Drug Consultation for Seniors, DePaul Rehabilitation Hospital, Milwaukee, Wisconsin 1983.
2. Comment, DePaul Rehabilitation Hospital, Spring 1981.
3. Blue Ribbon Study on Alcoholism and the Aging: Report of the Mini Conference, National Council on Alcoholism, Racine, Wisconsin, February 1981.
4. Fact Sheet: Alcohol and the Elderly, N.I.A.A.A., August 6, 1979.
5. Special Report: National Council on Alcoholism, N.I.A.A.A., August 6, 1979.
6. Snyder, J. Lorraine, Report for the Task Force on Aging, Alcohol and other Drug Abuse for Dane County Medison, Wisconsin, May 1983.
7. What Senior Citizens Should Know About Drugs and Alcohol, Do It Now Foundation, Phoenix, Arizona, February 1978.
8. Zimberg, Sheldon, "Two Types of Problem Drinkers: Both Can Be Managed", Geriatrics, August 1974.

Compiled by J. Lorraine Snyder, M.S.S.W.

Take the Risk - You Can Help

LET'S ALL START TELLING THE PEOPLE WE LIKE AND
CARE ABOUT HOW THEIR DRINKING BEHAVIOR EFFECTS
US WHEN WE DISLIKE IT.

A few guidelines to being effective when talking to the alcoholic may be
helpful . . .

1. Be certain your motive is not to punish, criticize, but to show genuine
    concern, so that he may have an opportunity to see it as a problem
    requiring his attention.
2. Wait until the next day or your first opportunity to call or see him or
    her, when you are reasonably certain he or she is sober.
3. Explain that you are concerned about certain specific behavior, and
    then describe exactly WHAT THE PERSON SAID OR DID THAT was
    objectionable to you. Try to avoid general descriptions or judge-
    ments, such as "you were obnoxious," or "it was disgusting."
4. Emphasize the contrast between the person's sober behavior which
    you like and the drinking behavior you dislike.
5. Do not get into discussions about anything else that detracts from the
    purpose of your talkk at least until your message is delivered. For
    example, if the alcoholic reminds you of a drinking episode of your
    own from years back, don't defend or justify it - simply go ahead with
    what you were talking about. In other words, try not to get pulled
    into an argument or allow yourself to be put on the defensive. Just
    remember your basic message is, "I like you, but I don't like your
    behavior when you drink." Nowhere is it truer that if you are not part
    of the solution, you are part of the problem.

Source: Northwest Treatment Center, Seattle, Washington

> **If there are problems and there is drinking,**
> **drinking may be the problem.**

13 Indices of the Elderly Problem Drinker

1. Drinks to the point of psychological and psycho-motor impairment at least once a week.

2. Stays intoxicated for several days at a time at least once a year, or for over 24 hours at least twice a year.

3. Exhibits withdrawal physiologically or is unable to consistenly control the time and/or the extent of drinking.

4. Shows symptoms of being dependent on alcohol to achieve everyday tasks.

5. Health problems as a result of drinking or existing health problems are complicated as a result of drinking.

6. Financial problems as a result of drinking.

7. Normal life style changes as a result of drinking.

8. Has accidents as a result of drinking; automobile, falls.

9. Has problems with relatives as a result of drinking.

10. Has problems with friends as a result of drinking.

11. Withdraws from normal social activites.

12. Becomes belligerent, hostile or unmanageable as a result of drinking.

13. Has problems with the law or the police as a result of drinking.

Source: Rutgers Center for Alcoholism Studies

Progressive Symptoms of Alcoholism

A.   Early Phase of Alcoholism
          Blackouts
          Preoccupations with alcohol
          Gulping
          Guilt feelings (start lying)
          Avoids reference to alcohol

B.   Middle Phase (Crucial)
          Loss of control
          Fabricating excuses
          Aggressive behavior
          Persistent remorse
          Going on the wagon
          Life becomes alcohol-centered
          Loss of outside interests
          Marked self pity
          Unreasonable resentments
          Early morning drunk

C.   Late Phase (Chronic)
          Benders (prolonged intoxication)
          Marked ethical deterioration
          Daytime drunks
          Solitary drinking
          Turns to inferior companions
          Drop in tolerance
          Indefinable fears (nameless dread)
          Psychomotor inhibitions (tremors, shakes)

Source: Rutgers Center for Alcoholism Studies

Chemical Dependency
The Road To Recovery

Phases: Early Stages — Crucial Phase — Chronic Phase — Rehabilitation

Descent (Early Stages / Crucial Phase / Chronic Phase)

- Occasional Relief Use
- Constant Relief Use Commences
- Increase in Tolerance
- Onset Of Memory Blackouts
- Urgency Of First Use
- Increasing Dependence On Drug (In Some Persons)
- Tolerance
- Defensive When Questioned About Use
- Concern/Complaints By Family
- Feelings of Guilt
- Decrease Of Ability To Stop Using When Others Do
- Preoccupation With Drug
- Memory Blackouts Increase or Begin
- Grandiose And Aggressive Behavior Or Extravagance
- Alibis For Use
- Persistent Remorse
- Efforts To Control Repeatedly Fail
- Telephonitis
- Promises Or Resolutions Fail
- Tries Geographical Escape
- Family And Friends Avoided
- Loss of Interest
- Unreasonable Resentments
- Work And Money Troubles
- Neglect Of Food
- Tremors And Early Morning Use
- Decrease In Tolerance
- Physical Deterioration
- Onset of Lengthy Intoxications
- Undeniable Fears
- Impaired Thinking
- Unable to Initiate Action
- Vague Spiritual Desires
- Obsession With Use
- All Alibis Exhausted
- Complete Defeat Admitted
- Obsessive Use Continues In Vicious Circles

Ascent (Rehabilitation)

- Honest Desire for Help
- Learns Chemical Dependency is an Illness
- Total Addiction Can Be Arrested
- Meets Happy Recovering Abusers
- Right Thinking Begins
- Onset of New Hope
- Start Of Group Therapy
- Stops Taking Drug
- Spiritual Needs Examined
- Appreciation of Possibilities of New Way of Life
- Diminishing Fears of The Unknown Future
- Regular Nourishment Taken
- Desire to Escape Goes
- Return of Self-Esteem
- Realistic Thinking
- Natural Rest and Sleep
- Adjustments to Family Needs
- New Interests Develop
- Appreciate Efforts
- Family and Friends
- Rebirth of Ideals
- Appreciation of Real Values
- New Circle of Stable Friends
- First Steps of Economic Stability
- Facts Faced with Courage
- Care of Personal Appearance
- **Increase of Emotional Control**
- Group Therapy and Mutual Help Continue
- Confidence of Employers
- Enlightened and Interesting Way of Life Opens Up With Road Ahead to Higher Levels Than Ever Before
- Contentment in Abstinence

Treatment *Approaches for Older Alcoholics*

by SANDRA M. SCHIFF

Older alcoholics have long been underrepresented in the psychotherapeutic treatment programs across the nation. The problems of misdiagnosis with this population have contributed to the small numbers of referrals to such programs. Concerns about traditional versus nontraditional approaches and the inaccessibility of programs for the older adult are some of the reasons that these individuals do not end up in appropriate treatment. Additionally, the bias against labeling a 70 year-old person an alcoholic and the belief that traditional treatment programs do not work with this type of patient also prevent successful intervention. A variety of treatment approaches is available for use with the older adult. I will mention and highlight several, identifying the modalities that I have found to be most successful in assisting the ongoing recovery of these patients.

To define recovery, the two types of elderly alcoholics referred to in the literature will be defined. The first type is the early-onset alcohol abuser, the survivor, the older adult who has been drinking heavily for 20-30 years. The prognosis for this type of patient is guarded based on the number of previous attempts at treatment and the physical as well as mental health of the individual. The second type of alcoholic is the late-onset, the reactive drinker, the social drinker who has probably increased his or her drinking patterns because of a recent loss. These losses could be role losses as well as loss of spouse and/or friend. The losses associated with sensory changes or health problems can also be devastating. The prognosis for this patient is good. Chances are that this patient has not been through any type of treatment program. Reference to both of these types of patients will be made throughout this article.

Treatment Approaches

As discussed elsewhere in this issue (see the article by Lamy), the older person is more susceptible to the effects of both alcohol and prescribed drugs and is particularly likely to suffer harmful interactions of drugs and alcohol. With any treatment approach, the danger of such interactions deserves attention that can only be provided by a thorough drug regimen reviews coeducted by a pharmacist or physician. After such a careful evaluation, an appropriate treatment regimen for the alcoholism problem can be selected.

Alcoholics Anonymous. It has been estimated that only 15 percent of alcoholics over the age of 60 are receiving treatment (Bloom, 1983). One reason may be the physician's hesitancy to recommend psychotherapy for older patients. Certainly, another is the fact that specialized older adult treatment programs are rare. Therefore, one of the first approaches that these patients turn to is Alcoholics Anonymous (AA). This is a self-help group that offers support, understanding, and a place where the alcoholic is not alone. Some older adults do not like the idea of attending AA. There are myths and stigmas that surround the group that are unappealing to them. Many patients have confided in me that they feared for their anonymity and felt different from "those alcoholics." In time and after coming to understand the benefits of the group as an additional support system, these patients formed their own AA group. With the help of the local AA office, a specialized group was formed called Golden Years. While anyone could attend these meetings, the name certainly atrracted older adults. With a largely age-homogeneous group, then, the AA experience became apositive one for older alcoholics who had felt uncomfortable in a group of alll ages.

Aversive conditioning treatment. Aversive conditioning treatment is one method used at the Raleigh Hills Hospital in Portland, Oregon, and consists of associating the sight, smell, taste, and thought of alcohol with an unpleasant reaction (Wiens et. al., 1982-83). The patient has a negative response to alcohol and then transfers the avoidance of alcohol from the clinical situation to nonclinical situations. This is not a common approach to treating the older alcoholic, and I would not recommend it on an outpatient basis.

Inpatient treatment. This approach is necessary for safe and quick detoxification. Cases where there may be organic impairment require longer inpatient stays. These patients may not be able to care for themselves. Inpatient treatment is also more common for the early-onset, chronic drinker to help ease probable withdrawal symptoms.

Psychotropic drugs. Tricyclic anti-depressants and major tranquilizers, such as the phenothiazxines (for example, Thorazine and Mellaril), have proven useful as adjuncts to treatment, especially in patients where depression follows detoxification (Khantzian, 1978). My own experience, however, has been negative with most uses of psychotropic drugs for my patients. For example, Serax, an anti-anxiety drug used widely in outpatient tretment programs, has a psychopharmacologic effect similar to alcohol. That is, while it does relax the patient, it also has a depressant effect on central nervous system function and may itself produce dependency. In addition, compliance with the doctor's instructions in taking medications is sometimes difficult for older adults, and the dependency problems of the alcoholic only complicate the process. When patients appear to require some type of medication get them through the initial phase of abstinence, a geriatric physician who prescribes geriatric dosages and monitors complicance very closely is required.

Behavioral psychotherapy. Behavioral psychotherapy is a structured therapy that concentrates on behavioral goals and a time frame to complete those goals. According to Ruben (1986), behavioral psychotherapy seeks (1) total abstinence, (2) increases in adaptive functioning, or (3) moderate-to-controlled drinking. Some of the positive aspects of behavioral psychotherapy cited by Ruben are the "integration" interventions. These processes are described as linking all the relevant factors in the older persons life that contribute to excessive drinking. Integration can also be viewed as a holistic, networking approach, a prcoess that is necessary to maintaining recovery. This approach requires medical, behavioral, historical, cultural variables, not unlike any thorough psychosocial therapy.

My experience has not been positive with any goal of moderate-to-controlled drinking. Older patients are often unable to distinguish what moderation is, because of the normal aging process. For example, the slowing down of the metabolic system that occurs with normal aging works to keep blood-alcohol levels high for an extended period, heightening the effects of even a small amount of alcohol.

Psychosocial approach. This approach, with its many varieties, is the most widely used in treatment programs. Zimbert (1978) refers to this type of treatment as sociopsychologic in nature and argues that the treatment is more likely to be successful if directed at the social and psychological stresses associated with aging. Therefore, much of the treatment can transpire in the social milieu of the nursing home or senior reisdent center or within the home healthcare programs. This approach can be effective with both the early-onset and late-onset alcoholic.

Many different modalities can be utilized within this approach. Individual, couple, family, and group therapy are viable treatment options for the older patient. Individual therapy begins with getting acquainted, and through several sessions the patient learns to trust the therapist. The result is a therapeutic alliance that is necessary for treatment to continue. Sometimes patients dicucss their history, while others deal with the here-and-now situations. Once there is a climate of trust, the idea of group therapy is introduced. Zimberg (1978) states that in an outpatient geriatric program the use of group socialization and antidepressant medication help to eliminate alcohol abuse. He also feels that older patients are unlikely to go to specialized programs for the elderly because of their denial of their problem and that the traditional approaches such as AA and administration of disulfiram are not necessary with these patients. This has not been my experience; I feel that older patients will attend a specialized program once they understand how it will be helpful to them.

Denial is strong with older alcoholics because of their sense of independence. For someone to suggest that they need assistance with their alcohol problem makes them feel guilty and inadequate. Building a rapport and involving other support systems, such as family and other services, can help to motivate the individual to enter treatment. The church, social service workers, home healthcare nurses, and physicans are examples of sources that have been tapped. Often these supports need more information about alcohol problems, especially the appropriate assessment techniques that can circumvent strong denial (see the article in this issue by Willenbring and Spring).

Families can be very helpful, but their help can also be "enabling." In the addiction field, enabling means to foster the dependency and perpetuate the problem. The typical enabler is the spouse who is referred to as the co-dependent. The co-dependent has tremendous control and investment in keeping the family together. Some families want no involvement with the process of therapy, and their resistance can prevent successful intervention. Alcoholism is a family disease, and it would seem that families would be encouraged to become involved in treatment. However, many older patients feel that their lives are run by their adult children. Those who live with their children feel themselves to be a burden to them and resent any intervention on the family's part. "Intervention" has a special meaning in the addiction field. This is a process where members of a family confront the alcoholic so that he or she will enter treatment. It is a powerful technique and should only be performed by a trained professional. So where does that leave the families of these patients? It depends on the relationship that the older person has with the family.

The following two clinical vignettes will describe the benefits and concerns of family involvement in treatment. John, a 42-year -old single male, came to see me because he heard that there was a special treatment program for older alcoholics. His mother, 78 years old, widowed for 40 years, was living alone in an apartment. Though legally blind, she continued to care for herself with her son's help during his weekly visits. He began to find his mother intoxicated, bruised from falls, and slurring her words. He had never thought that his mother could be alcoholic. He, himself, has been in recovery for four years. He asked me to talk to his mother and said that he would help in any way he could. I visited with her only to find a very lonely and scared woman. Her fears of growing old and feelings of isolation were overwhelming her. I explained what was happening to her as a result of the alcohol she was drinking. Though her immediate reaction was denial, I very slowly began to build a trusting relationship with her. She told me that her son had moved out three years ago, and she was stillgrieving. She had worked most of her life and valued her indpendence. She learned to recognize that her belligerent behavior and anger were triggered by alcohol. Gruadually she began to accept her problem. This process took six weeks of 45-minute visits and weekly phone calls. The relationship we developed and her new understanding of the effects of alcohol helped her stop drinking and agree to attend group therapy. (She as a late-onset, episodic drinker, and detoxification was not necessary.) She is currently in recovery an attends a weekly group therapy session faithfully. Her son's visits are more frequent, and he takes her to church every Sunday. She is proud of her accomplishment. She is enjoying her new freedom and feels more useful to others. In this case example, the son was an important factor in initiating treatment for his mother. He did not "enable" her to continue drinking, and he offered support as needed.

The next case example illustrates how family involvement ended in tragedy. Mildred, 80 years old, was living in a senior high-rise residential structure. Her son lived far away in another part of the state. Her granddaughter lived near her reisdence. The administrator of the facility called me to discuss her concerns about Mildred falling in the halls and acting "weird." The administrator thought that an evaluation might be in order since she had smelled alcohol on Mildred's breath. I came to visit her and found a very proud and private woman who looked much younger than her years. She was confused about why I was there, but I quickly told her that people were concerned about her recent behavior. She knew what I meant and told me that she had not been feeling well and that her new medication might be to blame for her problems. We agreed that she should inform her physician so that he could evaluate any possible side effects. I began to ask her about social drinking in the center, and she openly admitted tha she had a nightly shot of brandy in her apartment to help her sleep. After talking with her more and learning about her family, I decided to end that meeting but asked her if she would talk with me again. She agreed for the following week, and we set up an appointment. I assured the administrator that I would continue to meet with Mildred and evaluate her condition and that, after I gained Mildred's permission, I would discuss my recommendations with the administrator. The day before my next appointment with Mildred, however, her granddaughter called me and canceled. I asked what the problem was, and she responded by saying, "Butt out. We don't need anyone helping my grandmother to stop drinking. She doesn't have many years left, so why not let her enjoy them?" Why not? This is one of the prevailing myths of our society. Why rehabilitate an 80-year-old alcoholic? Three months later, Mildred died. Whether her death was related to alcoholism, I don't know; but I do know that recovery would have helped enhance her life.

Group Treatment

Group treatment has always been a treatment of choice for the chemically dependent patient. This is the treatment modality I have found to be most successful with older patients. This modality is effective because the group confronts the alcoholic's denial and keeps the person in reality. While the traditional confrontation that is used with the younger alcoholic does not usually work with the older patient, the group can address the denial in a nonthreeatening manner. Group psychotherapy has proven effective for both early-onset and late-onset alcoholics.

The dynamics of the group can enhance self-image, allow member to share anxieties associated with their aging, test their judgement, and learn to communicate with others. The group environment provides a safe place for catharsis by allowing the release of suppressed feelings. Reminiscence, also referred to as life review, helps to facilitate closeness among members. Horton (1986) asserts that, although psychotherapy may have beneficial effects, it is not possible to say that one particular brand of psychotherapy is better than another. He does, however, recognize the value of life review methods.

One of the important functions of the group is to restore the member's capacity to enter into relationships. Compatibility of group members is considered very important, so groups are usually best if they include a limited number of people (six to eight is ideal) of the same sex and similar marital and health status. While both sexes can be treated in the same group, I have been most succesful by having a women's group and a men's group. The only exception might be a separate group for married couples. Usually the male partner is the recovering patient and the female the co-dependent. Issues that are dealt with in this kind of group would not usually arise in individual therapy. For example, in my experience, people find it easier to disucss some of the sexuality issues in the couple's group than in same-sex groups. Participants in my couples groups discovered that, of the six couples prsent, none slept together in the same bed. While their reasons for sleeping separately differed, the catharsis resulting from these revelations was quite therapeutic.

Since age-focused groups are the type in which older poeple feel most comfortable, these will probably be most successful. Certainly, groups composed of people of different ages can function, but the variance in ages can be a disservice to older patients, since their younger counterparts are not likely to possess the same perspective on life as the older, more experienced patients. Since these guidelines are based on my own experience, it might be beneficial for other therapists to explore alternative types and copmpositions of groups.

Some of the main components of group treatment are discussed below

Self-image. Alcoholism carries such a strong social stigma that alcoholics generally experience a great deal of guilt and strong feelings of inferiority as a result of their dependency. Many older people also suffer problems with self-image and a decline in their sense of self-worth because of bodily deterioration and the many social losses associated with aging (for example, job, income, spouse, and social respect). When an alcoholic also has to deal with the stigma of growing old, damage to self-esteem is doubled; in the case of an older female, it may be tripled by the additional burdens of being female, old, and alcoholic.

Rebuilding of self-concept and redevelopment of social roles supportive of self-esteem need to be the focal points of group treatment. The group brings together patients who are experiencing negative feelings about themselves so that they have an opportunity to confront those feelings and, with group support, achieve a more realistic and positive self-image.

Communication problems. Many older alcoholics have learned not to express their feelings, but this only increases their sense of loss and isolation. They are passive and fearful of saying what is on their minds. Group experience can facilitate listening and speaking skills.

Catharsis. Any group that comes together for apurpose experiences a catharsis. There is a mood, a common goal, a peaceful feeling that develops. The common problems of alcoholism and aging combined with a commitment to the common goal of sobriety brings about catharsis. This is an intense feeling that is created within the group.

Reality testing. Alcoholism helps to distort perceptions of self and perceptions of others. Group work can help to correct these distortions. A group member has an opportunity to look at the world more accurately through the eys of fellow group members. Older persons can test the commonality of their circumstances and the reality of their aging-related problems. One reality for many older alcoholics is that they have many health and personal problems and little purpose in their lives. These realities must be dealt with because, without the motivation to live, there is no desire for abstinence.

Conclusion

A tremendous gap exists in the literature regarding treatment of older minorities. If special programs exist in areas where the population is made up of minority groups, research needs to be conducted to help us recognize the similarities and difference of these groups.

Many treatment approaches appear to be suitable for older alcoholics. However, without careful analysis and application of alternatives, failure may occur. Group treatment as a modality in a psychosocial approach seems to be the most effective. Because of the social networking that occurs simultaneously with treatment, there is less chance of relapse. All of the support systems should work collaboratively to provide as sound backup for these patients. And, finally we must examine our attitudes toward older alcoholics and evaluate our commitment to this population if we are to bring them to treatment and if we are to be able to deal appropriately and successfully with them once they arrive.

Sandra M. Schiff, M.S.W., A.C.S.W., is manager of the Employee Assistance Program, Oakwood Hospital, Dearborne, Mich., and has directed several geriatric programs specializing in treatment of substance abuse.

REFERENCES

Berger, H. 1983: "Alcoholism in the Elderly." *Postgraduate Medicine* 73 (1): 329-32.

Bienfield, D., 1987. "Alcoholism in the Elderly." *American Family Physician* 36 (2): 163-69.

Blazer, D.G., 1982. *Depression in Later Life* St. Louis, Mo.: C.V. Mosbey Co.

Bloom, P.J., 1983. "Alcoholism after Sixty." *American Family Physician* 28 (2): 111-13.

Horton, A.M., 1986. "Alcohol and the Elderly." *Maryland Medical Journal* 35 (11): 916-18.

Khantzian, E.J., 1978. "Organic Problems in the Aged: Brain Syndromes and Alcoholism." *Journal of Geriatric Psychiatry* 11 (2). 191-202.

Kola, L.A., Kosberg, J.I. and Joyce, K., 1984. "The Alcoholic Elderly Client: Assessment of Policies and Practicies of Service Providers." *Gerontologist* 24 (5): 517-21.

Morse, R., 1984. "Alcoholism and the Elderly." *Geriatrics* 39 (12) 28-29.

Ruben, D.H., 1986. "The Elderly Alcoholic: Some Current Dimensions." *Substance Abuse* 5 (4): 59-70.

Wiens et al., 1982-83. "Medical-Behavioral Treatment of the Older Alcoholic Patient." *American Journal of Drug Alcohol Abuse* 94 (4): 461-75.

Zimberg, S., 1978. "Diagnosis and Treatment of the Elderly Alcoholic." *Alcoholism: Clinical and Experimental Research* 2 (1). 27-29.

Zimberg, S., 1978. "Treatment of the Elderly Alcoholic in the Community and in an Institutional Setting." *Addictive Diseases* 3 (3): 417-27.

Zimberg, S., 1983. "Alcoholism in the Edlerly." *Postgraduate Medicine* 74 (1): 165-73.

Sexuality and Older People

by Bonnie Genevay

"Why is there a tendency to look upon the sexual activities of the aged with aversion? . . . I have the impression that sex does not end as long as you don't want it to end . . . there is no doubt that some old people masturbate until their death . . . what you cannot do is to stop for a long time because then it is very hard to start up again. So you always have to keep the engine running. It is something I'm dealing with in this book."

Above are thoughts from Gabriel Garcia Marquez, author of One Hundred Years of Solitude, as he contemplated his new book about a love affair between two very old people (Simons, 1985). To write the book, Marquez has been anticipating his own sexuality in old age, and he has been reflecting on the sexual activity and expression of his grandparents and parents, who are models for the book. These two endeavors - anticipation of one's own aging and reflection on family and person al sexual history and values - are also critical for human-service helpers to engage in if they are to be sensitive to and helpful with sexual issues of older patients and clients.

In staff training, a wide array of professionals - case managers, counselors, volunteers, nurses, social workers, doctors, in-home and institutional care staff - demand answers: "What do I do when an older person makes a pass at me? "How do I deal with the nursing home patient who constantly touches herself and drives her roommate to distraction?" "What can I say to the older man who demands sex with his wife when she believes it should be over. When this 80-year-old started hugging and kissing me and calling me by her dead daughter's name, was I wrong to terminate service?" "Should an 80-year-old who has sexual delusions and talks constantly about them be medicated so he won't make the others uncomfortable?" "How should I respond to an older woman who tries to give me gifts - money, her dead husband's underwear, and pictures of herself when she was twenty?" "How can I help a family whose grandfather shows lewd, nude pictures to them and doesn't seem to know it's not appropriate?"

Obviously these situations faced by service providers are not solely sexual in nature, and many indicate that the older person is undergoing mental and physical changes disguised in a sexual cloak. Even from the standpoint of sexual assessment, these quotes show only the tip of the iceberg, for beneath the external behavior lie core sexual identity and history, affectional and touch deprivation, losses, low self-esteem and pain. But because the behavioral manifestation is sexual, it scares us. We human service providers too quickly jump to the questions of what to do because the behavior makes us uncomfortable. An alternative is to allow our discomfort and ask ourselves, "How shall I understand this in the context of everything else that's going on with this older person?" A good example of other possible factors in the person's life is depression. Weiner and White (1982) link depression with sexual expression and observe that in the older person depression represents a loss of self, while the opportunity for sexual expression represents an affirmation of self.

Service providers bring to each interaction with old people their own family values, personal sexual experience - or lack of it - and cultural biases about old age and sex. This interface between personal and professional thoughts, behavior and feelings in regard to human sexuality may be either unconscious and conflictual or intentional and highly therapeutic for all concerned. The helper who is able to imagine his or her old age without sexual satisfaction, and without affection or touching, can be a strong enabler of the older client who needs to resolve, grieve over, or let go of longstanding sexual-affectional issues. In addition to anticipation and reflection, the following forms of professional behavior are useful when helping older adults with their sexual and intimacy needs:

1. Assume nothing about what appears to be sexual behavior until you check out the meaning to that particular older person. (Example: A case manager was appalled when an elderly woman asked her if she wore panties. The worker assumed this was a sexual innuendo until the woman explained, "You see, I don't wear them any more because I can't get to the bathroom on time." This was a statement about incontinence, not a proposition.)

2. Remember that as a helper you may be the only "significant other" in the life of an older person who is alone or whose family lives far away. When this role becomes oppressive and adds to your own emotional overload, you may find it easier to terminate service or to transfer the client to another professional. It takes more time to work through the meaning of this personal-professional relationship, and it may be more threatening to the service provider. (Example: An outreach worker asked her supervisor to transfer a long-term client because the client was getting too fond of her, inhibiting her effectiveness. The supervisor recommended confronting the issues of transference, intimacy, and boundaries, and redefining goals.)

3. Talk, one adult to another, about sexuality and intimacy. This practice is difficult when the older person treats you as an age-inferior. (Example: "You know, honey, you look just like a teenager! You're so cute.") When you ignore or succumb to this agist behavior, however, you lose the power to confront honestly and deal directly with the adult sexual issues that give pain and need clarification. The reverse is also true: When you condescend to the older person it prohibits him or her from any in-depth disclosure of sexual self and needs.

4. Understand, as a helping person, that you do not have to have all the answers about sexual activity and expression - no matter what age you are. (Example: Service providers often feel inadequate to respond

to specific sexual questions regarding such issues as inadequate lubrication, impotence, or masturbation.) Even if you had an encyclopedic knowledge of geriatric sexuality, it would not necessarily help a specific older client. Personal values and habits, family rules, and emotional needs may influence a client far more than statistics and facts. Asking the painful questions, and listening patiently for the answers without judgement, may be far more helpful than citing norms that may not even apply.

5. Be the advocate for the older person in matters sexual. This advocacy sometimes means interpreting a new relationship to the family or encouraging sexual expression, fantasies, and feelings that adult children may not be able to condone. The sexual fabric of family is sometimes so fragile, and the early experiences of adult children so negative, that it is impossible for families to discuss sexuality. You may need to champion massage, friendship skills, and even such benign acitivites as shared TV watching with another older person, when these prove a threat to adult children. (Example: A nurse who approved of two lonely older people becoming close.)

6. Risk talking about and relating to older people in terms of sensory, sensual, affectional, companionship, and sexual needs. It helps if you are clear about your own sexual needs and identity, but if you are not - learn from your clients. Let them tell you how it is. Listen to their past history, honor their preferences, see them as men and women, value their experience in living, and encourage them to initiate contact with human beings of all ages. It takes all of this support - plus anticipation and reflection on the part of the service provider - to enable older people to cope with their deep needs for intimacy at the end of life.

Bonnie Genevay, A.C.S.W., is a trainers, consultant, and counselor in the areas of older people and their families, caregiving, intimacy, loss and bereavement. She is director of Facing Aging Concerns Together, Family Services of Seattle, Wash.

Reprinted from <u>Generations</u>, 1990

References
Simons, M., 1985. "Love and Age: A Talk with Garcia Marquez." <u>The New York Times Book Review,</u> April 7.
Weiner, M. and White, M., 1982. "Depression as the Search for the Lost Self." <u>Psychotherapy: Theory, Research and Practice</u> 19(4): 493.

Intimacy & Aging

"I always thought sunsets were more spectacular than sunrises, anyway," says Dexter, 83, looking adoringly at Liz, his 81-year-old wife. "Now we're having some beautiful times in the evening of our lives." After each had been widowed and lived alone for some time, Liz and Dexter met at a dance for older adults. Now, after having been married for two years, Liz says, "This is the most well-rounded relationship I've ever had. Dexter and I are intellectual equals and we have a lot of laughs together. I feel we're fortunate that we've reached this point in life, and our story shows that it's never too late to find love and sex."

Love and sex are among the most important social and personality issues throughout life, including old age, and they can go far to help the elderly enjoy these years. The losses that Dexter and Liz suffered from widowhood are typical at this time of life. But then so are the vigor and interest in life that enabled them to find and be open to a relationship with each other. As we note in this chapter, while the losses of old age are considerable, so are the strengths displayed by many elderly persons in dealing with them.

While the problems of old age are important, we need to be aware, too, of some of the positive aspects of having lived a long time. Old age is a unique developmental stage, as gerontologists Robert N. Butler and Myrna I. Lewis (1982), point out: During childhood, we gather and enlarge our strength and experience; during old age, we clarify and find use for what we've learned over the years. Growth and adaptation can occur in old age, as in all other stages of the life cycle, if old people are flexible and realistic, if they learn how to conserve their strength, how to adjust to change and loss. and how to use these years productively. At this time of life certain feelings come to the forefront of many old people's lives - a new awareness of time and the life cycle, a desire to leave a legacy to their children (or the world), and a wish to pass on the fruits of their experience (to validate their lives as having been meaningful).

People who feel well, who have opportunities to demonstrate competence, and who feel in control over their lives are likely to have a strong enough sense of self that they will be able to cope with the losses that tend to accompany these years - the deaths of loved ones, the loss of work roles, and the loss of bodily strength and sensory acuity. Successful aging is possible and many people do experience the last stage of life positively.

My life is in the background of my mind much of the time; it cannot be any other way. Thoughts of the past paly upon me; sometimes I play with them, encourage and savour them; at other times I dismiss them.

Source: R.N. Butler, (1963). The life review: An interpretation of reminiscence in the aged. Psychiatry, 25, 65-76.

LAUGHTER-HEALER FOR THE STRESSED

STRESS

People always have said that laughter is the best medicine and, they're right. Psychologist Rod Martin, Ph.D., and Herbert Lefcourt, Ph.D., both at the University of Waterloo, in Ontario, Canada have taken laughter into the lab and tested its benifits on mind and mood. They gave their subjects various tests of stress and mood, as well as several tests of sense of humor: ability to respond with humor in real life situations: how often they saw humor around them; how much they liked humor; and how often they used humor as a way of coping with stress. Then the researchers did two behavioral studies: in one they asked volunteers to make up a three-minute comedy routine; and, in the other, they asked volunteers watching a stressful film to make up a funny narative as they watched. Martin and Lefcourt found that humor is a terrific buffer between stress and negative moods. People who recognize the absurdity in events and who laugh a lot are less prone to depression, anger, tension and fatigue than are people who lack the healing power of humor.

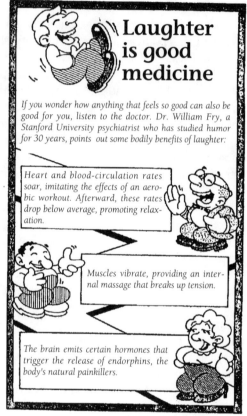

Laughter is good medicine

If you wonder how anything that feels so good can also be good for you, listen to the doctor. Dr. William Fry, a Stanford University psychiatrist who has studied humor for 30 years, points out some bodily benefits of laughter:

Heart and blood-circulation rates soar, imitating the effects of an aerobic workout. Afterward, these rates drop below average, promoting relaxation.

Muscles vibrate, providing an internal massage that breaks up tension.

The brain emits certain hormones that trigger the release of endorphins, the body's natural painkillers.

by John Sherlock, USA TODAY

• FOUR WAYS TO REELIEVE STRESS:

1. LIFESTYLE = modify/change habits . . . eating, smoking, drinking, drugs . . . whatever is causing anxiety and stress.

2. RELAXATION = meditation and relaxation methods, biofeedback techniques, etc.

3. GET EXERCISE = get physical - aerobics, running, swimming, etc. Get those endorphins working!

4. LAUGHTER = use the healing power of laughter and play. Get in the habit of looking on the bright side.

WHAT STRESSES ME THE MOST IS: _____

How to Discover Your Humor Potential

THE "DO-BEES"

(1) <u>Be Open</u> to all the humor around you. Keep an open mind. Avoid being judgemental. If you are receptive, you'll see potentially humorous situations or things everywhere you go.

(2) <u>Be Willing to Choose</u> the lighter, positive, more optimistic side of life. It's much easier to be cheerful than tearful. Make a CHOICE to be happy every day.

(3) <u>Be Ready to Risk</u>. Every day has it's risks - and it's rewards.Using humor has an element of risk; the alternative is boredom. Stretch yourself.

(4) <u>Be Appropriate</u>. Always remember there's a right-time, right-place to use humor. If your " inner voice" says "don't say it," heed it. Never use humor as a weapon.

(5) <u>Be Outrageous</u>...because it's not crowded there! The world is full of colorless people. Allow yourself to be one of it's loveable "characters" and you'll create friends wherever you go.

(6) <u>Be Playful</u>. Let your "kid" come out and play. It's never too late to have a happy childhood. Not to be childish - but to be child-like. Strive for spontaneity.

For information about
Humor Workshops,
speeches, presentations to
your club
or organization,
contact: Joe Jenkins,
3002 - 30th Ave. W.
Seattle, WA 98199
(206) 282-5441

©1985, Jenkins & Associates

"Oh, I just *love* it, Mr. Maxwell, when you get into one of your silly moods."

"H.A.L.F.:" Assessment Tool for Aged Abuse

Adult Child

Health
- Has been abused or battered as a child.
- Poor self-image.
- Limited capacity to express own need.
- Alcohol or drug abuser
- Psychologically unprepared to meet dependency needs of parent.
- Denies parent's illness.
- Shows evidence of loss of control, or fear of losing control.
- Presents contradictory history or one that does not or cannot explain the injury.
- Projects cause of injury onto third party.
- Has delayed unduly in bringing the aged person in for care.
- Over-reacts or under-reacts to the seriousness of the situation.
- Complains continuously about irrelevant problems unrelated to injury.
- Refuses consent for further diagnostic studies.

Attitudes Toward Aging
- Views parent as different.
- Negative attitude toward aging.
- Has unrealistic expectations of the aged person.

Living Arrangement
- Socially isolated.
- Has no one to provide relief when uptight with the aged person.

Finances
- Financially unprepared to meet dependency needs of parent.

Aged Adult

Health
- Poor health.
- Overly dependent on adult child.
- Has been extremely dependent on spouse who is now deceased.
- Persists in advising, admonishing and directing the adult child on whom he/she is dependent.
- Has an unexplained or repeated injury.
- Shows evidence of dehydration and/or malnutrition without obvious cause.
- Has been given inappropriate ood, drink and/or drugs.
- Is notably passive and wit drawn.
- Shows evidence of overall poor care.
- Has muscle contractures due to being restricted.

Attitudes Toward Aging
- Insistent upon maintaining old patterns of independent functioning.

Living Arrangement
- Intrusive, allowing adult child no privacy.

Finances
- Uses gift money to control others, particularly adult children.
- Refuses to apply for financial aid.
- Has money and refuses to spend it.
- Savings have been exhausted by medical expenses.

Aged Adult - Adult Child Interaction

- Is the aged adult fearful?
- Are their postures relaxed?
- Does the adult child touch, talk, look at or listen to the aged parent?
- Is the aged parent excessively dependent on the adult child?
- Does the adult child blame the aged parent?

Primary Prevention

Goal: Decrease Abuse Risk Factors
Strategies:
1. Teach non-violent coping behavior early in life.
2. Educate family to normal aging process.
3. Develop extended kinship network.
4. Develop tool to assess family dynamics.
5. Provide day-care or other support services.

Secondary Prevention

Goal: Promote Early Diagnosis of Abuse Dynamics and Provide Prompt Treatment for Family
Strategies:
1. Assess role change in family members.
2. Identify role conflicts.
3. Clarify expectations about the needed roles.
4. Strengthen the family members' abilities to enact the new roles.
5. Assist the family member to perform new roles (plan schedule).
6. Reward the new role taking (describe the outcome of new roles).
7. Help the family members to modify the new roles.

Tertiary Prevention

Goal: Reduce the residual effects of abuse.
Strategies:
1. Respite care.
2. Boarding homes.
3. Nursing home placement.

Source: Ferguson, Doris and Beck, Cornelia, University of Arkansas for Medical Sciences College of Nursing, 4301 W. Markham, Little Rock, Arkansas 72205

Suicide and the Suicide Rating Scale

"I've been doctored for ten years, but I keep getting worse. I can't do for myself anymore and I hate to be a burden. I've been thinking about death and it would just be a relief."

"I'm probably wasting your time. You can't get my job back for me or bring back my wife. It doesn't seem worth it. But what can I expect at my age? There's nothing to look forward to."

Support Group Helpers, like others who work with troubled people can expect to encounter suicidal situations. The suicide rate among older adults increases with age, especially for males. Suicide can offer a moral choice - the right to a preferred time and manner of dying. Usually however, an examination of the histories of most suicides points to psychological, physical and cultural causes which drive the individual to seek an ultimate escape - the person feels no other way out and no sense of choice at all. Also, potential suicides who have been counseled often report that their wish to die was a mistake. Because of these factors and the finality of death, the responsibility of the helper is specific: suicidal individuals that come to a helper's attention are assumed to be requesting help. It is important to be able to recognize the risk potential and to be aware of the resources available for effective intervention.

Common issues in the histories of suicide victims are poor physical health, unemployment and lack of resources, and psychological adjustment contemplating or attempting suicide. Suicidal thoughts and gestures should be regarded as attempts to reconnect and communicate with the significant people; attempts to overcome this isolation. A SGH often works to facilitate the connections with rescuing resources, and in cases where the suicide potential is high, the immediate response is to connect the individual with specialized community resources (mental health centers, hospitals and crisis centers).

At any point in the course of talking to an individual, the SGH may begin to sense a hopeless or morbid trend. As soon as the question is raised in the Support Group Helper's mind, the issue should be approached directly with inquiries such as "Do you think about the suicide?" or "Does it seem like it's just not worth it?" Such questions may appear to suggest or plant a suicidal idea, but in this situation a complete examination of the possibility of suicide is considered a more critical factor. In the course of this evaluation (rating the suicidal potential), the SGH should provide acceptance, support and optimism for a satisfactory resolution of whatever problems are leading the individual toward self-destruction. This attitude may be expressed to the individual with phrases such as: "You certainly do have a lot to contend with, and you are doing the right thing to get some help. There are some very good ways of getting over this and you soon be looking back at all this and feeling a lot better."

Source: Support Group Helpers

COUNTERTRANSFERENCE ISSUES AND
CLIENT AND PROFESSIONAL BEHAVIOR

Client Behavior	Countertransference Issues	Professional Behavior
Family resentment, grief, fear of abandonment	Denial	Interrupt, avoid and deny client's expression of feelings
Client's agitation, anxiety, inability to communicate	Fear of growing older, being helpless	Produce more concrete answers", over-identify with family's guilt, overcompensate
Client's and family's fear of being alone	Fear of dying, the unknown, and contagion	Reduce opportunities for grief work, focus on "curing," not caring.
Client's and family's emotional lability, anger	Anger	Fail to schedule appointment, deal with facts, not feelings, terminate service
Client's aphasia, wandering, excessive demands	Need for control and professional "omnipotence	Become parental in approach, fail to trust wisdom of client system, miss appointment
Client's and family's helplessness	Need to be needed	Produce practical suggestions, structure interventions more rigidly

Source: Renee S. Katz & Bonnie Genevay, <u>Older People, Dying and Countertransference.</u>
Reprinted from <u>Generations</u>, 1992.

Rational and Irrational Thinking and Stress

Basic Tenets of Thinking and Stress:

1. Humans are both rational and irrational in their thinking.
2. A stress response is a result of irrational thinking.
3. Happiness and unhappiness are results of self-verbalization.
4. Unhappiness continues as a result of self-verbalization.
5. Negative and self-defeating thoughts need to be attacked by logical and rational thinking.
6. Humans are verbal, therefore, thinking accompanies emotions.

Irrational Thoughts that Contribute to Stress :

1. I must be loved and approved by everyone.
2. I must be competent, adequate and achieving to be worthwhile.
3. Some people are bad, wicked, and should be blamed and punished.
4. It is catastrophe if things don't work out like I want and expect.
5. I have no control over my happiness and unhappiness.
6. I must worry about all the bad that can happen.
7. It is easier to avoid difficulties and self-responsibilities.
8. I should be dependent on someone who is stronger.
9. I am a product of my past and I can't change.
10. I need to worry about and get upset about other people's problems.
11. There is always a right and perfect solution to every problem.

Adapted from <u>Rational Emotive Therapy</u> by Albert Ellis.

Whatcom Pain Management and Psychiatric Services
1229 Cornwall, Suite 313
Bellingham, Washington 98225
676-5060

Physical, Physiological and Psychological Feelings, Actions, and Images Related to the Breathing Rhythm

	Exhalation	Inhalation	Holding the Breath
Physical and Physiological	Relaxation	Increase of Tension	Maintenance or Increase of Tension
	Heaviness	Lightness	Unstable Equilibrium
	Calmness	Stimulation	Restlessness
	Warmth	Coolness	Variability
	Darkness	Brightness	Variability
	Softness	Hardness	Rigidity
	Moisture	Dryness	
	Weakness, Weariness	Strength, Invigoration, Refreshment	Momentary Conservation of Strength
Psychological	Patience, Endurance	Speed, Being Startled	Anxiety, Oppression
	Contemplation	Ready Attention	Strained Attention
	Equanimity	Courage	Cowardice
	Deep Thought, Concentration	Openmindedness, Creativity	Closedmindedness
	Introversion	Extroversion	
	Boredom	Excitement	Keen Interest
	Satisfaction	Curiosity	Uncertainty
	Depression	Cheerfulness	Nervous Tension
	Comfort	Exhilaration	Uneasiness
	Generosity	Greed	Stinginess
Actions	Relax, Release, Let Go, Loosen	Tense, Bind, Tighten, Grasp	Hold On
	Release Pressure, Stream or Flow Out	Increase Pressure, Stream or Flow In	Maintain or Increase Pressure
	Liquefy	Solidify	Maintain Consistency
	Expand, Widen, Open	Contract, Narrow, Close	Dimension Unchanged or Congestion
	Sink, Descend, Fall Asleep	Ascend, Levitate, Rise, Wake Up	Maintain Level
	Lengthen	Shorten	Maintain Length
	Move or Swing Forward, Strike, Kick, Punch, Reach Out	Move, Draw, Pull or Swing Backward, Haul In	Stop, Stand or Hold Still
	Send, Give, Help,	Receive, Take,	Keep, Interrupt

Source: Dr. Douglas Uhl, Ph.D., 1990

Symptom Effectiveness Chart

Now that you have identified your stress-related symptoms, it is time to choose the one or two that bother you the most, and to select the techniques that you will use to relieve them. Since everyone reacts differently to stress, it is hard to say which stress reduction techniques will be best for you. However, this chart will give you a general idea of what to try first, and where to go from there.

Chapter headings for each stress reduction method are across the top , and typical stress-related symptoms are listed down the side. You may have only one or several of these symptoms.

As you can see, more than one stress reduction technique is indicated as effective in treating most symptoms. The most effective techniques for a particular symptom are marked with a boldface X, while other

| *Symptoms* | *Techniques* | | | |
	Progressive Relaxation	*Breathing*	*Autogenics*	*Imagination*
Anxiety in specific situations (tests, deadlines, interviews, etc.)	X	X		X
Anxiety in your personal relationships (spouse, parents, children, etc.)	X	X		
Anxiety, general (regardless of the situation or the people involved)	X	X	X	X
Depression, hopelessness, powerlessness, poor self-esteem	X	X		
Hostility, anger, iritability, resentment		X	X	
Phobias, fears	X			
Obsessions, unwanted thoughts		X		
Muscular tension	X	X	X	X
High blood pressure	X		X	
Headaches, neckaches, backaches	X		X	X
Indigestion, irritable bowel, ulcers, chronic constipation	X		X	
Muscle spasms, tics, tremors	X			X
Fatigue, tired all the time	X	X	X	
Insomnia, sleeping difficulties	X	X		

Source: W. Douglas Uhl, Phy., Ph.D., 1990

The Alzheimer Caregiver's Disease

Although much has been said and written about the stages and progression of Alzheimer's Disease in relation to the patient, little mention has been made of the stages and progression of Alzheimer's Disease in relation to the caregiver. The Caregiver's Disease, described below, outlines the impact of Alzheimer's Disease on the primary caregiver - that vulnerable and concerned spouse, family member or friend who is committed to the constant care of the Alzheimer patient.

<u>Stage One</u> - **Pre-Diagnosis** *(from onset to diagnosis - one to ten years, or more)*

During this period the Alzheimer patient may experience a variety of symptoms — all attributed to the normal aging process by doctor, family, friends, and associates. These symptoms may include forgetfulness; memory loss; problems with alcohol; problems with drugs, prescribed and over-the-counter; personality changes; confusion; lethargy; withdrawal; facades.

These symptoms may cause family and social disruptions through stress, depression, abuse, divorce, job changes, automobile accidents. The undiagnosed Alzheimer patient and the caregiver may go from doctor to doctor and be treated for numerous 'in' diseases, or some rare disease, or be told "what do you expect? Your husband is old - he's senile."

Finally someone - generally not a close family member - suggests the problem needs a thorough investigation. A "yearly physical" is an accepted practice. Why not a "yearly mental"? Presently this would be an expensive procedure but a less expensive diagnostic procedure can and must be developed.

<u>Stage Two</u> - **Diagnosis** *(immediately before and after diagnosis - six months to a year)*

For the caregiver and family it is a time of shock, confusion, questioning, fear, guilt, nonacceptance, inane rationalization, and of hiding the diagnosis from the patient, other relatives, friends and society ("Insanity doesn't run in my side of the family"). There are many unanswered questions: What will happen to my spouse? my relative? my friend? What will happen to me? my savings? my health? my friends? my world? my everything? Who pays? Who lives? Who dies? Society's insensitive and ignorant response seems to be: Too old! Too sick! Too bad!

After a diagnosis of Alzheimer's disease, one Seattle physician thought and thought, tied a weight around her body, and drowned.

Luckily, if the diagnosis has come early, much can be accomplished with the help of professional counseling for the family with respect to the medical, psychiatric, and behavioral, social, legal, and financial implication of the disease. The post-diagnostic stage is a time for understanding, information-seeking, and for learning about how to slow down the deterioration of the Alzheimer patient and the Alzheimer caregiver.

Stage Three - Planning *(one to two years, post-diagnosis)*

Planning is directed to maintaining both the patient and the caregiver at the highest possible functional levels. Planning must include the help of professionals, family support, self-help groups, and public agencies.

Too often, the patient is institutionalized prematurely because of the caregiver's frustration, health, or "to hell with it" attitude, or due to the witless advice of the kind doctor, other family members, or friends. The decision to "put" the patient in a nursing home will be a most devastating and traumatic event for the caregiver because even in the past phases of Alzheimer's disease, some cognitive function remains. Unable to express in words, the patient looks in bewilderment at the caregiver and asks, "My life? My love? My friends? My confidante? What have I done to be "put" away after all these years?" and seems to say "If you must shorten my life, do it here and not in a strange land." And, after years in a nursing home, a patient, with all verbal communication seemingly lost, will ask, "What am I doing here? When can we go home?" That is a heavy load for the caregiver.

Is breathing life? When does death arrive? When can we no longer "feel dawn, see sunset glow?" One caregiver writes, "My husband has been in a nursing home for eleven years. My money has all been spent and I will have to bring him home. I am only sixty-one years old and would like to do something with my life. But my children, my church, and my town keep me tied to a corpse. Sometimes I feel like stealing away in the night forever."

To the caregiver, the last breath often comes as a relief but not as a release. The funeral began when the patient was "put" in the institution, or the warehouse, or the mausoleum - or whatever term seems suitable. Nor has the funeral ended with the last urn of earth on the grave, nor the last flickering flame of the crematorium.

Stage Six - Healing the Caregiver *(six months after patient's death to death of caregiver)*

The healing process for the caregiver is influenced by a variety of "if" circumstances:

    If there has been early diagnosis and death comes quickly,
    If there has been acceptance,
    If there has been strong family support,
    If there has been strong community support,
    If there has been caring and knowledgeable professional assistance,
    If there has been no excessive conflict in the marriage,
    If there has been a life of integrity and not of despair,
    If there has been an understanding of the disease process,
    If there has been no serious caregiver health problems.
    If there has been less me and more you,
    If there has been no fear . . . no guilt . . . no anger . . . no blame . . .
        no hiding,

If you are not already dead, then you, the caregiver, will emerge from the ordeal, the furnace, the battle, unscathed and undaunted.

If, otherwise, the caregiver may well be a candidate for:
early death,
the psychiatrist's couch to be treated for depression, neurosis, or psychosis,
murder,
suicide,
poverty,
physical deterioration,
abandonment,

and you, the caregiver, will become the spitting image of an Alzheimer patient, sans hope, sans grace of tribute, sans tears.

Source: letter by Warren Easterly from reprint from articles in
Alzheimer's Caregiver Support Materials, 1981.

The "Other Victims": Working with the Families of Cognitively Impaired Elders

Case Studies

Mr. Jones is a 75-year-old gentleman who is living with his 72-year-old wife in Seattle. He was diagnosed with Alzheimer's Disease three years ago, but his wife notes that she has been observing changes in him for the last six years. At this point in time he needs help with eating and dressing, but is still able to walk. He frequently walks around the block with his wife. At times he does this without his wife and has gotten lost. His wife has had to call the police several times to bring him home. When he returns each time he states: "I was looking for home."

The Jones's have two daughters . . . Mary who lives in Chicago, Ill. and Marcy who lives three blocks away. Both are willing to be helpful, but feel that their mother "shuts them off" from what is really going on in the household. Mrs. Jones has just been told by her doctor that she has breast cancer and needs to have treatment. She is very upset, because if she goes to the hospital for this, there will be no one to care for her husband.

The Jones family has very limited income. Social security and a small pension from the company where Mr. Jones worked for 25 years as watchman are the only monthly income for the family.

Miss Smith is 80 and lives in Spokane. For many years she was an elementary schoolteacher, and now draws a small teacher's pension as well as social security. Miss Smith has been living with her 68-year-old sister, Mrs. Thomas, who is a widow. Mrs. Thomas moved in with her sister when Miss smith was diagnosed as having Alzheimer's disease 7 years ago. Her children were against it, saying that she had cared for her husband through his terminal illness, and that she needn't sacrifice her whole life to her sister's needs. Mrs. Thomas did not see that that was the problem. When she was a child Miss smith had become "the mother" for the family when their mother had died in childbirth, so Mrs. Thomas feels responsible to her sister as if she were a mother.

Miss Smith attends a day health center, but the staff there reports that her behavior, which includes hoarding all of the butter off the table at lunch, is becoming inappropriate. This is upsetting the other participants. Also, Miss Smith is becoming more and more incontinent, a problem which keeps Mrs. Thomas doing great amounts of laundry. They have suggested that Mrs. Thomas look into a nursing home for her sister, an idea that she is rejecting. Mrs. Thomas's children are also reinforcing the idea, because they are very concerned about her physical and mental health.

Dr. Doe has been a highly respected school principal for many years. He is now 65, but he was diagnosed with Alzheimer's Disease at sixty when his colleagues noticed that he was not able to carry out decisions that he had made. His 45-year-old divorced daughter, Joan, and her 15-year-old son, John, now live with him in his small home.

Because Joan works daily, a live-in companion has been hired to stay with Dr. Doe during the day. This woman has been very responsible, and Dr. Doe has enjoyed her company. She has just informed that family that she has to leave because her husband has just taken a job in a distant city. Joan does not feel that she can leave her job, and it is difficult to find home helpers in the area. Also, her son John is expressing some concern that grandpa is getting worse and that he cannot bring his friends over to listen to records any more. He complains that "grandpa just yells at us for being too loud."

Dr. Doe has a good retirement income and several thousand dollars in savings. He has, up until this point, been doing very well in his home environment. Joan, John and the helper have put up cue cards all over the house, and Dr. Doe's unusual behavior of getting up at night and rummaging through the house has not been a bother to anyone, nor has it created any safety hazards. He needs a bit more care in hygiene and dressing in recent days.

Mr. Kay is a 65-year-old man who recently came to the adult day center. He was chairman of the board of his own very successful company. He was diagnosed with Alzheimer's Disease five years ago and his illness has progressed quite rapidly. His wife was exhausted from 24-hour caregiving, so he came to the center. He has a daughter and a son who live near by who have been involved in his care. The center's social worker's goal was to provide some relief care for Mrs. Kay and some socialization activities for her husband. Today he was swearing and abusive to the other's. The worker called the daughter to let her know that he was not appropriate for the day center, and that she better start thinking about a nursing home for her father, because that is the kind of care he really needs to help him and to help the family. The daughter became very upset, and said that the worker was being judgmental of her father . . . that he might swear a bit, but that he was not abusive. He was not abusive to her and she was sure he didn't even know how to be abusive. The wife and the daughter have both told the worker that before the crisis of the Alzheimer's Disease, all of them communicated very well.

Mrs. Ajax had been admitted to the nursing home following surgery for the repair of a fractured hip. She also has a diagnosis of Alzheimer's disease. Her husband had been caring for her in their large home prior to the hospitalization. They had received some help from the Volunteer Chore visitor from their church where they have been active members for many years. Mr. Ajax has told the nursing home staff that he is exhausted. Yet he felt very strongly that it was "terrible" to have his wife in a nursing home. Mr. Ajax has a comfortable monthly income and many assets, yet he is reluctant to spend them as he and his wife always were saving for a "rainy day."

Besides Mr. Ajax, the family consists of a daughter and son-in-law who live next door to the Ajaxs's, and a 20-year-old grandson away at college, who has always been Mrs. Ajax's favorite. Both the son and daughter-in-law work full time. All of them would like to see Mrs. Ajax come home again following her recuperation from surgery. The nursing home staff feels that there is no way that Mrs. Ajax can go home and are trying to find a way to convince Mr. Ajax of that.

Guidelines for Providing a Facilitative Environment for the Elderly Patient with True Dementia

1. Make change very slowly. The patient must be well prepared for any physical, emotional, drug, nutritional, personnel, or geographic change.
2. Keep the patient ambulatory as long as possible with daily exercise routine, including a walk in the sunshine.
3. Maintain a routine. A dependable world and a structured existence are essential.
4. Provide social stimulation without overload. Maintain communication through every possible channel.
5. Avoid crowds or large spaces without boundaries. Avoid sensory overload.
6. Assist in organizing the personal aspects of the client's affairs, safekeeping of treasures, obtaining legal aid of attorney or ombudsman, and setting up file of personal papers.
7. Monitor use of health measures, including good nutrition, attention to mouth and teeth, and adequate shoes. Avoid use of drugs.
8. Do not expect the patient to understand or participate in complex activities or conversations.
9. Maintain positive input, such as reinforcement for any worthy act., to maintain the patient's self-esteem and encourage self-participation in activities of daily living.
10. Ensure that information is available to the patient about time and place landmarks that provide reality - calendars with huge figures, clocks with all numbers for hours, reality boards for institutions, and reminders of special events such as birthdays, anniversaries, and holidays.
11. Make bowel and bladder control consistent, using a routine. As the patient's mind becomes more hazy, use clothing with simple fasteners, or elastic waistbands.
12. Support the family, who in turn support the patient, by simple reinforcement of their efforts with a special commendation. Respite care from the daily watching may enable them to care for the patient in the home and visit him in the institution long after internal rewards have ceased to exist.

Source: Carnevali, D., and Patrick, M., Nursing Management for the Elderly, Philadelphia: J.B. Lippincott, Co. 1979.

Global Deterioration Scale

Alzheimer's Disease Parallels In Reverse The Developmental Stages of Childhood

Approx. Age	Abilities Acquired		Stage of Disease	Abilities Lost
12+ years	Hold a job		Borderline	Hold a job
7-12 years	Handle simple finances		Early	Handle simple finances
5-7 years	Select proper clothes		Moderate	Select proper clothes
5 years	Put on clothes		Severe	Put on clothes
4 years	Shower unaided			Shower unaided
4 years	Go to toilet unaided			Go to toilet unaided
3-4-1/2 years	Control urine			Control urine
2-3 years	Control bowels			Control bowels
15 months	Speak 5/6 words		Late	Speak 5/6 words
1 year	Speak 1 word		(Stage 6)	Speak 1 word
1 year	Walk			Walk
6-9 mos.	Sit up			Sit up
2-3 mos.	Smile			Smile

Source: Dr. Barry Reisberg - New York University Medical Center and Moyra Jones Resources, Burnaby, B.C., Canada.

Part VII

Bibliography

Annotated Bibliography

1. Alzheimer's Disease and Related Disorders Association (ADRDA), 360 North Michigan Avenue, Chicago, IL 60601, 1-800-621-0379.
   Publishes "The Alzheimer's Disease and Related Disorders Newsletter, "useful to family members, caregivers and professionals. Provides up-to-date information on current research and treatment.

2. Hoyman, Nancy R. and Wendy Lustbader, <u>Taking Care of Your Aging Family Members: A Practical Guide</u> (New York, N.Y.: First Free Press 1986).
   Excellent book designed for use by family members, caregivers and professionals. Presents typical problems and models strategies for their resolution in a variety of caregiving situations.

3. Phillips, Alice H. and Caryl K. Roman, <u>A Practical Guide to Independent Living: For Older People</u> (Seattle: Pacific Search Press, 1984).
   An up-beat book about healthy aging. Safety tips, good health care practices and resource guide designed for the older person. Large print.

4. Torrey Fuller R., <u>Surviving Schizophrenia: A Family Manual.</u> (New York, N.Y.: Harper and Row, 1983).
   An excellent, complete book for families of schizophrenics. Deals with the origins of illness, treatment, institutionalization, and an invaluable chapter on what families can do, however it is limited in terms of aging issues.

5. Edinberg, Mark A., <u>Talking With Your Aging Parents</u> (Boston: Shambhala, 1988).
   A must book for anyone struggling with how to raise a range of important issues related to aging and well-being. All about communication and caring.

6. Moore, Pat and Charles Paul Conn, <u>Disguised</u> (Texas: Word Books, 1985).
   A fascinating story about a young woman's personal exploration into the world of aging by disguising herself as an older woman to try to understand the limitations of advanced age in a sympathetic way.

7. Luke, Helen M. <u>Old Age</u> (New York, Parabola Books, 1987)
   The author presents six essays which highlight various aspects of older age. She is particularly interested in symbolism as a Jungian and explores works of Shakespeare, T. S. Eliot and concepts from Christianity and Jung's work. The writing provides food for thought and a different perspective on some familiar themes of aging.

8. Mace, Nancy F. and Peter Robins <u>The 36-Hour Day</u>, Baltimore, John Hopkins University, 1981
    A useful account of the caregivers world. Helpful to professionals, as well as family members, to give support for the many issues involved in care for, or working with dementing illnesses. Essential reading for Peer Counseling Program workers.

9. <u>Generations</u>, Journal of the American Society on Aging, <u>Mental Health issue, Spring, 1986 Alcohol and Drugs Abuse and Misuse</u>, Summer, 1988.
    These two journals speak clearly of the two areas of aging that Peer Counseling Programs often deal with. The individual articles are written by experts in their areas. It offers suggestions, new views and references for both the paraprofessional and professional.

Annotated bibliography compiled by Lizabeth Bandy, B.A., certified in Geriatric Mental Health, Skagit Mental Health and Susan Gardner, M.S.W., Skagit Mental Health.

Suggested Reading for Program Development

Egan, Gerard. The Skilled Helper, Third edition. Belmont, CA. Brooks/Cole Publishing, 1986.

Ivey, Allen and Norma Gluckstern. Basic Attending Skills, Microtraining Associates, Inc., North Amherst, Mass., 1976.

Bridges, William. Transitions, Philippines, Addison-Wesley Publishing Co, Inc., 1980.

McKinney, Liz. They're Not Alone, Good Samaritan Hospital & Medical Center, Portland, Oregon, 1986.

Alpaugn P. and M. Haney. Counseling the Older Adult, Lenington Books, Lexington, Mass., 1985.

Freeman, Evelyn. Peer Counseling for Seniors, Senior Health & Peer Counseling Center, Santa Monica, CA, 1986.

Stevens, John. Awareness: Exploring, Experimenting, Experiencing, Real People Press, Moab, Utah, 1971.

Babic, A.L. "The Older Volunteer, Expectations, & Satisfaction." Gerontologist, Vol. 12, 1972, Pp. 87-93.

Becher, F. and Zarit, S. "Training Older Adults As Peer Counselors." Educational Gerontology, Vol. 3, 1978, Pp. 241-250.

Carkhoff, R.R. The Art of Helping, Amherst, Mass. Human Resource Development Press, Inc, 1977.

Comfort, A. A Good Age, New York, N.Y.: Simon & Schuster, 1976.

Harris L. and Associates. The Myth and Reality of Aging in America, Washington D.C.: National Counsel on Aging, 1975.

Suggested Readings for Aging

Anderson Barbara. The Aging Game, New York: McGraw-Hill, 1978.

Bloomfield, Herold. Making Peace With Your Parents, New York: Harper and Row, 1975.

Butler, Robert N. Why Survive? Being Old In America, New York: Harper and Row, 1975.

Cousins, Norman. Anatomy of an Illness, New York: W.W. Norton, 1979.

Kemper, Donald W., Molly Mettle, Jim Gruffre, Jim & Betty Matzeh, Growing Wiser, Boise, Idaho, 1986.

Kubler-Ross, Elizabeth. <u>On Death and Dying</u>, New York: MacMillin, 1969.

Mace, Nancy and Peter Robins. <u>The 36 Hour Day</u>, Baltimore: John Hopkins University Press, 1982.

Mandel, Evelyn. <u>The Art of Aging</u>, Minneapolis: Winston Press, 1981.

Walters, E., S. Fink and B. White. "Peer Groups Counseling for Older People" <u>Educational Gerontology</u>, Vol. 1, 1976, Pp. 147-150.

National Institute of Mental Health, <u>Plain Talk About...Mutual Health Groups.</u>

Maslow, Abraham. <u>Towards the Psychology of Being</u>, New York: Van Nostrand Reinhold, 1960.

Mustakas, Clark E. <u>Loneliness and Love</u>, Englewood Cliffs, N.J.: Prentice-Hall. 1972.

Rogers, Carl. <u>A Way of Being</u>, New York: Houghton Mifflin, 1980

Satir, Virginia. <u>Peoplemaking</u>, Palo Alto, Ca: Science & Behavior Books, 1972.

Willing, Jules. <u>The Lively Mind</u>, New York: Lively Mind Books, 1982.

DeCastillejo, Irene Claremont. <u>Knowing Woman</u>, New York: Harper and Row, 1973.

Kavanaugh, Robert. <u>Facing Death</u>, New York: Penguin Press, 1974.

Weininger, Ben, and Eva L. Menkin. <u>Aging is A Lifelong Affair</u>, Los Angeles: Guild of Tutors Press, 1978.

Zunin, Leonard, M.D. <u>Contact: The First Four Minutes</u>, Los Angeles: Nosh Publishing, 1972.

Suggested Readings for Memory

Cook, Thomas. <u>Clinical Assessment of Memory Problems.</u>

Gose, Kathleen & Gloria Levi. <u>Instructor's Manual For A Course in Memory Skills-Dealing with Memory Changes As You Grow Older</u>, Health Promotion Directorate, Western Region, Health and Welfare, Canada, 1986.

Garfunkel, Florence & Gertrude Landaw. "Memory Retention Course for the Aged: Guide for Leaders," Wash. D.C. National Counsel on the Aging, 1981.

<u>Helping Memory Impaired Elders: A Guide for Caregivers</u>, Corvallis: Oregon State University Extension Services, 1985.

Suggested Readings on Death

Becker, Ernest. The Denial of Death, New York: The Free Press, Division of MacMillian Publishing Co., Inc., 1973.

Henlin, David. Death As A Fact Of Life, New York N.Y.: Warner Paperback Div., 1973.

Grolbman, Earl A., Ed. Concerning Death: A Practical Guide for The Living, Boston: Beacon Press, 1974.

Manners, Marya. Last Rights: A Case for the Good Death, London: Millington L&D, 1975.

Anderson, Robert. I Never Sang for My Father, New York: J.B. Lippincott & Sons, 1973.

Suggested Readings for Grief

Hewett, John H. After Suicide, West Minster Press, 1980.

Freese, Arthur. Help for Your Grief, York: Schochen Books, 1977.

Mooney, Elizabeth. Alone: Surviving As A Widow, New York City: C.P. Putmans, 1981.

Tatelbaum, Judy. The Courage to Grieve, New York: Harper Books, Harper Row.

Pincus, Lily. Death and the Family, New York: Vintage Books, 1974.

Scarf, Maggie. Unfinished Business, New York: Random House, Inc. 1980.

Suggested Reading for
Psychotherapy with Older Adults

Abrahams, Joel, and Valerie Crooks Eds., Geriatric Mental Health.

Bradshaw, John, Healing the Shame that Binds You.

Butler, Robert and Myrna Lewis, Aging and Mental Health.

Carter, Elizabeth and Monica McGoldrick, Eds., The Family Lifecycle.

Erikson, Erik, The Lifecycle Completed.

Foucault, Michel, Madness and Civilization.

Garner, J. Dianne and Susan Mercer, Women as they Age.

Generations, Winter 1990.

Gido, John and Arnold Goldberg, Models of the Mind.

Lerner, Harriet Goldhor, Women in Therapy.

Herr, John J. and John Weakland, Counseling Elders and Their Families.

Hughston, Geo et al., Aging and Family Therapy.

Hussian, Richard, Geriatric Psychology. A Behavioral Perspective.

McGoldrick, Monica, Genograms in Family Assessment.

Sandler, Ann-Marie. "Psychoanalysis in Later Life: Problems in the Psycholanalysis of an Aging Narcissistic Patient," Journal of Geriatric Psychiatry, Vol XI, No. 1, pp. 5-36.

Practical Preparations for Death
A Bibliography

Antoniak, Scott, Worchester. Alone, Millbrae, California: Les Femmes Press, 1979, 204 pp.

Baer, Louis Shattick, M.D. Let the Patient Decide, Philadelphia: The Westminster Press, 1978.

Becker, Ernest. The Denial of Death, New York: The Free Press, Division of Macmillan Publishing Co., Inc., 1973, 315 pp.

Grollman, Earl A., Ed. Concerning Death: A Practical Guide for the Living, Boston: Beacon Press, 1974, 364 pp.

Hendin, David. Death as a Fact of Life, New York, N.Y.: Warner Paperback Div, 1974, 223 pp.

Kavanaugh, Robert E. Facing Death, Kingsport, Tennesse: Kingsport Press, Inc., Penguin Books, 1974, 226 pp.

Kubler-Ross, Elisabeth. Death - The Final Stage of Growth, Englewood Cliffs, New Jersey: Prentice-Hall, Inc., 1975, 175 pp.

Mannes, Marya. Last Rights: A Case for the Good Death, London: Millington, Ltd., 1975, 150 pp.

Stoddard, Sandol. The Hospice Movement: A Better Way of Caring for the Dying, New York: Vintage Books, 1978, 347 pp.

Death

Agee, James. <u>A Death in the Family</u>, New York: Avon Publishing, 1957.

Cousins, Norman. <u>Anatomy of an Illness</u>, New York: Bantam Books Inc.,1981. (mind control curing the body)

Davis, Richard (Ed.). <u>Dealing with Death</u>, Los Angeles: Andrus Gerontology Center, 1978.

de Beauvoir, Simone. <u>A Very Easy Death</u>, New York: Warner Books, 1964. (personal account of her mother's death)

Gonda, Thomas and John Ruark. <u>Dying Dignified - The Health Professional's Guide to Care</u>, Menlo Park, CA.: Addison-Wesley Publishing Co., 1984

Grollman, Earl (Ed.). <u>Concerning Death: A Practical Guide for the Living</u>, Boston: Beacon Press, 1974.

Horan, Dennis and David Mall. <u>Death, Dying, and Euthanasia</u>, Maryland: Maryland University Publications, Inc., 1980.

Humphry, Derek. <u>Jean's Way</u>, New York: Grove Press, 1984. (personal account of euthanasia)

Humphry, Derek and Ann Wickett. <u>The Right to Die - Understanding Euthanasia</u>, New York: Harper & Row, 1986.

Johnson, Christopher and Marsha McGee. <u>Encounters with Eternity - Religious Views of Death and Life After Death</u>, New York: Philosophical LIbrary, 1986.

Kalish, Richard. <u>Death, Grief, and Caring Relationships</u>, Monterey: Brooks/Cole Publishing Co., Inc., 1972.

Kastenbaum, R. and R. Aisenberg. The Psychology of Death, New York: Springer Publishing Co., Inc., 1972.

Kastenbaum, Robert. Is There Life After Death? New York: Prentice Hall Press, 1984.

Kavanaugh, Robert. Facing Death, New York: Penguin Books, 1977.

Kluge, Eike-Henner. The Ethics of Deliberate Death, National University Publications, Kennikat Press, 1981.

Kubler-Ross, Elisabeth. Death, The Final Stage of Growth, New Jersey: Prentice-Hall, Inc., 1975.

Bereavement

Caine, Lynn. Widow, New York: William Morrow & Co., Inc., 1974.

Colgrove. M., H. Bloomfield, and P. McWilliams. How to Survive the Loss of a Love, New York: Bantam Books, Inc., 1977.

Gatov, Elizabeth. Widows in the Dark, New York: Warner Books, 1985. (financial managementd)

Glick, I, Tobert Weiss, and Colin Murray Parkes. The First Year of Bereavement, New York: John Wiley & Sons, Inc., 1974.

Jackson, Edgar. Understanding Grief: Its Roots, Dynamics and Treatment, Nashville, Tenn: Abingdon Press, 1975.

Jackson, Edgar. When Someone Dies, Philadelphia: Fortress Press, 1984.

Lear, Martha. Heartsounds: The Story of Love and Loss, New York: Simon & Schuster, 1980.

Lewis, C.S. A Grief Observed, New York: Seabury Press, 1961. (a male's viewpoint of bereavement.)

Lindemann, Erich. Beyond Grief, New York: Jason Aronson, 1979.

Loewinsohn, Ruth Jean. Survival Handbook for Widows, Washington, D.C.: AARP, 1984.

Marshall, Catherine. To Live Again, New York: McGraw/Hill Books, 1967.

Moffat, Mary Jane (Ed.). In the Midst of Winter, New York: Vintage Books, 1982. (selections from the literature of mourning)

Parkes, Colin Murray. Bereavement, New York: International Universities Press, 1972.

Peterson, James and Michael Briley. Widows and Widowhood. Chicago Follett Publishing Co., 1977.

Pincus, Lily. <u>Death & the Family - The Importance of Mourning</u>, New York: Vintage Books, 1976. (for the mental health practitioner)

Slagle, Kate Walsh. <u>Live With Loss</u>, New Jersey: Prentice-Hall, 1982.

Stearns, Ann Kaiser. <u>Living Through Personal Crisis</u>, Chicago: The Thomas More Press, 1984.

Westberg, Granger. <u>Good Grief</u>, Philadelphia: Fortress Press, 1976.

Worden, J. William. <u>Grief Counseling & Grief Therapy</u>, New York: Springer Publishing Co, 1982. (a handbook for the mental health work.)

Wylie, B.J. <u>Beginnings - A Book for Widows</u>, New York: Ballantine Books, 1982. (how to cope financially, emotionally, spiritually.)

Suggested Readings for Families

Gray, Katherine. <u>Caresharing: How To Relate to the Frail Elderly</u>, Minneapolis; Ebenezer Center on Aging & Human Development, 1984.

Henig, Robin Marantz. <u>The Myth of Senility: The Truth About the Brain and Aging</u>, (An AARP Book) Scott, Foresman & Co., 1985.

Noyes, Lin. <u>"What's Wrong With My Grandma."</u> Distributed by ADRDA Northern Virginia Chapter, P.O.Box 2715, West Springfield, Virginia, 1982.

Roach, Marion. <u>Another Name For Madness</u>, New York: Houghton Mifflin Co., 1985.

Zarit, Stephen, Nancy Orr & Judy Zarit. <u>The Hidden Victims of Alzheimer's Disease: Families Under Stress</u>, New York: N.Y. University Press, 1985.

O'Conner, Kathleen and Joyce Prothero. <u>The Alzheimer's Caregiver: Strategies for Support</u>, Seattle: University of Washington Press, 1986.

Senior Peer Counselors of Skagit, Whatcom, Island & San Juan Counties
Winter 1992

Pat Agnew
Jan Allison
Shirley Assink
Agnes Bark
Beverly Bell
Sara Jane Bergstrom
Maurice Bisson
Florence Boden
Bette Bosman
Juanita Bravard
Claudia Case
Richard Case
Lucetta Cleveland
Joan Collins
Betty Craig
Ellen Einarson
Ann Emerson
Kathleen Everett
Corrine Garris
Frederica Gentilini
Sharon Haglund
Helen Hammers
Selma Handyside
Betty Jo Hanson

Mary-Alice Horner
Judell Harrsch
Dorothy Hembury
Iris Hicks
Dean Hillhouse
Avonelle Hines
Jack Hinton
Valda Holmes
Myrtle Hunnewell
Connie Hummel
Walter Hummel
Howard Jacobson
Bette Johnson
Carole Johnson
Esther Karlstrom
Leroy Karlstrom
Carol Kertson
Ariel Kuljis
Martha M. Larson
Vesta Lavin
Emma Leppala
Bert Lederer
Nelle McClenahan
George Meintel

Harriet Napiecinski
Elmyra Nelson
Helen Omdal
Theresa Parakh
John S. Read
Aristine Reinhart
Betty Richey
Betty Riddick
Joyce Reavis
Jeanne Ryan
Helen Sannyasin
Donna Sehlin
Charles Smither
Virginia Spray
Yvonne Talmadge
Alice Teeter
Marianne Titus
Lynda Thompson
Marilyn Thostenson
Bill Urschel
Virginia Walsh
Laura Vanderbeck
Frank Wili
Marlene Zei